Instructor's Manual with Test Bank

THE ART AND SCIENCE OF LEADERSHIP

SOUTH RIVER MEDIA

Instructor's Manual
with Test Bank

THE ART AND SCIENCE OF LEADERSHIP

Fourth Edition

Afsaneh Nahavandi

PEARSON

Prentice Hall

Upper Saddle River, New Jersey 07458

VP/Editorial Director: Jeff Shelstad
Product Development Manager: Ashley Santora
Associate Director Manufacturing: Vincent Scelta
Production Editor & Buyer: Wanda Rockwell
Printer/Binder: Offset Paper Manufacturer

10 9 8 7 6 5 4 3 2 1
ISBN 0-13-148542-3

CONTENTS

SECTION ONE: Course Outlines and Exercise Summary

SECTION TWO: Chapter Materials

Part I: Building Blocks

Part II: Contingency Models

Part III: Current Developments and Applications

Part IV: Looking Toward the Future

SECTION THREE: Video Guide

SECTION FOUR: Test Bank

SECTION ONE

COURSE OUTLINES AND EXERCISE SUMMARY

INTRODUCTION

The topic of leadership is challenging and stimulating for students and faculty. Whether the course is offered as part of an undergraduate curriculum, as a graduate business elective, in an educational leadership program, or in a public administration program, it is always popular. The newfound practitioner interest in the topic, which has led to the publication of many widely available books, is further bringing students back to leadership classrooms. It is easy for them to get frustrated and disappointed. Leadership may appear easy to define and interesting to write about, but it is difficult to teach. It is a field that contains many well-developed theories, is replete with empirical challenges, and continues to be highly divided.

The goal of the "Art and Science of Leadership" is to move beyond the differences and the divisions and to provide students with a theory-based, integrative, hands-on, practical view of leadership. The third edition of the book builds on the strengths of the first two editions and introduces some new emphasis and new features. The many debates and controversies within the field of leadership are presented in this third edition as they were in the first two. I continue to emphasize integration of the concepts and distilling useful and practical concepts from each theory while taking a cross-cultural perspective. The guiding philosophy and assumptions remain the same. These include:

The fourth edition of this book builds on the strengths of the first three editions while updating the research, the examples and many of the cases. The many debates and controversies within the field of leadership are presented in this edition as they were in the first three. I continue to emphasize integration of the concepts and distill useful and practical concepts from each theory while taking a cross-cultural perspective. The guiding philosophy and assumption remain the same:

- We can all learn to become better leaders.

- Application focus to help student apply what they learn.

- Cross-cultural focus that emphasizes that leadership is not a culture-free process.

- Looking at the future by addressing the dramatic changes that organizations are undergoing.

- Exercises and self-assessments with some revisions and additions.

- The features from the previous edition, although all present new research and examples. "Leadership on the Cutting Edge" presents current empirical or theoretical research studies. "Leading Change" highlights examples of innovative practices in organizations. "Leadership in Action Case" presents short case of a "real-life" leader at the end of every chapter. Five of the cases are new; one has been considerably updated.

In addition, I have updated several key areas extensively including:

- Detailed presentation of the Global Leadership Organizational Behavior Effectiveness (GLOBE) research findings from 0ver 60 countries in Chapter 1 and throughout this edition further expands the strong cross-cultural coverage.

- Discussion of emotional intelligence updated and expanded to reflect current strong research and interest in the area (in Chapter 3).

- I have revised the discussion of power and corruption in Chapter 4 to separate individual and organizational factors that contribute to power corruption.

- All new "Leading Change" profiles in every chapter includes a wide range of U.S. and global organizations such as Anne Mulcahey of Xerox, Semel and Sartain of Yahoo, Shirley Choi CEO of the Chinese company Seapower, Ricardo Semler of the Brazilian company Semco, and Sir Richard Branson of the U.K.'s Virgin group.

- Several new end of chapter cases including Jet Blue's David Neeleman, Ikea's Pernille Spears-Lopez, NYSE's Richard Grasso, Whole Foods' John Mackey, and Procter & Gamble's A.G. Lafley present in depth information on interesting leaders.

- An "almost new" pedagogical feature: Leading from the Grassroots" replaces "What does this mean for me?" in each chapter and provides examples of leadership at all levels of organizations emphasizing the theme that leadership is not the exclusive domain of those in top organizational levels.

- New updated web sites in "Searching the Web" section.

Additionally, the instructor resource manual for this edition includes:

- Test bank with multiple choice and True/False questions.

- A video guide.

- Summaries for the web sites presented in "Searching the Web" sites.

- Regular updates will be provided on www.prenhall.com/nahavandi

Regardless of the level at which leadership is taught, it is generally taught as an elective. Therefore, the content of the course remains very much up to the instructor. Most faculty who teach a leadership course have some degree of expertise in the topic. They are likely to have their own favorite materials and lectures. I developed the contents of this handbook based on those assumptions. In addition to the multiple choice and true/false questions that are provided for this edition, you will find potential assignments throughout the handbook. I also provide a summary and detailed outline of every chapter for quick review.

I focused on providing the instructor with directions and ideas for the exercises and other activities presented in the text. I have tested all of the exercises at the end of the chapters in my classes over the past 20 years. Many are appropriate for all students; some work better with students with more work experience. However, in spite of some differences, they are all accessible and relatively easy to use. The clear majority is designed to be used as a brief supplement to a topic; a few are lengthy enough to take up a whole class. I provide two brief course outlines along with a table of activities to help instructors in designing their courses and deciding which activities are appropriate for their class.

SAMPLE COURSE OUTLINES

Sample course outline for 15 weeks with one 150 minute period a week

Week	Topic	Reading and other assignments	Class activity
1.	Introduction: Definitions and functions		Exercise 1.1: What is leadership?
			Exercise 1.2: Images of leadership
			Exercise 1.4: Understanding the leadership context
2.	Cross-cultural models Impact of leaders	Chapter 1	Exercise 1.3: Narian bridges
			Case analysis: JetBlue
3.	History of leadership	Chapter 2	Exercise 2.1: Old wines
			Exercise 2.3: Leadership and gender
4.	Current approaches	Chapter 2	Exercise 2.2: The toy factory
			Case analysis: The caring dictator
5.	Individual differences and traits	Chapter 3 Self-assessments 3.1 to 3.7	Exercise 3.1: Your ideal organization
			Case analysis: IKEA
6.	Power	Chapter 4 Self-assessment 4.1: Views of power	Exercise 4.1 Recognizing blocks to empowerment
			Case analysis: Dick Grasso of NYSE
			Midterm examination
7.	Contingency models: Using resources effectively Fiedler's model	Chapter 5 Self-assessment 5.1: LPC Self-assessment 5.2: Assessing the leadership situation	Exercise 5.1: Changing leader's sit con

Week	Topic	Reading and other assignments	Class activity
8.	Contingency models: Using resources effectively Normative decision, and cognitive resource theory Contingency models: Introduction to exchange and relationship development models	Chapter 5 Chapter 6	Exercise 5.2: Using the normative decision model Case analysis: Mary Kay Ash and Bill Gates
9.	Contingency models: Exchange and relationship development Path- Goal, Attributional model, LMX	Chapter 6 Self-assessment 6.1: Identifying your in-group/out-group	Exercise 6.1: Removing obstacles Exercise 6.2: In-group/out-group
10.	Relationship management models (continued): Substitutes for leadership and situational leadership Participative leadership and leading teams	Chapter 6 Self-assessment 6.2: Leadership substitutes Chapter 7 Self-assessment 7.1: Delegation	Case analysis: Michael Abrashoff of the U.S. Navy Exercise 7.1: To delegate or not to delegate?
11.	Leading teams, and super leadership	Chapter 7 Self-assessment 7.2: Are you a team leader	Exercise 7.2: Strategies for becoming a superleader Case analysis: Whole Foods
12.	Change-oriented leadership	Chapter 8 Self-assessment 8.1: Building credibility	Exercise 8.1: Do you know a charismatic leader? Exercise 8.2: Charismatic speech Case analysis: Andrea Jung of Avon
13.	Strategic leadership	Chapter 9 Self-assessment 9.1: Strategic leadership type	Exercise 9.1: Understanding strategic forces Exercise 9.2: Your organization Exercise 9.3: The influence process Case analysis: A.G. Lafley of P&G

Week	Topic	Reading and other assignments	Class activity
14.	Looking at the future	Chapter 10	
15.			Final examination

Sample course outline for 15 week with two 75 - minute periods a week

Session	Topic	Reading	Class activity
1.	Introduction: Definitions		
2.	Functions of leaders	Chapter 1	Exercise 1.1: What is leadership?
			Exercise 1.4: Understanding the leadership context
3.	Role of leadership	Chapter 1	Exercise 1.2: Images of leadership
			Case analysis: JetBlue
4.	Cross-cultural models	Chapter 1	Exercise 1.3: Narian bridges
5.	History of leadership	Chapter 2	Exercise 2.1: Old wines
			Exercise 2.3: Leadership and gender
6.	Current approaches	Chapter 2	Case analysis: The caring dictator
7.	Current approaches	Chapter 2	Exercise 2.2: The toy factory
8.	Individual differences: Locus of control, Type A	Chapter 3 Self-assessment 3.1 to 3.7	
9.	Individual differences: MBTI, Self-monitoring, Mach	Chapter 3	Case analysis: IKEA
10.	Individual differences	Chapter 3	Exercise 3.1: Your ideal organization
11.	Understanding power	Chapter 4 Self-assessment 4.1: Views of powers	Exercise 4.2: Recognizing blocks to empowerment
12.	Changing faces of power	Chapter 4	Case analysis: Dick Grasso of NYSE
13.			Midterm examination
14.	Contingency models: Fiedler	Chapter 5 Self-assessment 5.1: LPC Self-assessment 5.2: Assessing the leadership situation	Exercise 5.1: Changing the leader's sit con

Session	Topic	Reading	Class activity
15.	Contingency models: The Normative decision model	Chapter 5	Exercise 5.2: Using the normative decision model
16.	Contingency models (continued) Introduction to exchange and relationship development models	Chapter 5 Chapter 6	Case analysis: Mary Kay Ash and Bill Gates
17.	Contingency models: Path-goal, attributional model, LMX	Chapter 6 Self-assessment 6.1: Identifying your in-group/out-group	Exercise 6.1: Removing obstacles
18.	Contingency models: LMX and substitutes	Chapter 6 Self-assessment 6.2: Leadership substitutes	Exercise 6.2: In-group/out-group Case analysis: Michael Abrashoff of the U.S. Navy
19.	Participative leadership	Chapter 7 Self-assessment 7.1: Delegation	Exercise 7.1: To delegate or not to delegate?
20.	Teams and superleadership	Chapter 7 Self-assessment 7.2: Are you a team leader?	Exercise 7.2: Strategies for becoming a super leader Case analysis: Whole Foods
21.	Change-oriented leadership concepts	Chapter 8	Exercise 8.1: Do you know a charismatic leader?
22.	Change-oriented leadership: Charismatic leadership	Chapter 8 Self-assessment 8.1: Building credibility	Exercise 8.2: Charismatic speech
23.	Change-oriented leadership: Transformational leadership	Chapter 8	
24.	Change-oriented leadership: Visionary leadership	Chapter 8	Case analysis: Andrea Jung of Avon
25	Strategic leadership	Chapter 9	Exercise 9.1: Understanding strategic forces
26.	Strategic leadership	Chapter 9 Self-assessment 9.1: Strategic leadership type	Exercise 9.2: Your organization Exercise 9.3: The influence process
27.	Strategic leadership	Chapter 9	Case analysis: A.G. Lafley of P&G

Week	Topic	Reading and other assignments	Class activity
28.	Looking at the future: What we know	Chapter 10	
29.	Looking at the future: What comes next	Chapter 10	
30.			Final examination

SUMMARY OF EXERCISES AND SUGGESTED ASSIGNMENTS

The table below presents a summary of all the self-assessments and exercises at the end of each chapter in the text. The table indicates 1) whether the activities require individual or group work - in some cases both, 2) whether they can be done in class, or require work at home, 3) the approximate time needed to complete the activity, 4) the complexity level, and 5) whether the activity can be used as a course assignment.

Individual or group

The rating of individual (I) or group (G) indicates whether students have to work on this activity by themselves or in groups. In many cases both are required, as students have to complete an individual section before moving to group activities (e.g., Exercise 4.1 "Recognizing blocks to empowerment"). Some activities require no prior individual work or are too complex for individual students to complete alone. Others, such as the self-assessments, require only individual work.

In class or at home

Some of the activities can be assigned as homework for students to complete outside of class. These are marked "H." Others require work in class either individually or in groups; they are indicated by "C".

Time needed

The time estimates provided are approximate minimum time required to complete an activity. Ten minutes is used as the base minimum, although many of the self-assessments are likely to take the students less than 10 minutes to complete. The majority of exercises requires around 30 minutes. The time needed often varies depending on class size.

Complexity level

A rating of 1, 2, and 3 is used to evaluate the complexity level of each activity.

- 1 = Low complexity

This rating indicates simple exercises that do not require a high level of skill or major time commitment. For example, the first two activities (Exercise 1.1 and 1.2) are both rated as a "1." They are both appropriate for getting the faculty and the student used to experiential exercises. Most of the self-assessments, which the students will be doing on their own, are also rated as low complexity.

- 2 = Moderate complexity

This rating indicates that the activity requires some skills, and generally a time commitment of 30 minutes or longer. For example, Exercise 4.1 "Recognizing blocks to empowerment," and 5.2, "When are you most effective?" are rated as a "2" because they require students to integrate information from the chapters in order to complete the exercise.

- 3 = High complexity

A rating of 3 indicates that the activity is complex and time consuming. Activities rated as a "3" either require complex role plays (e.g., Exercise 1.3 "Narian bridges"), or complex integration and application of course concepts (e.g., Exercise 5.3, "Using the Normative decision model," and 8.2, "Charismatic speech").

Course assignment

 This symbol in the table and in the Leader's Handbook indicates that the activity is well suited for use as a course assignment - graded or otherwise. The assignments are described throughout the handbook.

Activities and Assignments

Activity and page number	Individual (I) or Group (G)	Home (H) or in class (C)	Time needed	Complexity level	Appropriate for course assignment
Chapter 1					
Leadership challenge: Juggling cultures (p. 27)	I and G	H or C	15 minutes	1	✎
Exercise 1.1: What is leadership (p. 29)	I and G	C	25 minutes	1	
Exercise 1.2: Images of leadership (p. 30)	G	C	25 minutes	1	
Exercise 1.3: Narian Bridges (p. 31)	G	C	60 minutes	3	
Exercise 1.4: Understanding the leadership context (p. 33)	I and G	H or C	25 minutes	3	✎
Chapter 2					
Leadership challenge: Selecting team members (p. 54)	I and G	H or C	20 minutes for class discussion; may require preparation outside of class	1	✎
Exercise 2.1: Old wines in new skins (p. 56)	G	C	30 minutes	2	
Exercise 2.2: The toy factory (p. 57)	G	C	75 minutes	3	
Exercise 2.3: Leadership and Gender (p. 58)	I	H or C	30 minutes	2	
Chapter 3					
Leadership challenge: Using psychological testing (p. 88)	I and G	H or C	15 minutes	1	✎
Exercise 3.1: Your ideal organization (p. 90)	I and G	C	30 minutes	2	
Self-assessment 3.1: Value systems (p. 91)	I	H	10 minutes	1	✎
Self-assessment 3.2: Emotional intelligence (p. 92)	I	H	15 minutes	1	✎

Activity and page number	Individual (I) or Group (G)	Home (H) or in class (C)	Time needed	Complexity level	Appropriate for course assignment
Self-assessment 3.3: Locus of control (p. 94)	I	H	10 minutes	1	✎
Self-assessment 3.4: Type A (p. 95)	I	H	10 minutes	1	✎
Self assessment 3.5: Self monitoring (p. 96)	I	H	10 minutes	1	✎
Self-assessment 3.6: MBTI (p. 97)	I	H	10 minutes	1	✎
Self-assessment 3.7: Machiavellianism (p. 99)	I	H	10 minutes	1	✎
Chapter 4					
Leadership challenge: How much is enough (p. 125)	I and G	H or C	15 minutes	1	✎
Exercise 4.1: Recognizing blocks to empowerment (p. 127)	I and G	H or C	30 minutes	2	✎
Self assessment 4.1: Views of power (p. 128)	I	H	10 minutes	1	
Chapter 5					
Leadership challenge: Creating Crisis: Performance vs. morale (p. 151)	I and G	H or C	15 minutes	1	✎
Exercise 5.1: Changing the leader's sit con (p. 153)	I	H or C	15 minutes	1	✎
Exercise 5.2: Using the Normative Decision model (p. 155)	I and G	H and C	45 minutes	3	✎
Exercise 5.3: Creating an atmosphere that encourages participation (p. 159)	I	H	10 minutes	1	
Self-assessment 5.1: LPC (p.160)	I	H	10 minutes	2	
Self-assessment 5.2: Assessing a leadership situation (p.161)	I	H or C	15 minutes	2	✎

Activity and page number	Individual (I) or Group (G)	Home (H) or in class (C)	Time needed	Complexity level	Appropriate for course assignment
Chapter 6					
Leadership challenge: The in-group applicant (p. 185)	I and G	H or C	15 minutes	1	✎
Exercise 6.1: Removing obstacles (p. 187)	I	H	30 minutes	2	✎
Exercise 6.2: In-group/ out-group (p. 189)	G	C	20 minutes	1	
Self assessment 6.1: Identifying your in-group and out-group (p. 191)	I	H	15 minutes	2	✎
Self-assessment 6.2: Leadership substitutes (p. 193)	I	H	10 minutes	2	✎
Chapter 7					
Leadership challenge: Who gets the project (p. 218)	I and G	H or C	15 minutes	1	✎
Exercise 7.1: To delegate or not delegate (p. 220)	G	C	45 minutes	3	
Exercise 7.2: Strategies for becoming a super-leader (p. 222)	I	H	45 minutes	3	✎
Self-assessment 7.1: Delegation scale (p. 225)	I	H	10 minutes	1	
Self-assessment 7.2: Are you a team leader (p. 226)	I	H	10 minutes	1	
Chapter 8					
Leadership challenge: Standing up to a charismatic but unethical leader (p. 250)	I and G	H or C	15 minutes	1	✎
Exercise 8.1: Do you know a charismatic leader? (p. 252)	I or G	H or C	10 minutes	2	
Exercise 8.2: Charismatic speech (p. 254)	G	H and C	60 minutes	3	✎

Activity and page number	Individual (I) or Group (G)	Home (H) or in class (C)	Time needed	Complexity level	Appropriate for course assignment
Self-assessment 8.1: Building credibility (p. 255)	I	H	15 minutes	2	✐
Chapter 9					
Leadership challenge: BODs and CEOs (p. 282)	I and G	H or C	15 minutes	1	✐
Exercise 9.1: Understanding strategic forces (p. 284)	G	C	30 minutes	2	✐
Exercise 9.2: Your organization (p. 286)	I and G	C	25 minutes	2	
Exercise 9.3: Influence process (p. 287)	I and G	C	30 minutes	2	✐
Self-assessment 9.1: What is your strategic leadership type? (p. 289)	I	H	15 minutes	1	
Chapter 10					
Self-assessment 10.1: My personal mission statement (p. 306)	I	H or C	30 minutes	2	✐

SECTION TWO

CHAPTER MATERIALS

PART ONE

BUILDING BLOCKS

CHAPTER 1

DEFINITION AND SIGNIFICANCE OF LEADERSHIP

Chapter Overview

This chapter introduces students to the concept of leadership and leadership effectiveness by providing working definitions and by emphasizing the cultural limitations of the concepts. It presents several cultural models that are used throughout the text to explain cross-cultural difference in leadership. The applicability and limitations of existing models and theories are discussed. Obstacles to effectiveness and the differences between leadership and management are presented. Roles and functions of leaders are outlined followed by a presentation of the arguments regarding the importance of leadership in organizational performance.

Chapter Objectives

OBJECTIVES	THROUGH BASIC TEXT	THROUGH FEATURES, TABLES, FIGURES, AND EXAMPLES	THROUGH EXERCISES
Define leadership and effectiveness	✓	Lorraine Monroe, Mary Sammons, Mitt Romney, Joyce Wycoff (p. 4) Barbara Waugh, John Hickenlooper, Father Francis Kline, Chik-fil-A (p. 5); New York Times, Hugo Chavez, and Bill Clinton (p.6) "Leading Change: Samll Dog Electronics" (p. 7)	Exercise 1.1 (p. 29) Exercise 1.2 (p. 30)
Identify the cultural values that have the potential to affect leadership Hall Hofstede Trompenaars GLOBE	✓	New York Times, David Peterson, Richard Tuck and Roger Abramson, (p. 9); Bill Clinton, G.W. Bush, and Vincente Fox (p. 10) Figure 1.1 (p. 8); Table 1.1 (p. 11); Figure 1.2 (p. 13); Table 1.2 (p. 15) "Leadership on the cutting edge: New iviews of culture in management" (p. 16)	Leadership Challenge (p. 27) Exercise 1.3 (p. 31)

Discuss major obstacles to effective leadership	✔		Exercise 1.4 (p. 33)
Compare and contrast leadership and management and understand their similarities and differences	✔	Carol Hymowitz and Carol Bartz (p. 17) Table 1.3 (p. 18)	Exercise 1.2 (p. 30)
List the basic roles and functions of management, and be aware of cultural differences in the use and application of those functions	✔	Francis Hesselbein,, Nancy Bador, Barbara Grogan, Meg Whitman, Gerry Laybourne, Cherri Musser, Darla Moore (p. 20) Ben Cohen, and Jerry Greenfield, Tyler Winkler (p. 21) Figure 1.3 (p. 21) Bob Ladouceur; Jack Welch (p. 22) "Effective Leadership from the Grassroots" Using culture to be effective" (p. 23)	Exercise 1.1 (p. 290 Exercise 1.2 (p. 30) Exercise 1.3 (p. 31)
Summarize the debate over the role and impact of leadership in organizations	✔	Robinson, Anne Mulcahy, and Hugo Chavez (p. 23) Table 1.4 (p. 25)	Exercise 1.4 (p. 33)

Chapter Outline

1. What is an effective leader?

    a. Who is a leader?

    A leader is defined as any person who influences individuals and groups within an organization, helps them in the establishment of goals, and guides them toward achievement of those goals, thereby allowing them to be effective.

    The definition includes three elements: 1) group process; there are no leaders without followers, 2) goal orientation, and 3) hierarchical relationship

    b. What is effectiveness?

    Definition includes internal stability and health, external adaptability, and goal achievement.

    A leader is effective when his or followers achieve their goals, can function well together, and can adapt to the changing demands from external forces

Leading Change: Don and Hapy Mayer are the owners and managers of Small Dog Electronics, the largest reseller of Apple computers in New England. The father and son team built their company around the love of animals and have created a company with a highly informal and effective culture. Small Dog not only takes care of it its customers and employees, it also is highly profitable and considered to be one of the best in its industry, and an active community contributor. With high profits and very low turnover, the company provides an example of how a company based on the leaders' passion can address multiple stakeholders well.

2. Culture and Leadership

   Culture consists of the commonly held values within a group of people and includes norms, customs, values, and assumptions that guide behavior.

   a. Three levels of culture are identified. These are: national, ethnic or other cultural groups within a nation, and organization culture (Figure 1.1).

   b. Four models for understanding culture are presented. These are: Hall's high and low context framework, Hofstede's five cultural dimensions (Table 1.1), Trompenaars dimensions of culture (Figure 1.2), and GLOBE (Table 1.2)

   Power points slides provide additional information about a further addition to the Hofstede's concept of individualism/collectivism proposed by Harry Triandis. The concept of Vertical and Horizontal individualism/collectivism refines the dimension by introducing the issue of hierarchy vs. egalitarianism. Vertical cultures are hierarchy based, whereas horizontal ones are egalitarian.

   Leadership on the Cutting Edge presents the research of European researchers Anne-Marie Søderberg and Nigel Holder who suggest that the tradition view of culture as a relatively stable and consistent system that can be a barrier to interaction is inaccurate and outdates. Instead the researchers propose that our new definition of culture must consider how different national and organizational cultures continuously interact to create new cultures that are the result of the contexts where individuals and groups live and work. Individuals often have to make sense of multiple cultures and construct new identities that combine their national and organizational cultures.

3. Obstacles to effective leadership

   Discussion of obstacles to effective leadership focuses on the need to practice various leadership skills in an atmosphere that encourages experimentation and tolerates mistakes. Organizational rigidity, lack of opportunity for practice, uncertainty, organizational complexity, and inaccessible academic research are all obstacles to effective leadership

4. Leadership and management

   Arguments about the difference between leadership and management are presented. Leaders are considered by some to be visionary and future-oriented, whereas managers focus on day-to-day routine activities (Table 1.3). The section concludes that effective managers often perform many of the duties and activities ascribed to leaders thereby making the distinction between the two concepts somewhat unnecessary.

5. Roles and functions of leaders

   a. Managerial roles

      Section presents Mintzberg's research on managerial roles and discusses cultural and gender differences in those roles. Particularly research that has found that female managers work at a calmer pace with closer contact with their followers and a more reflective approach is

21

presented. The concept of web structure is used to describe the style and structure used by women managers.

b. Function of the leader in creation and maintenance of an organizational culture

The key role of leaders in the creation and maintenance of an organization's culture is discussed. The processes used by leaders to shape culture are: role modeling, setting up the reward system, hiring decisions, and decisions regarding strategy and structure (Figure 1.3).

Effective Leadership from the Grassroots outlines the key factors for managers to build the culture of their organization. They include: Clear definition of desired culture, sharing with employees, adjusting the reward system, attention to details, and "walking the talk."

6. Does leadership make a difference?

Arguments over the impact of leadership in organizations are presented in this section. In spite of strong popular beliefs that leaders are important, research findings have not been very supportive of the concept.

a. Arguments against the impact of leadership

Research findings with a strong sociological focus point to the minimal impact of leaders in organizations. External organizational factors, economic forces, and the leader's limited discretion are used as reasons why leaders have limited impact (Table 1.4)

b. Arguments for the impact of leadership

Brief review of research supporting the "leader has impact" theory is presented (Table 1.4)

c. Reconciling the differences

The impact of the leader is often affected by situational characteristics that limit his/her power and discretion. These factors are described in detail in chapters 6, and 9. The view that leaders impact their organizations directly through their actions and decisions, or indirectly through the vision they provide, is reaffirmed.

7. Summary and conclusion

Searching the Web

The Globe Web site

www.ucalgary.ca/mg/GLOBE/Public/

The GLOBE web site presents a summary of the research activities including a brief history, a complete list of 61 countries included in GLOBE and the researchers who contributed to the study. Additionally, the web site provides access to several full-text GLOBE related publications.

The GLOBE web site is an excellent starting point for students interested in further research about the GLOBE findings.

Mintzberg's managerial role

www.brunel.ac.uk/~bustcfj/bola/mintzberg/mintzberg2.html

> The web site provides information about the three managerial activities that Mintzberg has proposed and a detailed description of Minzberg's 10 managerial roles that fall within those activities. The activities include: interpersonal relationships, information processing, and decision making. The ten managerial role are: figurehead, leader, monitor liaison, disseminator, spokesman, initiator/changer, disturbance handler, resource allocator, negotiator.

Women leadership styles

www.winaz.org/female-leadership.html

> The WIN (Women in Networking) web site is a hands-on networking tool for women in business. It includes links to scholarship and community outreach opportunities and a member's only area for direct contact with other WIN members. It also includes an array of articles detailing a variety of topics including this article which discusses two unique qualities of women's leadership.

List and description of "Best Bosses"

www.winningworkplaces.org/services/award/bestbosses2004.php

> The Winning Workplace website features profiles of the 15 winners of the 2004 "Best Bosses" competition put on by FSB (Fortune Small Business), a subsidiary of Fortune Magazine. Students may follow hyper-links to a detailed profile of each leader including strategies, revenue, and leadership styles. In addition to the winners, many distinguished finalists are profiled, which offers further insight into leadership styles and team building.

Cross-cultural historical leader profiles

> A rich website brimming with everything from detailed profiles of histories most successful and effective leaders, to a pool of resources including articles, links, and book reviews all offering an abundance of practical leadership information. The following links below lead to detailed profiles on each specific leader including biographies, backgrounds, values, and how each leader did or did not use the 4 E's of leadership: Envision, Enable, Empower, and Energize.

> Genghis Khan: www.leader-values.com/Content/detail.asp?ContentDetailID=799

> Gandhi: www.leader-values.com/Content/detail.asp?ContentDetailID=795

> Miyamoto Musashi: www.leader-values.com/Content/detail.asp?ContentDetailID=801

Leadership and management

www.sba.gov/managing/leadership/leadvmanage.html

> Starting with an article that covers the sharp differences between leading and managing, this website features a variety of helpful resources for both novice and well seasoned small business owners alike. It includes a number of articles detailing Leadership Traits, Leading Change, and Business Ethics, plus an extensive how-to section for would-be small business start ups.

The Leadership Challenge

The leadership challenge for this chapter focuses on the impact of culture. The dilemma for the leader is to balance culture, organizational needs, fairness, and legal standards. Some of the issues that students must consider before making their decision are:

- **The Saudi culture.** Saudi Arabia is a Muslim country where because of religious traditions and requirements, women have practically no role in public life and business transactions. Women are not only covered from head to toe when out in public, they are also often segregated from men. Although these standards are not as strictly enforced on non-Muslim and Western women, they still find their freedom highly restricted when traveling or living in Saudi Arabia. In addition to the limited role of women the Saudi culture is generally high-context, collectivistic, power and status-oriented, ascriptive in that who you are is more important than your performance, and with a long-term orientation. Students should be directed to do some research regarding the culture. Web sites such as www.executiveplanet.com can provide a quick overview.

- **Legal requirements.** Depending on the country, there may be clear anti-discrimination laws protecting women and minorities. For example, anti-discrimination and equal opportunity apply to all U.S. companies, regardless of where they operate. Other Western countries do not have as specific legal requirements regarding discrimination. The argument that Saudi culture does not welcome women may therefore, in and of itself, not be legally defensible. Managers are required, at the very minimum to uphold the laws of the country in which they operate.

- **Company interest.** It is in the company's best interest to have its best and most experienced negotiator represent it. Sending an inexperienced person may be highly detrimental.

- **Fairness and equity.** Regardless of legal requirements, standards of fairness and equity should prevent discriminating against a person based on sex. Not sending in the female executive to Saudi Arabia, simply because she is female and she may encounter problems, is not fair or equitable and may set a bad precedence, as well as open up the company to legal action.

Given the complexity of these issues, a simple solution of is not likely to work. Sending the female executive to Saudi Arabia may not be feasible, although many foreign women function well in those environments. They are often treated as a "third gender," neither male, nor quite female. Whether this would work in this case depends on the existing relationship with the Saudi clients. Some possible solutions may be:

- Holding negotiations in another country, such as the United Arab Emirates, Egypt, or Lebanon which are all close to Saudi Arabia, but not as restrictive concerning the role of women may provide a comfortable compromise.

- Sending the female executive's manager, if it is a male, along as the front person. She could then provide "support" to her boss.

- Hiring a local or third party negotiator that would report to and work with the female executive.

Some solutions that students often propose but that are not workable are:

- Sending the junior male executive as the primary front person with the backing of the female executive, having her act as her subordinate.

- Ignoring culture altogether and telling the clients that discrimination against women is wrong

- Giving up the contract because Saudis discriminate against women

Chapter 1 Experiential Exercises

Exercise 1.1: What is leadership?

This exercise is designed to help students develop a personal definition of leadership and understand how their personal view of ideal leadership affects their assumptions and future behaviors as leaders. The exercise can be used in a variety of ways, from a cooperative learning exercise as presented in the text, to an individual assignment focusing on only the first step.

Total time: Minimum 25 minutes; Maximum time depends on number of students and groups.

Materials needed: Paper and pencil; use of board; flip chart can be useful for development of group definitions and presentations.

Part 1: Describe Ideal Leader (Individual work; 5-10 minutes)

Either as a homework assignment or as an in-class exercise, ask students to list the desirable and undesirable characteristics of their ideal leader. The desirable characteristics are sometimes easier than the undesirable ones. You can help students with the second category by asking them to consider characteristics and behaviors that their ideal leader would not have. For example "my ideal leader would not make arbitrary decisions, or would not be indecisive." Although some overlap is to be expected, students should be encouraged to avoid simply listing opposite characteristics in the two lists.

Examples of typical items listed by students

Desirable	*Undesirable*
Integrity	Autocratic leadership
Good interpersonal skills	No concern for others
Enthusiasm	Dishonesty
Decisiveness	Manipulativeness
Competence	Arbitrariness
Charisma	Self-centeredness
Good communication skills	Unresponsiveness
Openness to others' ideas	Closed-mindedness
Participative decision making	Unwillingness to accept feedback
Vision	

Option: The personal list developed by each student can be used as a basis for evaluating what students have learned in class and how their thinking has evolved, their assumptions have been changed or been reaffirmed. The lists can be collected by the instructor and handed back the last week of class.

Part 2: Develop Group Definition (Group work; 10-20 minutes)

As with all group exercises in the book, the instructor has the option of either assigning groups or allowing students to select their own groups. Groups of larger than six tend to be inefficient and often have trouble reaching a group decision in the limited time allocated in class. Ideal size is four to five members.

Ask students to keep their own list intact and write the group list on a separate piece of paper.

This part of the exercise often generates considerable in-group discussion as students compare their lists. Although some common items are listed by different students, there are also many that show up only on one or two people's lists. Through the discussion, students realize the highly personal nature of definitions of leadership. If the groups are culturally diverse, cultural differences in leadership may also surface. Similarly, there often is a gender difference in images of ideal leadership. For example, decisiveness and "in charge" characteristics are more often part of male students' definitions than part of female students'.

Option: Groups can be assigned based on gender or other cultural characteristics to accentuate cultural differences and focus discussion on the cultural elements of ideal leadership.

Part 3: Present and Defend (7 minutes per group)

Each group is asked to make a 3 to 5 minute presentation listing their ideal leader's desirable and undesirable characteristics and briefly explaining the reason for their choices.

Option Group presentations can be replaced by instructor asking each group for their first, second, third, etc.. characteristic in a round robin fashion until all items are recorded on the board.

Part 4: Common Themes (Class discussion; 10-15 minutes)

Part 4 focuses on in-class discussion of images of ideal leadership. The lists generated by the groups are used as the basis for this discussion. The focus should be on the complexity and diversity of leadership images and the implications for understanding the process of leadership.

With the recent push towards empowerment and participative decision making, common themes among students' list often include issues of participation, autonomy, having a vision as essential to ideal leadership. Undesirable characteristics often focus around lack of integrity, too much control, and inability to motivate followers.

The discussion can include cross-cultural differences in leadership. The instructor or the students can bring in material about how culture impacts our images of ideal leadership. Hosftede's cultural dimensions also provide a good basis for discussion. For example, in high power distance and uncertainty avoidance cultures, ideal leaders are likely to be expected to provide answers to all follower questions. Additionally, expectations of employee participation and empowerment are likely to be low. In masculine cultures, the element of taking care of followers is likely to be less pronounced than in feminine cultures. Concern for individuals and individual attention to followers is likely to be lower in collectivist than in individualist cultures.

Overall: This is a very simple exercise for both students and faculty. It can serve as a nice ice breaker the first week of class and help point out the richness of concept and process of leadership and prepare students for the broad diversity of topics and issues that will be discussed throughout the semester.

Exercise 1.2: Images of Leadership

As with Exercise 1.1, this exercise is designed to help students clarify their personal assumptions about leadership. It can be used alone or in conjunction with Exercise 1.1. Using images to clarify ideal leadership is generally appealing to students. Although the exercise has a group-discussion component, the exercise is not designed as a cooperative learning exercise. Group discussions help students fine-tune and clarify their personal definitions.

Total time: Minimum 25 minutes

Materials needed: Paper and pencil; use of board by instructor.

Part 1: Select your image (Individual work; 5-7 minutes)

Similar to the popular organizational metaphor exercise, students are encouraged to develop their personal image or metaphor of leaders. Commonly used metaphors include leader as:

Sport coach	Orchestra conductor	Head of family
Team facilitator	Jungle/safari guide	Therapist
Train engineer	Ringmaster	Obstacle remover

Ask students to pick an image/metaphor and list the implications of that metaphor for the role and behavioral expectations of leaders. For example, an orchestra conductor is the undeniable leader of the orchestra; nothing happens without his/her direction. He/she is in full control and often dictates the actions of others. The organization, on the other hand, is fully synchronized and acts in total coordination and unison. The head of the family is similarly in full control, although the sense of total cooperation and focused action is lacking. The head of a family has responsibility for the emotional and psychological well-being of members, a factor that is lacking from an orchestra. The issue of conflict is also part of a family much more so than an orchestra.

Students are often very creative with their images. The instructor's goal should be to guide them in the understanding of the implications of the image they select.

Part 2: Share and Clarify (Small group discussion; 10-15 minutes)

Small groups can be used as a sounding board for students to help them clarify the implications of the image that appeals to them.

Option: This step can be skipped to move directly to class-discussion, especially in small classes (under 25 students) where whole-class discussions are possible. Having small group discussions allows students to fine-tune their images and think about the consequences.

Part 3: Class Discussion (10-15 minutes)

The discussion questions allow for exploration of various images and their implications for organizations. Some images are becoming obsolete while others are gaining ground. For example, team facilitator is a very popular metaphor although students are often not fully aware of the implication of such an image for the structure of an organization or its potential short-comings. Namely, team facilitators do not make decisions for their teams; their role is to support, guide, and encourage. The implications of such a style in times of crisis when quick decision making is essential need to be explored.

Option: As with Exercise 1.1, discussion of cross-cultural differences in images of leadership is very appropriate. Particularly, the diversity of images that are used in the U.S. can be pointed out as resulting from the cultural diversity within the population.

Overall: As with Exercise 1.1, Exercise 1.2 is very simple and easy to execute. The development of images triggers lively and interesting discussion among the students and makes this an ideal ice breaker for the first week of class.

Exercise 1.3: Narian Bridges

Narian Bridges is a very engaging cross-cultural role play designed to allow students to experience the challenges of interacting with different cultures. Although no out-of-class preparation is needed for the students, the instructor needs to decide on team assignments prior to class. You can expect considerable frustration on the part of U.S. teams and lively discussion about how to deal with cross-cultural differences and conflicting goals.

Total time: Minimum 60 minutes.

Materials needed: Access to 2 separate rooms (quiet hallway or sitting area) to allow for separate planning for each cultural group.

Part 1: Background (Individual reading; 10 minutes)

Ask all students to read "Background" information on pp. 21-22.

Instructor's Preparation: The instructor needs to decide on team assignments prior to class. The only restriction is that Mr. Dafti has to be male; all other roles can be assigned to either male or female students. Selection of students to play Narian or U.S. roles can be made randomly or based on each student's personal characteristics. For example, students who show "typical" American characteristics, such as assertiveness and directness, can be assigned to the U.S. team to emphasize those roles, or they can be put in Narian teams to allow them to experience a different culture.

Both the Narian and US team can function with just two members. Depending on class size, some teams may have three members while others only two. Keeping the Narian and US teams at no more than three allows for all members to participate. Students assigned to teams larger than three are unlikely to have the opportunity to role play.

For each role-play group, assign:

Narian Team	U.S. Team
Mr. Dafti (male student)	U.S. team leader
Naran	Team member 1
Touran (optional)	Team member 2 (optional)

Call students' names and pair them up with their Narian and U.S. role play groups before you provide further instructions. There is no restriction on the overall number of role play groups.

Provide students with role play instruction sheets appropriate for their role (see end of this chapter).

Part 2: Role Play (Preparation: 15 minutes; Role play: 15-20 minutes)

Preparation: Separate the Narian and U.S. teams by sending U.S. team to another room. Review instructions on the role play sheets with Narians and US separately, reminding each group about basic role-play rules:

- Stay in the general guidelines provided by your role

- Improvise as needed while keeping goal in mind

- Practice role for a few minutes alone or with your team

- Provide rich role play so that others can respond to you

- Be as creative as you feel comfortable; some of the students will play roles more intensely than others; differences are normal

In helping each group of students prepare for their roles while answering their questions, the instructor can provide them with the following information.

Narian teams: The description of Narian culture matches that of a high power distance, feminine, vertical collectivist culture with moderate uncertainty avoidance. The culture has many elements of middle-eastern cultures. Students find the highly differentiated but equal gender roles both surprising and comfortable. Issues that need to be emphasized in preparing students to role play Narians are:

- Maintain good interpersonal relations in all situations

- Avoid open conflict and disagreement among yourselves and with U.S. teams

- Be very respectful and polite with one another and with U.S. team

- Appear confident, stick to your ground without being rude and confrontational

- Remember that you know the U.S. culture and language well

- Keep the social goal of the meeting in mind at all times; this is not a negotiation session

U.S. teams: Initially, the U.S. team members have an easier task since they are role-playing a culture with which they are familiar. The U.S. culture is moderate-to-low power distance, masculine, individualistic, and tolerant of uncertainty. Issues that need to be emphasized in preparing students to role-play U.S. team members are:

- Remember that your goal is changing the contract and that your success depends on getting Dafti to agree with the changes

- Appear confident and knowledgeable

- Rely on your relationship with the two Narian associates, Naran and Touran, and on your information about Narian culture

- Remember that the Narians speak English well and are familiar with U.S. culture

Once both groups are prepared (approximately 15 minutes), invite the U.S. team back and inform them that they have a maximum of 20 minutes for the role play. Each group of U.S. and Narian teams can sit in clusters to start their interaction.

Part 3: Debriefing (Class discussion; 20-30 minutes)

The role-play is likely to cause much frustration for US team members who will in most cases not achieve their goals. The Narian members are likely to observe the pushiness of US teams. Class debriefing can start with allowing each role-play group to describe the interaction and the outcome while students share their role-play instructions with their counterparts.

Discussion should include issues of goal differences, rudeness of one culture vs. the other's unwillingness to talk business, and potential solutions. Other discussion themes can include:

- **Leadership differences**: The Narians consider their leader to be the infallible head of their family. There is strong loyalty and sense of respect. As a result, they will not disagree with their leader and will not be co-opted by the U.S. team members even when their leader is "wrong." Such views sharply differ with those of the U.S. teams who have the "correct" solution and put the objective truth ahead of respect for the leader.

- **How to handle goal differences**: All role-play groups are likely to have been frustrated because of their divergent goals. Discussion of and solutions for how to handle such differences are often lively. Many U.S. teams find a partial solution that satisfies the Narians by focusing on long-term accomplishments.

Overall: The Narian Bridges is a powerful role-play that works even with students and instructors who have limited experience at role play or cross-cultural situations. The issues at play tie in directly with the cultural dimensions presented in the chapter.

Exercise 1.4: Understanding the Leadership Context

This exercise is designed to help students understand the various contextual factors that have the potential to affect leadership. It presents a fairly complex concept and may be difficult for younger and less experienced students to grasp. However, more experienced students with some work experience, should not have any difficulty picking a leader that they know or have known and to identify the various contextual factors that affect the person's leadership concept. This exercise can be used both individually and for a group activity. The group discussions often allow students to grasp the concept of context. It also can be assigned as part of graded class assignment.

Total time: Minimum 25 minutes

Materials needed: Paper and pencil; use of board by instructor.

Individual/Group work (15 minutes)

Student should select either a leader they know and have worked with or a business or political leader with whom they are familiar. This can be done individually or as group. Once the leader is selected, the students must consider the context in which the leader operates. Not all these factors may be relevant; however, students should be encouraged to explore the context may be relevant and influence how the leader makes decisions and acts.

1. *Long-term historical, political, and economic forces* include such factors as:
   - The history of the organization, if it has been around for a while
   - The national history, if relevant (for example, the organization may have a long-standing positive or negative reputation)
   - Political factors (for example, the organization may be tied to a particular political party or system)
   - Long-term economic factors (for example, the steel industry has long-term economic factors to consider

2. *Current contemporary forces* include such factors as:
   - Cultural diversity (changes in the demographic and cultural makeup of the organization's customers and other stakeholders)
   - Social values that may affect the organization, its products and services (for example, fast food companies are affected by the increase in obesity in the U.S.)
   - Technology (for example, many organizations are seeing competitors who operate on-line services similar to theirs; or organizations are expected to provide on-line services for their customers)

- The economy
- Social changes (for example, a more conservative political and social climate may affect the products and services an organization offers or how it advertises them)

3. *The immediate context* includes such factors as:
   - The organizational culture and climate
   - The structure of the organization
   - The organization's performance
   - The products and services delivered
   - The various suppliers
   - The followers (their abilities, strengths, and weaknesses)

Option: For students who have no or limited work experience, the instructor can assign a well-known leader using articles for current headlines. I have successfully used President G.W. Bush and asked students to identify the contextual factors that have affected his decision to launch the war with Iraq. You can also compare the context two years ago to the current context. While the long-term and contemporary elements remain the same, the immediate context has changes. The contextual factors to consider in this case are:

Long-term historical, political, and economic factors:

> The Middle-East situation (Arab-Israeli conflict; Iran)
> Oil
> History of Republican party
> The U.S. as the policeman of the world

Contemporary context
> The first Gulf war
> Conservative vs. liberals
> The U.S. as the remaining superpower
> Prior actions by Bill Clinton

Immediate context
> The terrorist attacks of 9/11
> The war in Afghanistan
> The Neo-conservative agenda
> The support and dissent from traditional allies
> The conservative agenda
> The concern of a legacy
> How the task is defined (easy victory; welcome by Iraqis)
> International goals
> Domestic goals
> Followers (voters on both sides of the political lines)

Discussion and presentation (10 minutes)

Each group is asked to present their leader and outline the contextual factors that impact the leader's decisions and actions. Similarities and differences between the leaders' different context can also be discussed. The instructor can highlight how some of the contextual factors strongly influence and limit a leader's ability to make decisions or take certain course of action. For example, with president Bush as the example, the first Gulf was, the 9/11 attacks, and the conservative agenda all provided a very strong context that determined many of his actions.

Overall: The Leadership Context exercise is a powerful way to focus students' attention on the importance of the leadership context instead of looking only at the leader characteristics.

Narian Bridges Role Play Instructions

Instructions for Mr. Dafti

Your culture focuses on harmony and respect for tradition and authority. You are taught from very early in life that disagreeing with others is rude and a sign of selfishness. Differences in points of view are expressed very gently and in an extremely roundabout way. As a result, business discussions are often veiled and lengthy. Leaders and bosses do not discuss the details of business deals. Even major contracts operate on a handshake from the leaders and there have been many conflicts with Western companies over the need to draft precise legal contracts. Narians find this aspect of Western business insulting and accept it very reluctantly.

You come from an old aristocratic Narian family with close ties to the monarchy. You have received your higher education in Europe and Austria. As is the case with many wealthy Narians, you have traveled extensively throughout the world and are very knowledgeable in the cultures and customs of European countries. Your family spends a good deal of its time in Europe every year, and your two daughters are currently going to college in France and Switzerland. However, you have less familiarity with the US, as you have only been there on two official trips.

Although you are aware of the importance of the US to your country's development, you are not very fond of their presence in Nari. You would prefer working with Europeans whom you find more cultured and more "civilized." The King, however, would like closer ties with the U.S. and has asked that U.S. companies be given every possible consideration. Americans seem to you to be rude, pushy, and unruly and lacking proper respect for tradition and authority. Your dealings with U.S. companies have led you to believe that their eagerness for contracts with your country often clashes with your culture and way of life. However, the construction company you have been working with on the bridge project has, so far, been easy to work with, and you have found the young engineer in charge of the project, whom you have met once at a cocktail party, to be charming.

The bridge project is particularly interesting to you because one of bridges that is planned is located near a number of historical and religious sites and its placement and design need to be in harmony with the environment. Therefore, you have personally made several key decisions regarding that one bridge. You are aware that the U.S. construction company is not happy about your choices, but that does not concern you as you believe that their role is to implement the wishes of your government. You have already made up your mind based on the needs of your country. Naran and Touran have been instructed to carry out your wishes and work on the details of the plans.

The head project U.S. engineer has asked for a meeting, and you are welcoming the opportunity to get to know him/her better, particularly in light of your positive first impression and your two associates' friendship with him/her.

During this meeting, your goal is to solidify the social relationship that is essential to a good business relationship.

Narian Bridges Role Play Instructions

Instructions for Naran and Touran

Your culture focuses on harmony and respect for tradition and authority. You are taught from very early in life that disagreeing with others is rude and a sign of selfishness. Differences in points of view are expressed very gently and in an extremely roundabout way. As a result, business discussion are often veiled and lengthy. Leaders and bosses do not discuss the details of business deals. Even major contracts operate on a handshake from the leaders and there have been many conflicts with Western companies over the need to draft precise legal contracts. Narians find this aspect of Western business insulting and accept it very reluctantly.

You are both from the higher levels of Narian society. You have traveled extensively around the world and are both U.S.-educated with a BS in Engineering and a Masters in Business. Like many young Narians, you find the excitement of the West, particularly the U.S., appealing. You have many American and other Western friends, and you enjoy the openness and relaxed interactions that you have with them. You have a good relationship with the U.S. project head whom you have met on a number of work and social occasions.

In spite of your interest in the West, you remain Narian at heart and you have no ambivalence about your loyalties to your culture and country. The focus on harmony and civility in your culture remains a key focus for you. Like all Narians, you have a strong respect for authority, particularly for Mr. Dafti who has been a mentor for the two of you. You also know his family very well.

You are both aware of the potential problem with one of the bridges. The head U.S. engineer has mentioned it to you. However, you have complete faith in Mr. Dafti's skills as an engineer and a manager. You have found the U.S. construction company's insistence on change irritating and have interpreted it as a typical sign of Western impatience and lack of knowledge of Nari. You have tried to explain the reasons to the U.S. engineer without being rude, but you are not sure that you were able to get through. You are welcoming the opportunity for Mr. Dafti to get to know the head project engineer in order to establish better relations. Your role as Mr. Dafti's associates is to hash out the finer details later.

During this meeting, your goal is to solidify the social relationship that is essential to a good business relationship. You also want to avoid any potential conflict that may jeopardize Mr. Dafti's trust of the new U.S. associates.

Narian Bridges Role Play Instructions

Instructions for the head U.S. engineer

The Narian Bridge Project is key to your company's success. Although your company has done a lot of business all over the world, this is the first time it has been able to win a contract in Nari by beating several European firms in what appeared to be a secret, very confusing negotiation process. You are still not sure why you were awarded the contract, but are confident that you can perform.

You have been with your company for eight years. As a result of your focus on international management in your MBA, your excellent technical skills, your outstanding performance, and your interest in foreign assignments, you have been put in charge of the key Narian project. You have already spent 3 successful years overseas, 6 months of which were spent in another middle-eastern country. You have been in Nari for 2 months and have very much enjoyed your stay. The culture is very warm and you have made friends with many young Western educated Narians who seem to share many of your values. You have even been trying to recruit several of them to leave Nari to join your firm, but have so far been unsuccessful.

You have instructions from your company to finalize the details of the bridges. Particularly, you need to change the design on one of the bridges. Although you have not had the opportunity to go to the site, your team has. Their analysis, and you agree with it, clearly shows that the location selected for one of the bridges and the design that has been proposed is unworkable. You are proposing to move the location by only three miles and build a much simpler and more functional bridge. Unless you can change the design, you will not be able to complete the project.

Your associates have also been in Nari for over 6 months. Like you, they speak a few words of Narian and have found the culture to be welcoming. Their background is more technical and they have the expertise to evaluate and change the design more than you, while you have expertise in international negotiations.

You are very optimistic about being able to achieve your goal of reaching a clear final agreement. You have had the contracts with the final changes drafted by your lawyers and reviewed by a Narian attorney. You have them ready for Mr. Dafti. You have met Mr. Dafti once before and found him to be charming. You are close friends with his two associates and, given their background, education and your conversations with them, you know that they are aware of the location problem. Although you have not been able to get a clear commitment from them, you think that they will support you. You were granted the meeting with Mr. Dafti within days of requesting it. You are ready to do some business!

Your goal is to obtain final agreements as soon as possible, including changes in design of that one bridge, and succeed in this contract in the hope of continued cooperation.

Narian Bridges Role Play Instructions

Instructions for the U.S. team members

The Narian Bridge Project is key to your company's success. Although your company has done a lot of business all over the world, this is the first time it has been able to win a contract in Nari by beating several European firms in what appeared to be a secret, very confusing negotiation process. You are still not sure why you were awarded the contract, but are confident that you can perform.

You each have been with your company for over five years. As a result of your excellent technical skills, your outstanding performance, and your interest in foreign assignments, you have already been assigned to several foreign countries as technical advisors on a variety of projects. You both tend to spend a limited time in each country, but you have gained considerably successful experiences. Nari has been one of your longer assignments. You have been here for over 6 months and have picked up some of the language. You have found the culture to be welcoming. You have made friends with many young Western educated Narians who seem to share many of your values.

Your role has been to hash out the technical details, and, in that capacity, you have worked with several Narian engineers and have met Naran and Touran on many occasions. Your analysis clearly shows that the location selected for one of the bridges and the design that has been proposed are unworkable. You have proposed to move the location by only three miles and build a much simpler and more functional bridge. Unless you can change the design, you will not be able to complete the project. Your attempts at discussing the problem with your Narian counterparts have not been successful. You hope that the new head U.S. engineer can negotiate the change during an upcoming meeting with Mr. Dafti.

During this meeting, your goal is to support the head U.S. engineer to obtain final agreements as soon as possible, including changes in design of that one bridge and succeed in this contract in the hope of continued cooperation.

Leadership in Action

JetBlue's David Neeleman Reinvents an Airline

Case summary

The case describes JetBlue, a small discount airline that serves mainly the eastern United States. The airline has been very successful while breaking all the rules of the industry. Its small size, dedicated staff, no-layoff policy, unusual routes, willingness to innovate have allowed it to achieve success. In spite of low prices, the airline pampers its customers with individual T.V. sets, chocolate chip cookies, and outstanding service. JetBlue's president David Neeleman relies on his employees for ideas and innovation. The airlines' "can do" attitude and its reliance on innovation play a great part in its success.

1. What are the key elements of JetBlue's culture?

   Focus on the customer, getting information from all sources, and maintaining a strong team spirit within the company are the key elements of JetBlue's culture. The company aims at pleasing its customers by pampering them and addressing their needs. JetBlue also listens to its employees, tries to create an egalitarian culture when participation is encouraged, and works on leaving the "we-they" attitude that typifies management and labor in most company behind.

2. What role does the leader play in the development and maintenance of the culture?

   Because JetBlue is still young, the impact of its founder, David Neeleman is still highly pervasive. His entrepreneurial, high-risk approach to business is evident in all aspects of the company. He is present and active in all aspects of the business. He serves as the formal leader, making key decisions, but he also serves as a role model, through his interaction with customers, his willingness to listen to his employees, his active engagement in the company, and his informal demeanor. The "image" of an effective and engaged leader is further communicated from customers and from employee to employee to reinforce his role and his power over the company. The company's creativity and willingness not to follow industry rules is also a reflection of Neeleman's entrepreneurial spirit.

The following are particularly useful references about JetBlue and David Neeleman.

Ford, R.C. 2004. David Neeleman, CEO of JetBlue Airways, on people + strategy = growth. *Academy of Management Executive*, 18(2): 139-143.

Salter, C. 2004. And now the hard part. *Fast Company* (May). Accessed online at pf.fastcompany.com/magazine/82/jetblue.html

Salter, C. 2004. Calling JetBlue. *Fast Company* (May). Accessed online at pf.fastcompany.com/magazine/82/jetblue_agents.html on October 1, 2004.

CHAPTER 2

LEADERSHIP: PAST, PRESENT, AND FUTURE

Chapter Overview

This chapter presents an overview of the history of the field of leadership by dividing it into the three eras of trait, behavior, and contingency. Recent research about leadership traits and their importance is discussed. Popular trends in leadership research and practice are also presented along with a discussion of the changes in the structure of U.S. organizations, and a review of the sources, causes, and barriers to change.

Chapter Objectives

OBJECTIVES	THROUGH BASIC TEXT	THROUGH FEATURES, TABLES, FIGURES AND EXAMPLES	THROUGH EXERCISES
Identify the three major eras in the modern study of leadership	✓		
Explain the methods, results, and shortcomings, and contributions of the trait and behavior approaches to leadership and identify their impact on current approaches	✓	Table 2.1 (p. 40)	Exercise 2.2 (p.57)
Present the elements of current contingency approaches to leadership	✓	"Effective Leadership from the Grassroots": Relying on modern leadership principles (p. 42)	Exercise 2.1 (p. 56) Exercise 2.2 (p. 57)
Discuss the current revival of trait research in understanding leadership	✓	Lisa Harper, Keith Blackwell, Steve Jobs, fumio Mitarai, Heidi Miller, Herb Kelleher, Goran Lindahl, Emilio Azcarraga, (p. 43) Michael Eisner, Andrew Nadel (p. 44)	
List the current changes in organizations and the new expectations and views of leaders	✓	Figure 2.1 (p. 46); Mitt Romney, Key Barnes,Rick Sapio, Jeff Imelt, Jane Cummins (pp. 46-47)	Exercise 2.3 (p. 58)

		"Leadership on the cutting edge: Leading for innovation" (p. 48) Figure 2.2 (p. 48) Bill Ford, Malaysia, Turkey, U.S. demographic changes (p. 49) Ted Childs. Joe Watson (p. 50) Table 2.2 (p. 50) "Leading Change: Young Female CEO in China" (p. 51)	
Barriers to change	✓	John Grundhofer, Al Dunlap, Bill George (p. 51) Marcus Buckingham, Tom Peters (p. 52)	

Chapter Outline

1. A Brief History of Modern Leadership Theory

   a. The trait era: Late 1800s to mid 1940s

   A review of the methods and results of the early scientific approach to leadership focused on identifying leadership traits is presented. The results of over 50 years of research indicate that, although some traits are correlated with leadership, no trait or combination of traits can be used to identify leaders.

   b. The behavior era: Mid 1940s to early 1970s

   The behavior approach to leadership with its focus on measuring leadership behaviors is presented. The results of the Ohio State research yielded the Leader Behavior Description Questionnaire (Table 2.1) are detailed.

   c. The contingency era: Early 1960s to present

   Elements of the currently dominant contingency approach to leadership are presented. They include:

   - There is no one best way to lead.
   - The situation and the various relevant contextual factors will help determine which style or behavior is most effective.
   - People can learn to become good leaders.
   - Leadership makes a difference in the effectiveness of groups and organizations.

   - Both the personal and situational characteristics affect leadership effectiveness.

   Effective Leadership from the Grassroots focuses on taking a contingency view and learning both about yourself and the situations where you lead. Acquiring tools of analysis are key.

2. The Present: Popular Trends

   a. Leader characteristics and traits revisited

Modern approaches to understanding the role leadership traits propose that although traits are not sufficient to make a leader, they are a precondition to effective leadership.

A fresh look at leaders' individual characteristics proposes key leadership traits that include: Drive and energy, motivation to lead, honesty, self-confidence, intelligence, and knowledge of the business.

Considering the demographic characteristics of leaders summarizes research about the demographic characteristics of U.S. business executives with a focus on their homogeneity in terms of ethnic and social background.

Leadership on the Cutting Edge presents a review by Mumford and Licuanan (2004) about the key findings regarding the role of leadership in creativity. The researchers indicate that the leader characteristics and how the leader interacts with followers and directs their activities are key to innovation. The researchers find that leaders can help innovation by being flexible and able to play multiple roles. While the leaders' technical expertise is important, they also must role model and encourage out of the box thinking. Furthermore, while developing intrinsic rewards for innovation is key, leaders must also be able to reward followers based on his or her own needs.

   b. Changes in organizations and expectations of leaders

The current trends and changes in U.S. and many other Western organizations are described with focus on the quality, empowerment and participative management movements.

The new roles for leaders are presented (Figure 2.1) and *factors fueling those changes* are summarized including demographic changes (Table 2.2), globalization, characteristics of a new generation of employees, increased level of education, and the quality movement (Figure 2.2).

Leading change discusses the case of Shirley Choi the CEO of Sea Power a Hong Kong company that operates a range of businesses in Asia. Choi, who gave up a lucrative job at Merril Lynch to take over her family's business, sees her role as a leader as that of an orchestra conductor. She also has had to battle many cultural and gender stereotypes and has developed her own team-based leadership style that blends Western and Asian values.

Barrier to change presents the difficulties faced by many organizations in moving towards new leadership and management models. Increased financial pressures, focus on individuals and absence of teams at higher levels of decision making, and the difficulty leaders have in giving up control after having been trained in a top-down style for many years are discussed as the primary barriers to change in organizations.

3. Summary and conclusion

Searching the Web

Leadership self-assessment

www.interlinktc.com/assessment.html

This website features a simple 25-point self-assessment designed to give a quick glimpse at personal skills in areas like Personal Stability, Productivity, Self-Management, Communication, Boundary Setting, Work Quality, Teamwork, and Leadership. The site also features a number of resources including tips on Executive Coaching, Leadership Development, and Team Communication.

Information about women on boards of directors in seven countries

www.globewomen.com/cwdi/cwdi.asp

Corporate Women Directors International

This site promotes increased participation of women in corporate boards globally. It features international and national reports that compare women's presence on corporate boards including a detailed chart that give specifics for women board activity and involvement in eight countries.

Information about women in corporate America and in the workforce

www.catalystwomen.org/

The Catalyst website features leading research and advisory organization that details, promotes, and expands opportunities for women at work. Catalyst conducts research on all aspects of women's career advancement and provides strategic and web-based consulting services on a global basis to help companies and firms advance women and build inclusive work environments. The site features a variety of resources that empower women in the workplace.

History of leadership

www.infinitefutures.com/essays/publichealth/leadershiphtml/tsld002.htm

Leadership in the 20th Century – a handy retrospective slideshow presentation that details leadership theory from Plutarch to Group, Trait, and Behavior theory concepts. Gets into modern concepts in detail by Kouzes, Postner, Rost.

The James MacGregor Burns Leadership Academy

www.academy.umd.edu/publications/presidential_leadership/sorenson_apsa.htm

Site features an article detailing the History of Leadership Studies and the role of James MacGregor Burns which includes a useful overview of the evolution of leadership concepts from the 1300's to current. The website also features resources for teachers, students, and trainers on a variety of topics related to the Burns Leadership Academy.

The Leadership Challenge: Selecting Team Members

The leadership challenge presents the difficulty of implementing change in organizations. The key dilemma is whether it is appropriate for a leader to use an authoritarian style to create a more participative organization. Some of the issues that students must consider and arguments they can use are:

- Is there a clear need for change? To persuade and convince followers, they must perceive a clear need for change. Use of objective data, emotional appeal, examples of other organizations, examples of performance gap, lost clients, and so forth can all be used to make the point.

- Why is there resistance to change? Fear of the unknown and job security are likely to be the key factors that lead to resistance to change. Styles and behaviors that have worked in the past are not easy to give up. Along with demonstrating the need for change, the leader must take the time to understand why resistance is happening, ascertain its sources and help followers deal with their resistance. Providing support, training, assurances of job security, etc., can all help.

The key issue in this scenario is that the style that the leader uses to implement the change will clearly demonstrate, more strongly than any words, the intentions. If the change is imposed without consultation, it will difficult to expect managers to use a team-based, participative style. By using an autocratic style of force followers to adopt the change, the leader will likely demonstrate the opposite of what is intended to happen.

On the other hand, the move to a new management style and philosophy that relies on teams and participation can be used as a demonstration of how effective that style can be in generating new ideas and building commitment and performance. The implementation of that change in effect becomes the first "team project" for the organization. The leader can use the opportunity to not only bring the followers on board and gain their buy in, but also to demonstrate the benefits of this new style in overcoming problems and resistance.

Chapter 2 Experiential Exercises

Exercise 2.1: Old Wines In New Skins

This exercise is designed to highlight the changes from old to new styles of leadership. The group-based, debate-style discussions can be used either as an introduction to the discussion of changes in organizations or as a conclusion to the topic. The goal is to inform students of the changes in leadership and their impact on organizations, employees, and individual leaders.

Total time: Minimum 30 minutes; Maximum time depends on number of students and groups.

Materials needed: Paper and pencil; use of board; flip chart can be useful for development of group definitions and presentations.

Part 1: Presentations (Group activity; 15 minutes)

Instructor preparation:

- Divide the class into an even number of groups. For classes under 20, two groups can be formed. For larger classes, you can use four or more groups

- Assign each group a presentation on either **traditional** or **new** leadership and management styles

- Direct the groups to include not only a description of the leadership or management style, but also its impact on organizations, employees, and their benefits and disadvantages

Option: Groups can be assigned in an earlier class and asked to come to class prepared for their presentations and discussion.

The Presentations:

Allow each group a maximum of 4 minutes to present their case. Allowing each side to question the other for 1-2 minutes livens up the discussion.

Part 2: Class discussion (15 minutes)

Class discussion should focus on the benefits and disadvantages of each style of leadership. In spite of the push to new participative leadership models, they are not appropriate in all situations. Particularly, they do not work well when:

- Employees are not ready

- Leaders are not trained in new methods and have trouble implementing them

- The organization's culture and climate is traditional

- There are genuine crisis and time urgency that require quick decision making

It is important to point out to students that new models are not cure-all, and that they require genuine buy-in and extensive support and training in order to be effective. Many managers and employees are not willing and ready to either give up or assume control.

It is interesting to note that, although students often state that they prefer to have their boss use new methods and include them in decision making, at the same time, many do not think that their own subordinates are ready and therefore prefer to use more traditional, top-down methods to manage their department. This dichotomy provides an immediate demonstration of the difficulty of implementing new leadership methods.

Overall: The Old Wines exercise is very effective in getting students to understand the differences between new and old leadership styles and the consequences of each style for organizations. The conclusion often reached as a result is to look at the new styles with a more critical eye.

Exercise 2.2: The Toy Factory

This exercise uses the making of origami toy wolves as a setting to demonstrate the effect of the three major leadership behaviors of autocratic, democratic, and laissez faire. Groups of students are assigned a leader who has instructions to act in one of the three ways. The groups then compete for the production of toys. The exercise is lengthy, but well worth the time. Issues of productivity, quality, and satisfaction of leader and followers under different leadership behaviors can be discussed. The different options in assignment of students (described below) can lead to a very effective demonstration for both leaders and followers.

Total time: Minimum 75 minutes

Materials needed: Paper, ruler, pencil/pen, and scissors.

Part 1: Preparation and leader training (10-15 minutes)

Instructor preparation:

- The instructor needs to become familiar with the steps in making the origami wolves (see instruction sheet) before class. He/she also needs to either ask students to bring their own paper or provide 20-30 sheets for each group.

- Group students in 6 teams of 4-6 (larger teams can be used in large classes), and select team leaders. Making the assignments before class allows the instructor to select certain individuals with particular styles and tendencies. For example, a student who has shown strong controlling and domineering tendencies can be selected to act as an authoritarian leader or as a democratic leader. Assigning him/her to either a comfortable or an opposite style yields different results and different experiences for both the team leader and the followers.

- If the class is small, laissez-faire style can be skipped using only democratic and autocratic leaders.

- One or two students can be selected to assist the instructor in training the leaders, in quality control, and as observers.

Leader training:

- The exercise starts with the instructor training the selected team leaders either before class or at the beginning of class. The leaders have to be trained in wolf-making without their group being present. Leaders can be trained by demonstrating wolf-making, sharing written instructions with team leaders, and allowing them to make a practice toy with the instructor.

- Provide each team leader with their Leader Style instruction sheet.

- Remind them that the Leader Style instructions are confidential and that they should not share them with their team or with other team leaders.

- Remind leaders that they should not provide their team members with the written instructions for toy making, but rather, that they should train them on how to make the toys. This step forces the leader to interact with followers rather than simply handing out the written instructions.

Part 2: Toy production (25-30 minutes)

Instructor needs to explain the purpose of the exercise as follows:

> The goal of this exercise is to make as many high quality toy wolves as you can in a 15 minute period. Your team leader has been trained in the skill of origami wolf-making and will provide you with instructions. You have 5 minutes to set up your teams and 15 minutes to produce the wolves.

The production run ends after 15 minutes. Instructor and assistant(s) check quality and count production of each group.

Part 3: Debriefing and discussion (25-30 minutes)

Instruct team members to complete the Toy Factory worksheet on p. 43.

Start discussion by asking each team, in a round-robin fashion to 1) describe their leader's behavior and style, 2) express their level of satisfaction, and 3) suggest improvements.

Ask each team leader to describe their style and express their views.

Focus class discussion around issues of differences among the leader behaviors and styles and their effect on subordinates' satisfaction, productivity, and quality.

In most cases, the exercise demonstrates, as research findings suggest, that:

- Followers of democratic leaders are more satisfied

- Teams led by autocratic leaders produce more

- Teams led by laissez-faire leaders are frustrated and are neither productive nor satisfied

If team leaders were assigned to styles that were "incongruent" with their personal style, they often express frustration and difficulty in implementing the required styles. In that case, discussion of the possibility of changing one's leadership style can be undertaken.

Concepts of contingency leadership can also be introduced or discussed by analyzing the leadership situation (short-term outcome, time pressure, no worry about follower satisfaction) and analyzing why one style may work better than others.

Overall: The exercise provides a vivid demonstration of the different leader behaviors and potentially of the difficulty and challenge leaders face when they attempt to change their behaviors.

Exercise 2.3: Leadership and Gender

In the U.S., as in many other, but not all, cultures, the images of leadership are closely tied to typical male behaviors. For example, leaders and males are supposed to be aggressive, dominant, and competitive. Females on the other hand are typically expected to be submissive, quiet, and cooperative. The female gender roles are generally inconsistent with the traditional views of leadership.

Although some students are aware of the link between gender and leadership, many assume that such links do not exist any longer. This exercise is designed to explore the relationship between gender roles and leadership.

Total time: Minimum 30 minutes

Materials needed: Paper, pencil, use of board or flip chart.

Part 1: Assign groups and develop list (Group work; 10-15 minutes)

- Divide class into three groups; the composition can be random or based on existing groups

- Assign each group to develop a list of ten characteristics using work sheet on p. 44 of the text based on one of the three instructions provided at the end of chapter

- Allow each groups 10-15 minutes to prepare their list

- Instruct them to be ready to make a brief 2-4 minute presentation to the class

Part 2: Presentation and discussion (In-class discussion; 10-15 minutes)

After the three groups have made their presentations, discussion should focus around:

- The relationship between leadership and the male and female gender roles

- Current changes in the definition of leadership and how they relate to gender roles

- Potential cross-cultural differences regarding views of both leadership and gender roles

In most cases, the majority of the traits and behaviors used to describe the male gender role are similar to those used to describe leaders. Traditional female gender roles are typically not associated with leadership. An interesting point of discussion is the similarity between many of the new leadership roles of facilitator, motivator, and coach and the female gender role. If Exercise 2.1 (Old Wines) was used, the descriptions can be contrasted with those generated by students for this exercise.

Overall: This relatively simple exercise can be a powerful demonstration of the strength of gender stereotypes. Focus on the future and changes in our views of leadership allow for a view of the future and the role of culture.

Leadership in Action

The Caring Dictator

Case summary

The case of Jack Hartnett is an excellent illustration of contingency leadership concepts. Hartnett owns 54 restaurant franchises with outstanding financial performance. Additionally, his turnover and training costs are lower that the industry average. Hartnett runs his organization as a benevolent dictator. He demands loyalty and obedience and he takes a personal interest in the personal lives of his managers and employees. The organization does not implement any of the current management methods and is, in many ways, an anachronism. Nevertheless, it is very effective and successful.

1. How would you describe Jack Hartnett's leadership style?

   Jack Hartnett is a highly authoritarian leader who tolerates very little dissent. He does not allow for participation and demands loyalty and obedience from his employees. While he is highly authoritarian, he also shows a high degree of care and concern about the lives of his employees. He does not hesitate to get involved in their personal problems. He runs his organizations like a traditional, patriarchal family where the father figure is both benevolent and the unquestioned leader.

2. Why is he successful? Would you work for him?

   The success of Hartnett's organization illustrates the concept of contingency leadership. Although his style of leadership may appear to be outdated, it works for his organization and for the restaurant franchise business. It is important to note that D. L. Rodgers Corporation is a small business. Additionally, the restaurant franchise business requires tight financial control and a strong focus on standardization and short-term results in order to be financially viable. Hartnett's style fits the industry and the culture he has created. Additionally, through careful recruiting and selection of employees, he assures the continuation of the culture he has created. He picks people who can work with him and in the organizational culture he has created. The key factor is the fit between the leader and the organization.

   Whether students decide that they would like to work for Hartnett or not is greatly dependent on their personality and individual values. These topics are discussed in the next chapter. The Hartnett case can be revisited after discussion of individual differences

Wolf-Making

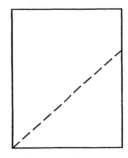

1. Fold up one corner
of rectangular paper to
make a square

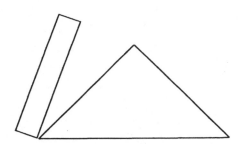

2. Cut off top and
Discard

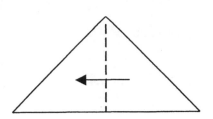

3. Fold to the left

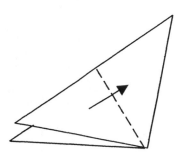

4. Fold one flap up

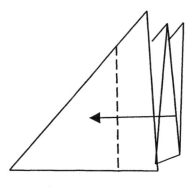

5. Turn over

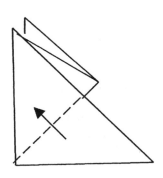

6. Fold other flap up

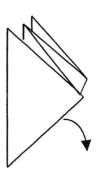

7. Rotate 45
degrees

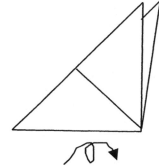

8. Fold ends to center

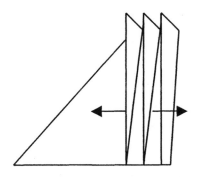

9. Separate flaps

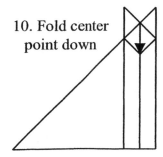

10. Fold center
point down

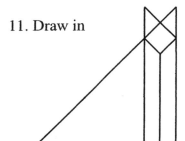

11. Draw in

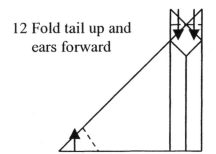

12 Fold tail up and
ears forward

Leader Style Instructions for TOY FACTORY

Democratic and participative

As the team leader, you are required to be open and participative. Consult with your team members, ask for their input, treat them as equals, and encourage them to participate and provide suggestions.

Remember not to share these instructions or the written wolf-making instructions with your team members.

Leader Style Instructions for TOY FACTORY

Autocratic and decisive

As team leader, you are the expert on this task. Provide the team members with directions and tell them what you expect of them. There is not much time for participation and suggestions. Focus on the task and get going.

Remember not to share these instructions or the written wolf-making instructions with your team members.

Leader Style Instructions for TOY FACTORY

Laissez-faire

As the team leader, simply provide instructions on how to make the toys and then leave your team alone to produce the items. Try to limit your contact with them and do not provide them with too many instructions. Let them do their job.

Remember not to share these instructions or the written wolf-making instructions with your team members.

Instructions for LEADERSHIP AND GENDER

Male gender roles

Your team's task is to list the typical personality traits and behaviors associated with the male gender roles in the U.S.

Be prepared to present your list to the class.

You have 15 minutes.

Instructions for LEADERSHIP AND GENDER

Female gender roles

Your team's task is to list the typical personality traits and behaviors associated with the female gender roles in the U.S.

Be prepared to present your list to the class.

You have 15 minutes.

Instructions for LEADERSHIP AND GENDER

Characteristics of leaders

Your team's task is to list the typical personality traits and behaviors associated with traditional leaders in the United States.

Be prepared to present your list to the class.

You have 15 minutes.

CHAPTER 3

INDIVIDUAL DIFFERENCES AND TRAITS

Chapter Overview

This chapter discusses the role that individual differences and traits play in leadership. Individual differences discussed include values, abilities (including intelligence and emotional intelligence) and skills, and several personality traits including the Big Five, locus of control, Type A, self-monitoring, MBTI, and machiavellianism. The chapter discusses how individual difference characteristics provide limits to leaders' behavior and ability and ease of learning new behaviors and styles. The focus is to view individual difference characteristics as a self-assessment and developmental tool for identifying strengths and weaknesses.

Chapter Objectives

OBJECTIVES	THROUGH BASIC TEXT	THROUGH FEATURES, FIGURES, TABLES AND EXAMPLES	THROUGH SELF-ASSESSMENTS AND EXERCISES
Explain the role of individual differences and traits in leadership	✓	Figure 3.1 (p. 63) and 3.2 (p. 65)	Exercise 3.1 (p. 90)
Describe the difference between the past and current approaches to leadership traits	✓		
Identify the impact of values on leadership	✓	Table 3.1 (p. 67)	Self-assessment 3.1 (p. 91)
Present the potential link between emotional intelligence and leadership Intelligence Creativity	✓	Table 3.2(p. 71) Scott Rudin (p. 69) Ken Chenault, (p. 72) Effective leadership from the grassroots (p. 72) Leadership on the cutting edge (p. 70) Donna Kacmar and Patrick Le Quément (p. 73)	Self-assessment 3.2 (p. 92-93)

Leadership skills		Table 3.3 (p 74)	
Highlight the role of the Big Five and other personality traits in leadership Type A Self-monitoring Myers Briggs Why leaders fail	✓	Table 3.4 (p. 75) Andy Grove, Lew Platt, Bill Gates (p. 75) Figure 3.3 (p. 78); Roger Abramson, Gerard Mestrallet, Tom DeMarco (p. 79) Herb Kelleher (p. 80) Figure 3.4 (p. 82) Pam Alexander (p. 84) Leading change (p. 85)	Self-assessments 3.3 through 3.7 (pp 94-96)
Understand cross-cultural differences in individual difference characteristics	✓	Culture and values (p 66 and 68) Gender and self-monitoring (p. 80); PRC managers and MBTI (pp. 81-82) Hong Kong managers and Machiavellianism (p.83)	

Chapter Outline

1. Elements of individual difference characteristics

    A framework for understanding individual difference characteristics is presented where the effect of both heredity and environment are emphasized. The major individual characteristics of personality, values, and abilities and skills are defined.

    a. The effect of individual characteristics

    The combined role of individual differences and the situation are clarified by proposing a model that defines behavioral zones of comfort and discomfort (Figure 3.1). Individual differences provide individuals with a zone of comfort that set limits of the zones of comfort.

    Individual characteristics play the strongest role in determining behavior when the situation does not provide clear guidelines. They also set limits and create a behavioral range, rather than dictate behaviors (Figure 3.2)

2. Values

    a. Value system and culture

    After defining values as long lasting beliefs about what is worthwhile and desirable, the impact of culture on values is discussed. Cultural values introduced in Chapter 1 are used to explain cross-cultural differences in value systems. The role of age and generational differences are presented (Table 3.1). The different view of ethics as a value are discussed.

1. Abilities and Skills

   The role of intelligence and technical, interpersonal, and cognitive skills are discussed.

   a. Intelligence and emotional intelligence

   The research on the link between intelligence and leadership is presented. Although intelligence and leadership are generally found to be related, the relationship is complex and moderated by many different factors.

   Although cognitive ability is important, emotional intelligence which includes ability to relate to others (Table 3.2) may have greater impact on leadership effectiveness.

   Leadership on the cutting edge presents a review by researchers T.A. Judge, A.E. Colbert and R. Ilies about the link between intelligence and leadership. While intelligence is one of the traits most often associated with leaders, research does not show a strong relationship between the two. Intelligence impacts leadership emergence and, most interestingly the perception of leadership effectiveness. How intelligent a leader appears to be is more important that how intelligent the person actually is. Additionally, intelligence impact a leader's effectiveness more in low than in high stress situations.

   Effective Leadership from the Grassroots discusses how EQ can be used as a leadership self-development tool.

   b. Creativity

   The four characteristics of creative people presented and their potential importance to leadership is discussed. They include: Perseverance in the face of obstacles, willingness to take risks, willingness to grow and openness to new experiences, and tolerance for ambiguity.

2. Skills

   As leader move up in their organization they require more interpersonal and conceptual skills and less technical skills (Table 3.3).

5. Relevant personality traits

   Six personality traits are presented.

   a. The Big Five personality dimensions

   The Big Five personality dimensions, which have been found to be consistent components of personality are described (Table 3.4). Although none are strong predictors of leadership, conscientiousness and extraversion have the strongest links to work-related behaviors

   b. Other personality traits

   Locus of control and the research regarding its impact on leadership and work-related behaviors are presented. Internals have been found to have higher self-confidence, more energy, more task-orientation, and less conformity to authority. The findings about CEOs' internal locus of control leading to more innovative strategies are also presented.

   Type A behavior pattern and its core element of need for control are described, and the research about work-related behaviors is presented (Figure 3.3). Specifically, the Type A's time urgency, competitiveness, polyphasic behaviors, and hostility and their related behavior of poor delegation, preference for working alone, action-orientation, high perception of stress, and harder work are discussed.

Self-monitoring is the degree to which people are capable of reading and using environmental and social cues. This ability to perceive and evaluate situations correctly is suggested to be key to leadership effectiveness.

The MBTI, which is a widely used leadership development tool, and the potential effect of style differences on leadership behavior are described. The focus of the section is on only the two dimensions of sensing/intuition and feeling/thinking (Figure 3.4). Cross-cultural research about the difference between Chinese and European managers is presented suggesting different MBTI profiles for the two groups. Implication of MBTI for upper-echelon leadership are also discussed.

The *Machievellian* personality, which consists of ability to manipulate and resist manipulation from others along with focus on personal goals and low integrity, is related to leadership effectiveness. Research findings suggest that moderate Machiavellian personalities are most effective as leaders. Cultural differences among Hong Kong, PRC, and U.S. managers are also presented, with the Hong Kong and PRC managers having been found to be more willing to use power to accomplish their goals. The implications of high Machs in positions of power are discussed.

6.   What about leaders who fail?

Individual characteristics of leaders who fail are described. They include: An abrasive style, arrogance, untrustworthiness, self-centeredness, poor performance, and inability to delegate.

Leading change describes how Steve Bennett of Intuit changes the informal and relaxed culture of the company. Intuit is the maker of popular software such as Quicken and Turbo Tax and faced a performance and financial slump in the late 1990. Bennett pulled the company out of its slump by focusing on performance, at the expense of the highly democratic and organic existing culture. Bennett instituted a strong customer focus and provided autonomy to managers to serve them. While the culture change was a shock, it allowed the company to survive and eventually led Bennett to also relax and reintroduce some of the old Intuit culture.

7.   Using individual difference characteristics

The limits of using individual difference characteristics in understanding and predicting leadership are emphasized. The major use should be for self-awareness and development.

8.   Summary and Conclusion

Searching the Web

Information about the corruption index for different countries

www.globalcorruptionreport.org

The web site presents a series of annual reports that details how companies around the world are fighting corruption in business. Each report includes case studies and in depth corruption research, statistics, and special articles such as "Corruption in post-conflict reconstruction" and "Political Corruption".

Transparency International Corruption Perceptions Index 2003

www.transparency.org/pressreleases_archive/2003/2003.10.07.cpi.en.html

The Transparency International Corruption Perceptions Index charts levels of corruption in 133 countries. Seven out of ten countries score less than 5 out of a possible score of 10, while five out of ten developing countries score less than 3 out of 10. TI, the only international non-governmental organization devoted to combating corruption, brings civil society, business, and governments together in a powerful global coalition.

Additional self-assessments

Mensa intelligence test: psychology.about.com/library/bl/bltest_mensa.htm

The Mensa test is based on questions created by Mensa's supervisory psychologist Dr. Abbie F. Salny, which are similar to those on the Mensa admission test. Mensa is the international high IQ society, whose members all have scored in the top 2% on intelligence tests. That is, every one of them has an IQ of 130 or higher.

Big Five: inst.santafe.cc.fl.us/~mwehr/X9PerT.htm

The Big Five Personality Traits test rates the five dimensions of personality, a normal distribution of scores on these dimensions, an emphasis on individual personality traits (the type concept is gone), preferences indicated by strength of score, and a model based on experience, not theory.

Type A: http://psychology.about.com/library/jv/bljv_pers.htm

The on-line Type A test provides a brief assessment of Type A behavior pattern designed for self-awareness. The site further provides many articles about Type and other personality traits.

Avoiding failure in times of crisis:

www.ccl.org/CCLCommerce/pdf/research/cclCreative.pdf

Center for Creative Leadership article discusses how a CEO's soft skills like trust, empathy, and communication can equip these leaders to improve their bottom lines despite hard economic times.

Psychological testing

psychology.about.com/library/weekly/aa072300a.htm

A list of online tests the American Psychological Association call "psychological and educational instruments developed and used by testing professionals in organizations such as schools, industries, clinical practice, counseling settings and human service and other agencies, including those assessment procedures and devices that are used for making inferences about people in the above-named settings".

The Leadership Challenge: Using Psychological Testing

The leadership challenge asks students to think about the use of psychological testing as a selection tool. The key point is to reinforce the idea that psychological testing is not a reliable tool for managerial decision-making regarding selection and promotion of employees. They should instead be used as a means of self-development. Factors students should consider:

- Depending on which tests are used and how they are administered, psychological tests of personality can vary in the degree of reliability and validity. While organizations use some tests that are well developed, valid, and reliable, they also often use tests that do not satisfy these criteria. In addition, even with well-developed tests, the link between personality and work related behaviors and performance is not well established and, in the case of management decisions, not full defensible if challenged.

- Because of these, psychological tests should be used with caution. Their primary and safest use is for development rather than selection or promotion. In this case, the test may be used to help the team become aware of the strengths and weaknesses of its members and as a springboard for team building.

- It is key to consider whether all the characteristics listed in the scenario are required for being a good team player. Particularly are assertiveness and competitiveness highly desirable characteristics for a team member. Although these characteristics may typically be important for those in sales and marketing, they may not be necessary, and even detrimental for a research team where cooperation and ability to compromise are key.

- While individual characteristics are one factor that leader must consider when selecting followers and team members, issues of diversity should also be part of the criteria. Building diversity is a social and managerial consideration that must be balanced with other needs.

Chapter 3 Exercises

Exercise 3.1: Your Ideal Organization

This exercise allows students to experience the impact of personality on various organizational factors first hand. It is most effective if Part I is assigned outside of class, prior to the students' either reading the chapter or completing the self-assessment at the end of the chapter. Part II can be completed after the students have taken the self-assessments. Discussion can then focus on why student preferences are different.

This exercise is very effective as an opener to the personality lecture.

Total time: Minimum 30 minutes in class; an additional 15 minutes required if Part I is assigned in class

Materials needed: Paper and pencil; board or flip chart can be useful.

Part I: Individual Description (Individual work; 10-15 minutes)

Assign students to complete Part I of this exercise prior to class and prior to reading the chapter or doing the self-assessments. Instruct them to focus on what they would like to see in their ideal organization rather than what they think is possible.

Part II: Group work (Group activity; 30-40 minutes)

The instructor needs to form groups based on the students' similar scores on the various personality constructs. Depending on class size and composition, you may be able to represent all constructs. For example, you could have a group of Type As and a group of Type Bs; a high- and a low-Mach group; an ST and an NF group...etc.

The constructs that work best are Type A, MBTI, and Mach. Locus of control can also be effective; self-monitoring does not lead to interesting discussions.

After the groups are assigned, ask each to focus on the similarities of their answers (inside the group) and draw up a brief description of their group's ideal organization using the questions in Part I. Each group then presents their ideal organization to the class.

Discussion items include the effect of personality on:

- Our world and organizational views

- Leadership styles and expectations

- Control, delegation, and structure

- The overall culture and climate of an organization

In most cases, the groups differ significantly on their organizational preferences. For examples, Type A groups create organizations that provide the leader control; structures are often centralized, whereas issues of control are not as central to Type Bs. High-Mach organizations reflect the group's suspicion of others. The ST groups' organizations focus on data, objectivity, and order, whereas the NFs are open and flexible with strong focus on interpersonal relations.

Overall: With some luck and the right personality mix in the classroom, this exercise can provide a vivid example of the impact of personality on organizations. As an introduction to the topic, it can be used to help students understand the individual differences by tying them to a personal experience.

Self-Assessment 3.1 to 3.7

The self assessments should be assigned to be completed prior to class. Students having their score on each of the scales allows for a much richer learning environment.

The instructor should take special care in the discussion of EQ, locus of control, and Machiavellianism. Students may be upset if their EQ score is low. Similarly, external locus of control often carries negative connotations, as does both being a high or low Mach. Type A, self-monitoring, and MBTI do not present the same challenge as there is no strong negative connotation associated with either end of the scale.

It is important to stress that these self-assessments are meant to develop a student's self-awareness. The EQ and Type A scales have not been scientifically tested and validated. They provide students with a general description of their behaviors and preferences.

 Course Assignment

All the self-assessments in this chapter can be used to develop students' self-awareness of their personal characteristics. Students can be asked to describe and analyze each of the characteristics measured in the self-assessments with a focus on identifying resulting strengths and weaknesses. Students should be reminded that the changing personality is not the goal, rather understanding should be their focus. By developing increasing self-awareness, they can build on their strengths and compensate for their weaknesses.

Leadership in Action

Pernille Spiers-Lopez assembles a winning team at IKEA

Case summary

Pernille Spiers-Lopez is the president of IKEA North America. IKEA is a Danish furniture maker that has experienced world-wide success with customers with its modern, convenient, and low priced furniture and home accessories. It has stores in 31 countries across the globe. IKEA North America is also experiencing continued success and growth partly due to Spiers-Lopez focus on nurturing coworkers and providing a family friendly work environment. Spiers-Lopez, herself a mother of two teens strongly believes in standing for what she believes in and being centered and self-aware. Her personal values focused on her family have led her to push IKEA to adopt an employee-centered culture that further encourages female employees to achieve their potential. Spiers-Lopez is very hard working and, has herself, experienced the negative impact of stress and working too hard. Her family and her team at work help her balance her life and her work.

1. What are Spiers-Lopez's key individual characteristics?

   Spiers-Lopez displays several of the individual characteristics that are related to leaders. These are described in Chapter 2 and include: Drive and energy, desire to lead, honesty and integrity, self-confidence, and knowledge of the business she is in. In addition, Reitz has both cognitive and emotional intelligence. Her ability to listen to and empathize with employees and customers is an indicator of her high EQ. Spiers-Lopez's high energy, task-focus, and ability to work to the point of exhaustion are typical characteristics of Type As. Her drive and proactive stance further indicate an internal locus of control.

2. What are the factors that contribute to her effectiveness?

   Spiers-Lopez strives to stay true to her personal values which include importance of family and providing a supportive work environment. She has a strong focus on keeping a balance between family and work for herself and for her employee. She is able to empathize with others while being passionate about getting the job done. While taking care of employees, she also has been able to deliver financial results that have made the company successful.

   Spiers-Lopez shows strong consideration behaviors paired with the goal-driven Type A behaviors. She provides a good example of how a Type A can also take care of people, negating the inaccurate but often held stereotype of Type As as uncaring and callous.

CHAPTER 4

POWER AND LEADERSHIP

Chapter Overview

The chapter presents power as a tool that leaders need to use wisely to influence their subordinates. The definition, sources, and consequences of power are presented. The traditional sources of individual power are described, along with power sources that depend on the organizational structure and the sources of power for top executives. The elements of power for teams and team leaders are discussed. The causes, consequences, and solutions to power corruption are presented along with the current views of power. The concept of empowerment is discussed as a new approach to leaders' power. The chapter has a strong cross-cultural flavor with many examples of how power is perceived and used differently in different cultures.

Chapter Objectives

OBJECTIVES	THROUGH BASIC TEXT	THROUGH FEATURES, TABLES, FIGURES, AND EXAMPLPLES	THROUGH EXERCISES
Define power and its key role in leadership	✓	Zingerman Community of Business (p. 103-104) National Hockey League (p. 104)	
Understand the cross-cultural differences in the definitions and use of power	✓	Australian, Chinese, European, and Mexican examples (p. 105) Leadership on the Cutting Edge (p. 110)	
Identify the individual and organizational sources of power available to leaders and describe their consequences for followers and organizations	✓	Table 4.1 (p. 106) Alan Greenspan (p. 106, 107, 102) Figure 4.1 (p. 107); Table 4.2 (p. 108) ZCoB (p. 108) What does this mean for me (p. 103) Effective leadership from the	Self-assessment 4.1 (p. 128)

		Grassroots (p. 112)	
Understand the role of power in the leadership and effectiveness of teams	✓	Mervyn's SWAT teams (p. 109) Table 4.3 (p. 110) Highsmith (p. 111)	
Identify the power sources available to top executives	✓	Dipak Jain and John Wood (p. 113)	
Explain the sources of power corruption and present ways to prevent its occurrence	✓	Enron, Tyco Conrad Black, Richard Grasso, Parmalat, WorldCom (p. 114) Table 4.4 (p. 115) Al Dunlap, Philp Agee (p. 115) Figure 4.2 (p. 116) Donald Carty, Richard Scrushy (p. 117) Gerard Arpey (p. 119)	
Trace the changes in use of power and explain their consequences	✓	Linda Ellerbee (p. 120) Table 4.5 (p. 120) Roy Vagelos and Kerry Killinger (p. 121) Leading change (p. 122)	Exercise 4.1 (p. 127)

Chapter Outline

1. Power in organizations: Definition and consequences

    Power is the ability of one person to influence another

    Authority is power vested in a position.

    a. Consequences of using power

    Commitment, compliance, and resistance are discussed as the three possible follower reactions to a leader's use of power.

    a. Distribution of power

    The concentration and distribution of power in organizations is discussed as source of effectiveness.

    Hofstede's concept of power distance and tolerance for diversity and Trompernaars' cultural organizational model are used to explain cross-cultural difference in power. On the one hand, the Chinese, Mexican, French, Italian, and German cultures all attribute considerably more power to their leaders than do U.S. subordinates. On the other hand, Swedes have little need for hierarchy and authority and as a result can function easily in leaderless team environments.

2. Sources of power

    a.   Sources of power related to individuals

Sources and consequences: French and Raven's five sources of individual power are described (Table 4.1) and potential reactions to the use of each source by a leader are discussed (Figure 4.1). The sources are: legitimate, reward, coercive, expert, and referent power. While the first three depend on the organization and are more likely to lead to either compliance or resistance, the last two depend on the individual and are more likely to lead to follower commitment.

Using Individual sources of power: Power and influence are compared, and influence tactics and their consequences are discussed. Research outlining the effect of influence tactics available to leaders is summarized (Table 4.2) and the work of Kotter on career stages and use of different power sources is presented. In early career stages, leaders develop a base of power by building broad networks and establishing credibility through their expertise and demonstration of competence. In middle career stages, the challenge is to use power wisely and ethically, whereas in later stages the issue becomes letting go gracefully.

    b.   Sources of power related to organizational structure

The sources of power stemming from organizational structures are presented. These sources are suggested to be key to teams, and team leaders' ability to achieve their goals (Table 4.3).

Leadership on the Cutting Edge presents research about cross-cultural differences in the use of influence tactics. Oana Branzei (2004) compared use of influence in the U.S., Romanian, and Japan using a sample of 223 MBA students. The study showed some, but not very strong differences in how people use power. Employees with more experience preferred legitimate tactics; Romanians used rational and ingratiation; U.S. and Japanese preferred rational inspirational, and consultation. Women tended to use ingratiation more than men.

Coping with uncertainty: The first structural source of power for teams is their ability to help others cope with uncertainty through obtaining information that they need, through preventing uncertainty by predicting and forecasting events, and through absorption of uncertainty by preventing change from affecting other parts of the organization.

Centrality: The second source of power for teams is the degree to which the team's activities are key and central to the overall mission and goals of the organization

Dependability and substitutability: The third source of team power is the extent to which the team's expertise is needed by others.

    c.   Special power sources of top executives

The sources of power of CEOs are described. These include: distribution of rewards and resources, control of decision criteria, and centrality in the information flow.

Effective Leadership from the Grassroots presents guidelines for the use of the different sources of power. The focus is on the development of personal power based on competence and relationship building.

3. The dark side of power: Corruption

The growing number of examples of abuse of power in organizations points to a potential problem with having too much power without much accountability. Power tends to increase the distance between leaders and followers and sets the stage for potential abuse.

a. Causes and processes

Both leader and organizational characteristics contribute to abuse of power (see Table 4.4 for a summary)

Leader characteristics include factors such as arrogance, inflated view of self, inflexibility, ruthlessness, and concern with power. Researchers have suggested that "evil" or destructive narcissist managers are more likely to have these characteristics and therefore abuse their power.

Organizational factors include the culture of the organization, hiring practices, and centralized structure along with short-term rewards based on limited criteria.

Corruption Cycle: The leadership and organizational factors combine to create a corruption cycle presented in Figure 4.2. Follower compliance, dependence and submission play a role.

b. Consequences

Poor decision making due to poor information is one of the major consequences of excessive power. The development of a separate morality by the leader can also lead to unethical actions. Finally, devaluation of subordinates can create a self-fulfilling prophecy that prevents delegation and empowerment and leads to further isolation and poor decision making.

c. Solutions

In order to prevent power corruption organizations must: encourage open communication, involve leader in day-to-day activities, reduce followers' dependence on the leader, use objective measures of performance, involve outsiders in decision-making, and change and monitor the culture.

4. Empowerment: The changing face of power

a. Steps to Empowerment

Empowerment is defined as the giving away and sharing of power with those who need it to perform their job. Factors involved in empowerment are presented in Table 4.5.

Leadership factors: To encourage empowerment, the leader must create a positive atmosphere, set high standards, encourage initiative, reward followers, practice equity and collaboration, and have confidence in followers.

Organizational factors that contribute to empowerment include: decentralized structures, training for leaders and followers, removing bureaucratic barriers, appropriate reward structure, and fair and open policies.

Impact of empowerment: Much anecdotal evidence supports the positive benefits of empowerment. Empirical research is not as clear. However, the concept is well established in the U.S. and several other Western countries.

Leading change presents the case of Brazilian businessman Ricardo Semler who has championed the concept of open book management and practices power sharing, participation management, and empowerment in his company Semco. These practices require extensive training and have led to high performance for the company.

6. Summary and conclusion

Searching the Web

Power and influence

http://www.gov.sk.ca/psc/MgmtComp/Impact_Influence.htm

Site features definitions of influence with a number of helpful exercises designed to improve personal influence abilities. There are five levels of developmental activities that students may use either in a classroom or professional environment. They include specific hands on activities that are useful for measuring and improving managerial impact and influence in leaders.

Corruption

www.transparency.org/

The Transparency International website features a wealth of information provided by a unique international non-governmental organization devoted to combating corruption in business. The site contains helpful research tools and indices like the National Integrity Systems Country Studies, the Bribe Payers Index (BPI), and an assortment of other resource material. There are a number of tools like the Business Principles for Countering Bribery link, which includes a practical guide to avoid bribery and corruption and a revealing Q & A section.

www.worldbank.org/fandd/english/0398/articles/010398.htm

From the Finance and Development website, a quarterly publication of the International Monetary Fund and the World Bank, this revealing article provides details about spotting corruption, how to know it, and what steps are needed to improve understanding of corruption and enhance the governments' effectiveness in combating it.

Executive compensation

www.rileyguide.com/execpay.html

The Riley Guide presents a website chock full of information regarding Executive compensation and severance packages. Articles and links on corporate contracts from The Corporate Library, the Ecomp Exectutive Compensation Database and much more.

www.aflcio.org/corporateamerica/paywatch/index.cfm

Article listing the top 10 highest paid CEO's and their wage form the American Federation of Labor and Congress of Industrial Organizations (AFL CIO) website. Site includes a long list of articles that examine executive pay like "2004 trends in CEO pay" and "What is wrong with CEO pay and what can be done to fix it?"

bwnt.businessweek.com/exec_comp/2002/index.asp

BusinessWeek's website featuring Executive Compensation Scoreboard article. The Scoreboard examines how closely pay matches performance. It compares an exec's total compensation with the company's total return to shareholders (appreciation + dividends) over three years, to minimize one-year windfalls.

Empowerment

humanresources.about.com/od/glossaryofterms/l/bl_empowerment.htm

About.com article with definitions, links, and other resources detailing the enabling effects of Empowerment. Includes links to Empowerment Mag.com, which features a host of articles, interviews, and resources detailing the subject.

The Leadership Challenge: How Much is Enough?

The leadership challenge presents the highly controversial issue of executive salaries which, particularly in the United States, have reached astronomical proportions. The key issues for students to consider in the debate are:

- The reasons for high salaries. These include: market forces and competition for executive talent, the need to retain top talent, the high risk and high responsibility that top level executives shoulder, compensating executives in a way that is commensurate with the performance of their organization and that encourages them to perform their best.

- The question of fairness and equity when compared to middle level management and lower level salaries and wages is highly subjective. Students should be encouraged to debate what fairness means. Their responses will reflect their personal values. The class is unlikely to come to a consensus on what is fair; however, the exploration of various points of views is key.

- The need to attract the best talent to help an organization out of crisis.

- The impact of high salary differential on the morale of others in the organization.

In preparation for this assignment students should be encouraged to read articles about executive salaries. Useful information can be found in several of the web site listed at the end of the chapter:

http://www.rileyguide.com/execpay.html

http://www.aflcio.org/corporateamerica/paywatch/index.cfm

http://bwnt.businessweek.com/exec_comp/2002/index.asp

Chapter 4 Experiential Exercises

Self-assessment 4.1: Views of power

This is an individual exercise that allows students to identify their views towards the various sources of power. The assessment should be completed before the class on power and used for discussions regarding the consequences of each source of power. Debriefing should include a strong contingency viewpoint whereby not one source is assumed to be better than others. However, it is essential that students understand that the use of each source has consequences for their ability to influence followers.

Exercise 4.1: Recognizing blocks to empowerment

This exercise allows students to assess their organization's readiness for implementation of empowerment by identifying the leadership and structural blocks. It works best if completed after the discussion of empowerment so that students have a clear understanding of the concept. It can also be a very effective conclusion to the power lecture.

Option: The exercise can be used as an individual assessment to help students understand empowerment better *or* as a group exercise (after the individual ranking). The group exercise focuses on devising strategies for removing obstacles to empowerment. This type of activity works best with more mature students who have some work experience. I have used it very successfully with part-time MBAs. The group activity is not as effective with traditional undergraduates who have limited or no work experience. The description below is for the group-based exercise.

Total time: Minimum 30 minutes in class

Materials needed: Paper and pencil; board or flip chart can be useful.

Part I: Individual Description (Individual work; 5 minutes)

Ask students to rate their organizations on the 16 questions and to calculate their score. They may need your help with the reverse-scored items.

Part II: Strategies for removing obstacles (Group work; 15-20 minutes)

In this part of the exercise, groups of students select one of their members' organizations, clearly identify the blocks to empowerment, and develop strategies for their removal. Issues that they need to consider before they embark in their search for strategies relate to readiness for change and include:

- Is the leadership of the organization ready for moving towards empowerment?

- Are employees and managers ready for empowerment?

- Is empowerment appropriate given the culture, strategy, performance levels, etc.?

- Would the stress and pain of moving toward empowerment be worth the potential benefits?

If the group feels that the answer to these questions is generally positive, then they should develop strategies to help move the organization towards empowerment.

The Instructor needs to point out to the students that their strategies do not have to solve all the problems; each group can set priorities in what can and should be done.

Each group can be given 4-5 minutes to present their organization and their solutions or a general class discussion of the solutions can take place.

Overall: This exercise is very effective with students who already have some experience with teams, quality circles, or empowerment. Working on this exercise allows them to identify the obstacles and understand, why the strategies their organization has been trying to implement may not be working. Discussions invariably turn towards the role of the leader in setting and encouraging a culture that would support sharing of power.

 ### *Course Assignment*

This exercise can be used as an assignment for the course. The assignment uses the students' organizations as live cases. The questionnaire is used as a tool to analyze the situation; other analysis can be required along with a description of the organization or departments the student is rating. The strategies portion involves developing and evaluating various alternatives for implementation of new management techniques.

Leadership in Action

The powers of Dick Grasso of the New York Stock Exchange

Case summary

Richard (Dick) Grasso is the former chairman of the New York Stock Exchange (NYSE) who was fired in 2003 after news about his $180 million dollar compensation package became public. Grasso accumulated power carefully over his many years at the NYSE by working harder than most, learning everything there was to know, developing powerful friends through networking and favors, and finally earning the title of chairman. While Grasso charmed many executives and other powerful people, he is accused of having been ruthless and vindictive with subordinates who crossed him, throwing temper tantrums, threatening them and demanding absolute obedience. His supporters point to his outstanding performance record and defend the benefit package with exceeded that of the previous chairman by $178 million. His detractors accuse him of abusing power and even unethical and illegal activities regarding trading favors.

1. What are the sources of Dick Grasso's power?

   Grasso based his power on developing considerable expertise early in his career. He also build a strong network of friends to give him referent power. As he gained official positions in the NYSE, he accumulated legitimate power and considerable reward and coercive power along with the official position. He, very astutely, used all the sources of power to build on one another. He used his legitimate position and the privileges it brought to further develop friendships and contacts. He used the same power to intimidate those who disagreed with him and reward those whom he liked.

2. What elements of power corruption are present in this case?

   Dick Grasso shows many of the individual characteristics that may lead to corruption. As his success increased, he developed an inflated view of himself and became arrogant and highly controlling. His temper further contributed to this. His treatment of subordinates shows his rigidity, sense of entitlement, and willingness to use his power to achieve his goals. Examples of abuse of followers further indicate his ruthlessness and viciousness. All the while, Grasso was extremely charming with those who had power over him, showing his ability to ingratiate himself with his superiors.

   The organizational factors that lead to corruption are also present. Grasso created a culture of intimidation and fear inside the organization, centralized decision-making, and focused on his own goals. Interestingly, the people who were supposed to provide a check on his power, the member of the NYSE board, were among his most ardent supporters, having been cultivated by Grasso for many years. The scandal in the case was that the rewards that Grasso received were partly determined by these friendships rather than by what would benefit the organization.

   While the individual and organizational factors that contribute to corruption were present, and Grasso is accused of having to abuse his power, especially with subordinates, the performance of NYSE under Grasso was stellar.

PART TWO

CONTINGENCY MODELS

CHAPTER 5

USING RESOURCES EFFECTIVELY

Chapter Overview

This chapter presents Fiedler's contingency and Vroom and Yetton's normative decision models, and Fiedler and Garcia's Cognitive Resource theory (CRT) of leadership. The three are combined in the chapter because they focus on how the leader uses various available resources, most importantly the group of followers, to achieve the goals. Effectiveness depends on understanding the situation, identifying the leader's style, and matching the two. Fiedler's model uses the Least Preferred Coworker (LPC) and situational control to measure leader style and situational characteristics. The normative decision model focuses on leader's decision style and the quality requirements of the decision at hand. Cognitive Resource theory uses leader intelligence and experience and level of stress or interpersonal conflict as a situational factor. While all three models suggest that the leader and the situation need to match in order to achieve effectiveness, the Contingency Model recommends that the leader needs to focus on changing the situation, while the Normative Model suggests changing the leader's style. The CRT focuses on the role of stress in leadership.

Chapter Objectives

OBJECTIVES	THROUGH BASIC TEXT	THROUGH FEATURES, TABLES, FIGURES, AND EXAMPLES	THROUGH EXERCISES
Explain the importance of effective use of resources to leadership	✓		
Distinguish between a task-motivated and a relationship-motivated leader and identify the elements of situational control used in Fiedler's Contingency Model of leadership	✓	Table 5.1 (p. 135) Marilyn Moats Kennedy, Marissa Peterson, Bernard Ebbers, Mort Meyerson, and Darlene Ryan (p. 135)	Self-assessments 5.1 and 5.2 (p. 160-164)

Present the Contingency Model's predictions and explain how to use it to improve leadership effectiveness	✓	Figure 5.1 (p. 137); Table 5.2 (p. 138) Presidents Richard Nixon, Jimmy Carter, Ronald Reagan, and Bill Clinton (pp. 138-139) Effective Leadership from the Grassroots (p. 140) Leadership on the Cutting Edge (p. 141) Leading Change (p. 143)	Exercise 5.1 (p. 153-154)
Present the four decision styles used in the Normative Decision model of leadership	✓	Junku Yoshida (p. 142 Table 5.3 (p. 144)	
Understand the role of decision quality and follower acceptance in the choice of leadership styles and how to use the Normative Decision model to improve leadership effectiveness	✓	Table 5.4 (p. 145); Figure 5.2 (p. 146)	Exercise 5.2 (p. 155-158); Exercise 5.3 (p. 159)
Discuss the Cognitive Resource theory and its implications for leaders	✓	Al Dunlap and Anne Mulcahey (p. 149)	

Chapter Outline

1. Fiedler's contingency model

    a. Leader's style

    The Least Preferred Coworker scale (LPC) is presented as the measure of leader style in the contingency model (Table 5.1).

    Task-motivated/low LPC individuals are described as being primarily motivated by task accomplishment.

    Relationship-motivated/high LPC individuals are described as primarily motivated by good interpersonal relationships.

    The socio-independent/middle LPC individuals are described as generally being unconcerned with others' opinions.

    b. Situational control

    Leader-member relations is the first and most important element of situational control in the contingency model. It is defined as the overall level of trust and cohesion in the group. Without good relations, the leader's ability to act is seriously affected.

Task structure, which is the second element of situational control, refers to the degree to which the task has clear goals, a clear answer, the number of possible solutions, and the availability of feedback.

Position power is the least influential element of situational control and refers to the leader's ability to hire and fire and reward subordinates.

Putting it together: Situational control. The three elements described in this section are combined to provide an indicator of the amount of control the leader has over the situation.

c. Predictions of the model

The contingency model predicts that different leadership styles will be effective in different levels of situational control. The task- and relationship-motivated leaders act differently in different situations (Table 5.2). In high- and low-control situations, the task-motivated leader groups perform best, whereas in moderate control, the relationship-motivated leader groups perform well (Figure 5.1).

d. Evaluation and applications

Critiques and support for the contingency model are presented.

Using the contingency model presents the Leader Match Concept which is the training method based on the contingency model. The focus is on learning to recognize the various elements of situational control and on adapting the situation to match the leader's style. Fiedler assumes that the leader's style is stable and not easily changeable; however leadership situations can change either randomly or as a result of the leader's actions. The leader's efforts should be to adapt the situations to fit his/her style.

Effective leadership from the grassroots provides guidelines for taking advantage of various leadership training programs to practice and learn more about how to implement the contingency model.

Leadership on the cutting edge presents research by Miller, Btler and Cosentino (2004) about adapting the LPC scale to followers' rating their Least Preferred Leaders (LPL). They found that the Contingency Model predictions can be extended to followers. High LPL followers performed better in moderate control, whole Low-LPL followers did better in low situational control. Additional High LPL believed they performed better when they got along with their leader. The study reinforces the concept of match proposed by Fiedler.

1. The Normative Decision Model

The Normative Decision Model focuses on decision-making, assumes that the leaders can change his or style, and is concerned with decision quality as the criterion for effectiveness.

a. Leader's decision styles

This section provides a description of the major leader decision styles and sub-styles used in the normative decision model (Table 5.3). They range from autocratic, to consultative, to group decision making.

Leading change describes the two very different leadership styles at Yahoo! Terry Semel, the CEO, who successfully re-energized the company, is highly detailed oriented and task-focused. Libby Sartain, the VP of HR and chief of people focuses on people and providing meaningful work.

b. Contingency variables: Defining the problem

The quality of the decision and follower acceptance are the two situation variables in the normative decision model. The questions and decision rules that used to understand the leadership situation are discussed (Table 5.4).

   c.   The Normative Decision model's predictions

The normative decision model is presented (Figure 5.2). The leader should make decisions alone when there is no time, he or she has all the information that is needed, the leader has support from the group, or followers cannot agree among themselves on a course of action. In other situations, the leader should rely on participation to varying degrees.

   d.   Evaluation and application

Critiques and support for the normative decision model are presented. The model has a narrow focus on decision making, but has been well supported and has broad application to real-life leadership decision making. The focus is on teaching the leader to understanding the leadership situation.

2.   Cognitive Resource Theory

   a.   Leader characteristics and contingency factors

CRT considers intelligence and experience as the two leader characteristics. Level of stress, primarily defined as interpersonal conflicts and concerns about performance, is the key situational factor.

   b.   CRT's predictions

The leader's intelligence contributes to group performance when the leader is directive. However, intelligence is an asset mostly when the situation is not stressful. Leader experience helps group performance in high-stress situations. In low stress situations, intelligence rather than experience is helpful.

   c.   Evaluation and application

The CRT needs further research, but the model points to the importance of stress in leadership situations and recommends paying attention to both intelligence and experience as leadership characteristics.

3.   Contingency Models and Culture

This sections discusses the application of contingency models cultures other than the United States. Because of limited research in other cultures, such models should be used with caution.

4.   Summary and conclusion

Searching the Web

Fiedler's Contingency Model

www.stfrancis.edu/ba/ghkickul/stuwebs/btopics/works/fied.htm

Site that features the article "Fiedler's Contingency Theory of Leadership" by Patrich Antoine which illuminates the theory that explains that group performance is a result of interaction of two factors: leadership style and situational favorableness. These two factors are discussed along with other aspects of Fiedler's theory.

www.css.edu/users/dswenson/web/LEAD/vroom-yetton.html

> Site features a helpful article with that details the Vroom-Yetton-Jago model, a decision making tree that enables a leader to examine a situation and determine which style or level of involvement to engage. The article features a series of questions that follow a detailed chart that will help readers how decision are made, even at an unconscious level.

Mary Kay

www.marykay.com/Headquarters/MaryKayBiography/MaryKayBiography.asp

> The site provides information about Mary Kay Ash, her biography, her principles, and accomplishments.
> It also provides links to the Mary Kay company web site to provide information about the culture of company.

www.brainyquote.com/quotes/authors/m/mary_kay_ash.html

> The site provides a series of quotes by Mary Kay Ash. The quotes provide insight into the person, her   values, and her leadership style.

Microsoft

www.microsoft.com/careers/mslife/whoweare/default.mspx

> Microsoft website, features links to company profile, history, their vision for the future including seven core businesses, corporate missions, and tomorrow's frontiers.

www.microsoft.com/careers/mslife/essence/default.mspx

> More future innovations and plans from tech pioneers Microsoft.

The Leadership Challenge: Creating Crisis: Performance vs. Morale

The challenge presents students with a dilemma of how to deal with the leader of a high performing group whose followers appear to be dissatisfied. Issues students must consider include:

- The possibility that the leader is a low LPC who either consciously or unconsciously know that he performs best in crisis, low situational control, than in moderate control. He therefore creates a situation that allows him to feel in control and perform well.

- While group performance is a key criteria of effectiveness, other dimensions of effectiveness such as follower satisfaction and development of followers must also be considered. Focus on performance only is likely to backfire in the long-run, as the organization loses key high-potential employees.

- Students should consider whether it is possible to change the leader's style or whether they can be more successful in changing the situation.

One of the most successful strategies in this case is the help the leader learn to change a moderate situation into a high control one rather than a crisis one. This would allow the low-LPC leader to be feel in control and his group to be effective without creating the negative feelings and employee dissatisfaction. The focus can be on building a cohesive team, providing the leader and the team with more task training, or increasing the leader's power.

Chapter 5 Experiential Exercises

Self-assessment 5.1: Determining your LPC

This self-assessment is the LPC scale that students can use to determine their task or relationship-motivation within the contingency model. It is beneficial for students to have completed the scale prior to the lecture on the contingency model. However, they need precise instructions on how to fill out the scale. These should mention:

- Select your LPC carefully; if you have several people in mind, select the one with whom you had the most difficulty working

- Select an LPC who is a real person; don't make up an imaginary one

- Your LPC has to be someone with whom you have worked on a task; it could be a work or social situation

- You may or may not like your LPC as well as not being able to work with them

- Rank your selected person based on your own perception; do not to worry about how he/she may appear to others

These instructions are important to assure that students complete the scale properly.

The score is interpreted as follows:

- If your score is 73 or above, you are a relationship-motivated (high-LPC) person

- If your score is 64 or below, you are a task-motivated (low-LPC) person

- If you score is between 65 and 72, you are a socio-independent (middle-LPC) person

  Relationship-motivated/high LPC

The students sometimes have trouble making the jump from describing another person to describing their own style. It helps to point out to them that their perception and description of their LPC is a reflection of their motivational preferences.

Self-assessment 5.2: Assessing a Leadership Situation

The three scales in this self-assessment measure leader member relations, task structure, and position power. The students can use them to determine the level of situational control they face as a leader. The scale can be used either before or after the lecture on the contingency model. Students who have no or limited work experience should be encouraged to use a school work group, sports team, community or church group where they have been the leader as the basis for their self-assessment. This self-assessment works well as a simple individual task to help students understand their leadership style and the importance of situational contingencies in leadership effectiveness.

- It is important to remind students that the leader's perception is important

- Check on student's rating for the task structure scale to assure that they complete Part II correctly

Option: The self-assessment can be used as the basis for a group exercise. Students' self-assessment can be used as the basis of class discussion about the various aspects of the contingency model.

Total time: Minimum 35 minutes in class (15 minutes for completing self-assessment), 20 minutes for group discussion); depends on the number of teams (5 minutes per team)

Materials needed: Paper and pencil; board or flip chart can be useful.

Step 1: Individual Description (Individual work; 10 minutes)

Assign the self-assessment to students preferably before class as a homework assignment or during class. As noted above, it is most effective prior to the discussion about the contingency model.

Step 2: Group Discussion (Group work; 20 minutes)

The group portion of this exercise should be done after the discussion of the contingency model. Students should have a good understanding of the model's assumptions and predictions in order to analyze each member's leadership style, situational control, and the issue of fit.

The goal of this portion is to allow students a critical look at the contingency model. In some cases, and for some students, the model predicts leadership effectiveness well. In other cases, the model does not fit well. The focus of the discussion should not be to either propose the contingency model as the "cure-all," or to discard it if it does not fit. Instead, the instructor should encourage students to use the model as a tool to understand their leadership situation and their style. Particularly, students can discuss:

- What important components of each member's leadership situation were (i.e., was having good relations with subordinates more important than the leader's power? What caused the most stress? etc.)

- The factors that made the effective situations effective and what made the ineffective ones difficult

- Could each leader have behaved different? Why or why not?

Step 3: Group Presentations (5 minutes per team)

Ask each group to prepare a brief 5-minute presentation that outlines:

1.   What they have learned

2.   What they find most useful about the contingency approach

3.   What other information is lacking from the model that might have helped them

Overall: This exercise, used as an individual assessment or as a group exercise can provide a hands-on conclusion to the presentation of the contingency model. Given the complexities of the model, such applied focus is very helpful to most students. In some cases, the situations described by the students do not support the predictions of the model. I have used those situations as a springboard to presenting other leadership theories such as the normative decision model, the LMX, or transformational leadership, pointing out that no one theory or model will fit all situations.

 Course Assignment

> This self-assessment can be used as an assignment for the course. Students would complete the self-assessment and provide an analysis of their own style and the situations in which they were effective and ineffective.

Exercise 5.1: Changing the leader's Sit Con

This exercise provides a checklist of the types of actions a leader can take to adapt the situation to his/her style. It is designed as an individual training tool to be used after a leader determines his/her

LPC and level of situational control. It works best after the reading and discussion of the contingency model.

Exercise 5.2: Using the Normative Decision model

The scenarios in this exercise are designed to demonstrate the various situations described in the normative decision model. The questions following each scenario walk students through the problem identification questions prescribed by Vroom and Yetton (see Table 5.4). The exercise works equally well as an individual assignment after students have read chapter 5 or as a group exercise to demonstrate how to use the model.

<u>Scenario Solutions</u>

1. Centralizing Purchasing

1. What type of problem is it?

Group problem; decision will affect all purchasing managers

2. Problem identification questions:

- Is there a quality requirement?

   Yes; some decisions regarding both process and outcome are clearly better than others.

- Does the leader have enough information to make a high-quality decision?

   Maybe, although individual managers may have other information that, at this point, is not available to the manager.

- Is the problem clear and structured?

   Yes; cost reduction and economies of scales are needed

- Is employee acceptance of the decision needed for its implementation?

   Yes; acceptance and buy in of all individual managers are absolutely key.

- Would subordinates accept the decision if the leader makes it alone?

   No; managers are used to independence and autonomy, they can drag their feet forever and sabotage any decision they don't agree with.

- Do subordinates share the organization's goals for the problem?

   Probably yes; the organization's overall efficiency is at stake.

- Is there conflict among subordinates (are they cohesive) regarding the problem?

   Probably yes; the larger facilities would like more autonomy than others

3. Which decision rules apply?

   The leader does not have all the information (AI is eliminated)

   Subordinates have enough information and expertise and quality is important (CII and GII are acceptable)

   Quality is important, leader lacks information, problem is somewhat unstructured, and interaction among subordinates is important (AI, AII, and CI are eliminated).

Subordinate buy-in is essential (AI, AII, and CI are eliminated).

Buy-in is important and subordinates are likely to disagree over solution; interaction among them is encouraged (AI, AII, and CI are eliminated).

Quality and buy-in are both important.

Acceptance is important but not guaranteed and subordinates share the goal of the organization (AI, AII, CI, and CII are eliminated)

4. What are the acceptable decision styles?

GII, which applies to group decision and requires involvement of the group in decision making, is the acceptable decision style. With some management of process and egos, CII may also be an option, especially if managers cannot agree on a solution after extensive discussions.

Why? The subordinates (managers in this case) have power and information and share in the organization's goals. Their expertise and buy-in are key to a successful decision.

5. What are unacceptable decision styles?

AI, AII, CI which apply to group decision, but involve leader making the decision alone, are not acceptable.

Why? The managers can easily sabotage the outcome through various direct and indirect means. The potential change in the purchasing process affects their autonomy and constitutes a major change for them. Such a change cannot succeed without their buy in.

2. Selecting the Interns

1. What type of problem is it?

Individual decision

2. Problem identification questions:

- Is there a quality requirement?

  Yes; it is important to have good interns.

- Does the leader have enough information to make a high-quality decision?

Yes; the leader and the assistant know the job requirements and the candidates.

- Is the problem clear and structured?

  Yes; the job is simple.

- Is employee acceptance of the decision needed for its implementation?

  Not really; acceptance is likely to happen anyway.

- Would subordinates accept the decision if the leader makes it alone?

  Yes; previous interns have been good and the position is temporary.

- Do subordinates share the organization's goals for the problem?

  Yes.

- Is there conflict among subordinates (are they cohesive) regarding the problem?

  No.

3. Which decision rules apply?

The leader and assistant have all the information.

Subordinate, in this case the assistant, has all the necessary information and expertise.

Subordinate has the same goal as the leader and the organization.

Subordinate buy-in is likely regardless of decision.

There is no conflict among the subordinates; only one person is really involved.

Quality is important and buy-in guaranteed.

Acceptance is important and very likely.

4. What are the acceptable decision styles?

All styles are acceptable in this case. AI and AII are more efficient ways of making the decision. DI is probably the best style.

Why? The assistant has all the information and the expertise. Delegation of the decision would free up the leader's time and provide a growth opportunity for the assistant while guaranteeing a quality decision.

5. What arc unacceptable decision styles?

There really are no unacceptable styles, although group decision in this case would be unnecessary, and inefficient.

3. Moving to a New Location

1. What type of problem is it?

Group problem; decision will affect all employees.

2. Problem identification questions:

- Is there a quality requirement?

   No; both locations are equally acceptable.

- Does the leader have enough information to make a high-quality decision?

   Yes; there are reports available.

- Is the problem clear and structured?

   Yes; the two possible decisions are equally attractive.

- Is employee acceptance of the decision needed for its implementation?

   Not really; the leader has the power to make the decision.

- Would subordinates accept the decision if the leader makes it alone?

   Yes, although there may be some initial unhappiness.

- Do subordinates share the organization's goals for the problem?

   Probably yes; the overcrowding problem is recognized and a solution is desired.

- Is there conflict among subordinates (are they cohesive) regarding the problem?

Yes; there is no agreement as to who should stay and who should move; there are also individual differences within departments.

3. Which decision rules apply?

   The leader has all the information and the expertise.

   The subordinates are not likely to have all the information from all the departments.

   Although there is agreement on the overall goal, there are differences on who should move.

   Quality is not a central issue and the leader has information.

   Subordinate buy-in is not required.

   There is disagreement over the solution.

   Quality is not a central factor and buy-in will follow.

   Acceptance is desired and likely to happen given eventual outcome.

4. What are the acceptable decision styles?

   AI, AII, CI are likely to be the best styles in this case. The leader needs to make a final decision.

   Why?

   The leader has all the necessary information and expertise; there is a genuine time pressure, subordinates are not likely to agree on one solution while they will accept the leader's decision. CI may not be viable given the time pressure.

5. What are unacceptable decision styles?

   CII and GII are not desirable.

   Why?

   Group decision making is inappropriate given that subordinates conflict on the desired outcome and given the time pressure to make a quick decision.

Exercise 5.3: Creating an atmosphere that encourages participation

This exercise provides a checklist for students to use in situations where increased participation is appropriate. The assumption is that participation is not always required or necessary; however, when it is needed by the group, a leader should be able to use the strategies described in the checklist to encourage more active involvement from the group.

Although the exercise can be used as a basis for discussion of participation either after this chapter or after chapter 7, the exercise is primarily designed as a self-development tool for students.

Leadership in Action

The Cosmetic Queen and the Software King

Case summary

The case describes the leadership styles of Mary Kay Ash of Mary Kay Cosmetics and Bill Gates of Microsoft. The emphasis is on showing how both leaders are highly effective and how they lead successful organizations while they have very different styles of leadership. Both organizations have achieved considerable financial success, while they have different missions. Ash focused on building relationships, taking care of her employees, and providing them with a second family. Gates focuses on performance and innovation and tends to be more impersonal. Each organization's culture is a direct reflection of its leader's style and personality. The case provides an excellent example of the contingency approach to leadership where clearly different leadership styles are effective in different situations.

1. How would you describe each of the two leaders?

   Based on the available information provided it is difficult to clearly establish the two leader's LPC. However, it appears that Ash was highly concerned with building relationships and has made taking care of people the core of her organization. This style matched her background and religious beliefs. It is tempting to simply classify her as a high-LPC, relationship-motivated leader. This is clearly a possibility; however, it is also possible that Ash focused on building relationships as a way of getting her task done. Based on such interpretation, relationship were not her primary motivator; they were the way she could achieve her goals, making her a task-motivated leader. Mary Kay Cosmetics' culture has the same elements. Even after the Death of Ash, the organization continues to emphasize and reward financial performance and encourage building good relationships (including relationship with one's spouse) as the way to achieve success.

   Gates is more easily classified as a low-LPC, task-motivated leader. His focus is clearly on his task. Working on new problems and enjoying the task, working hard, and keeping busy are the factors that motivate him. Microsoft reflects its leader's focus on performance with little concern for other factors.

2. How are they similar? How are they different?

   Ash and Gates are both driven and highly motivated. Both have considerable passion for what they do. They work hard and demand that others around them do the same. Ash achieved her goals by focusing on relationship. Gates simply focuses on the task. Their styles may be partially due to generational and gender differences. There is no doubt that working with the two leaders would be a very different experience for followers. While in both cases, there is the push to perform and succeed, Ash demonstrated considerable care and concern for her employees and used that interest as a way to motivate them. Gates challenges his followers to do better by role modeling hard word and focusing on performance first and foremost. Both leaders use their groups to achieve the goals.

3. What makes each effective?

   Each leader has a style that matches their industry, their followers, and organization they have created. It is the fit that makes each highly effective and successful. The majority of Mary Kay's employees is women, many of whom with limited education and form traditional background and holding traditional values regarding the role of family and work. The organization continues to attract employees with those values and the leader assures that they needs are satisfied and their values reinforced and affirmed.

Gates' organization is one of the most powerful and successful organizations in the U.S. in a dynamic industry. Many of his followers are young and educated. Microsoft's focus on performance fits their style and need for autonomy.

The key to both leaders' effectiveness is the match between their style and the situation.

CHAPTER 6

EXCHANGE AND RELATIONSHIP DEVELOPMENT AND MANAGEMENT

Chapter Overview

This chapter presents five contingency views of leadership that all focus on the way the relationship between leaders and followers is established, develops, and is managed and on the process by which the leader guides subordinates to become effective rather than on how resources are used to make the group effective. Path-goal theory considers the leader's ability to remove obstacles for subordinates to be key to their satisfaction. The attribution models consider the way a leader's interpretation of subordinates' behavior affects the relationship between them. LMX focuses on the dyadic relationship between a leader and each follower and the creation of in- and out-groups around the leader. Leadership substitutes model presents various organizational and team variables that replace the relationship between the leader and followers. Finally, the situational leadership model, in spite of its serious limitations, is briefly reviewed because of its extensive use in training.

Chapter Objectives

OBJECTIVES	THROUGH BASIC TEXT	THROUGH FEATURES, TABLES, FIGURES AND EXAMPLES	THROUGH EXERCISES
Explain the key role of relationship development and management in effective leadership and use the concepts in improving leadership effectiveness	✓	Table 6.3 (p. 184)	
Discuss the Path-Goal Theory of leadership and explain the role of the leader in removing obstacles in followers' paths	✓	Figure 6.1 (p. 169)	Exercise 6.1 (p.187-188)

Understand the role of attribution in the relationship between leaders and followers and how it can be used to manage relationships	✓	Canadian vs. Jordanian attribution about leaders (p. 171) Effective leadership from the grassroots (p. 172)	
Present the Leader-Member Exchange Theory of leadership and clarify how the creation of in-groups and out-groups affects the leadership process	✓	Figure 6.2 (p. 172) Use of in-groups in Asia and the Middle East (p. 175-176) Leadership on the cutting edge (p. 175) Table 6.1 (p. 176) Alan Canton (p. 177) Michael Eisner and Michael Ovitz (p. 178) Maggie Widerotter (p. 178)	Exercise 6.2 (p. 189-190) Self-assessment 6.1 (p. 191-192)
Summarize the impact of leadership substitutes and identify situations in which the leader's impact is decreased	✓	Ricardo Semler (p. 179) Table 6.2 (p. 180) D.G. Yuengling & Sons (p. 181) Leading change (p. 185)	Self-assessment 6.2 (p. 193-194)

Chapter Outline

The chapter focuses on a second group of contingency models that addresses the exchange between the leader and his or her followers and the way in which the relationship is established, develops, and is managed.

1. Path-Goal theory

    a. The framework

    The path-goal theory of leadership is presented with focus on the role of the leader to clear paths for subordinates to accomplish goals. The exchange between the leader and followers centers around this obstacle removal role and the exchange of guidance or support from the leader for performance and satisfaction from followers (Figure 6.1).

    The two central hypotheses of the model are discussed. These are: when the task is structured, the leader's supportive behavior leads to follower satisfaction, whereas when the task is ambiguous, the leader's structuring behavior leads to satisfaction.

    b. Limitations and applications

    Lack of consistent research findings is suggested to be one of the major limitations of path-goal theory. However, the model's focus on followers' perception of the task and the role of the leader as obstacle remover provide interesting areas of applications.

2. Attributional models

The way the leader interprets followers' behaviors and uses that information to make decisions regarding future interactions with followers is the basis of attributional models of leadership. The factors that affect the way a leader interprets an employee's poor performance are presented

The role of culture in the way people make attributions regarding leader behavior is discussed. The example of a Canadian manager working with a Jordanian subordinate is used to illustrate the point.

a. Limitations and applications

Attributional models have limited application to the way leaders interpret their followers' actions. However, the model has received strong empirical support and points to an important area in the relationship between leaders and followers.

Effective leadership from the grassroots for me provides several practical guidelines to help leaders avoid biases that may affect their judgment of their followers.

3. Leader-member exchange (LMX)

The LMX model (vertical dyad linkage) is presented with the focus on the impact of existence of in-groups and out-groups on organizational performance and leadership effectiveness (Figure 6.2). The three stages of development of the relationship between leaders and followers are described (Table 6.1).

The effects of culture on in-group membership is presented. In many cultures in-group membership is assumed to be based on performance. In collectivistic cultures such Malaysia and many middle-eastern countries, in-group membership tends to be based on family and clan membership.

Leadership on the cutting edge focuses on research by Janssen and Van Yperen (2004) that tested how the followers' goal setting approach affects the quality of their relationship with their leader. The results indicate that a mastery goal setting orientation (those who believe that their effort leads to performance and take an intrinsic interest in their task) is positively correlated with LMX, job performance, and satisfaction. Followers with a performance goal-setting orientation (those who do not see a strong link between effort and performance) had lower quality LMX, lower performance, and lower satisfaction.

a. Limitations and applications

The model's lack of clarity regarding the factors that lead to the development of an out- vs. in-group relationship and the scarcity of research regarding the impact of in- and out-groups on organizations are presented as its major limitations.

The strength of the model is in its intuitive appeal and its potential use for making in- and out-groups effective. Particularly, the use of in-groups can be highly beneficial when membership is fluid and based on performance rather than personal factors.

Examples of the danger of selecting in-group members who are highly homogeneous are presented with focus on top level executive teams. This homogeneity can be partially blamed for the recent lack of performance of many large U.S. businesses.

4. Substitutes for leadership

The leadership substitutes model is presented (Table 6.2).

a. Limitations and applications

The need for more extensive testing of the model and its components is suggested to be one of the major limitations of the substitutes model. However, the model can be very useful in the current environment of self-managed teams and empowerment where the leader may intentionally use the model's findings to set up organizational and team substitutes to replace the traditional leadership functions.

Leading Change presents the case W.L. Gore which has a unique organizational culture and leadership development. The company operates with little hierarchy, no bosses, and few rules. Informal communication leads to mentoring relationships and the development of natural leadership whereby leaders are those who actually have willing and eager followers.

5. Situational leadership

    The situational leadership model (life cycle) is presented because of its extensive use in leadership training.

    a. Limitations and applications

        In spite of its widespread use in leadership training, the model suffers from serious theoretical and empirical problems, highly inconsistent findings, and very limited research.

6. Summary and conclusion

    Table 6.3 presents a comparison of the contingency models of leadership discussed in Chapters 5 and 6. The models are contrasted based on their use of leader and follower characteristics, task and effectiveness criteria, and the inclusion of other factors in the understanding of leadership.

Searching the Web

The W. L. Gore corporate culture

www.gore.com/en_xx/aboutus/culture/index.html

An article on leadership techniques from W. L. Gore & Associates, one of the most successful automotive, engineering, and textile manufacturers. This article and the site highlights the Gore policy of avoiding traditional hierarchy, opting instead for a team-based environment that fosters personal initiative, encourages innovation, and promotes person-to-person communication among all of our associates. This kind of unique corporate structure has proven to be a significant contributor to associate satisfaction and retention, and continues to be a factor in our inclusion in the magazine's annual list of top companies.

Path-Goal Theory

www.css.edu/users/dswenson/web/LEAD/path-goal.html

Detailed resource featuring questions and charts that examine different leadership models like Directive leadership, Supportive leadership, Participative leadership, Achievement-oriented leadership. Other links include a Locus of Control survey and an investigation into how environmental and subordinate contingency factors may moderate leadership behaviors to produce task and interpersonal outcomes.

Leader-Member Exchange Model

www.siop.org/Instruct/LMXTheory/sld001.htm

> Site features a great teaching tool, a slide show that details the LMX model including the precursors of LMX, how gender influences fairness in LMX relationships, and the role of perspective taking in LMX. In a theoretical overview, goes into detail about the series of exchanges or interactions like Role-taking, Role-Making, Role Routinization that make of the development of LMX. Many resources and links in addition to slide show.

Substitutes for Leadership Model

www.css.edu/users/dswenson/web/LEAD/substitutes.html

> In this comprehensive study dissecting Substitutes, Neutralizers, and Enhancements, charts and graphs detail the nuts and bolts of dealing with flawed leadership. Similarly, includes strategies for improving effective leadership, a feasibility overview, and a detailed table covering Substitutes and Enhancers for leader direction & support.

Commander Abrashoff (video clip)

http://www.grassrootsleadership.com/new/

> For a web cast of Commander Abrashoff go to the site above and then select videos under CLIENT RELATIONS.

www.watsonwyatt.com/strategyatwork/articles/2001/2001_05_tl.asp

> Commander Michael Abrasoff discusses leadership and his successful style of letting go of control in order to establish it when he took over command of the USS Benfold. The now famous Naval Commander details the winning leadership styles he employed that skyrocketed retention on his ship, the Benfold from 28 percent to 100 percent.

The Leadership Challenge: Creating Crisis: Performance vs. Morale

The role of culture in the creation of an in-group is explored by presenting students with a cross-cultural situation that by U.S. standards involves unfair advantage and maybe even unethical behavior. Students from the United States and other cultures that are primarily performance-focused rather than ascriptive, and individualistic rather than collectivistic tend to react strongly to the case and find the action of the Indian employee highly objectionable. Students should review the Hofstede and Trompenaars models to prepare for discussion. Issues that they must consider include:

- India is an ascriptive and vertical collectivistic culture where individual performance is less important than your personal background and connections with the family or clan. Additionally, power distance is high. In such culture, the in-group even for business setting is likely to determined by the family and clan membership more than individual achievement and performance.

- The Indian office manager is acting in good faith and in a reasonable and appropriate way based on his culture. He is supporting and protecting his supervisor.

- Not hiring the "cousin" may be highly insulting, causing your assistant to lose face and the manager to lose the trust of his Indian office manager. Therefore, the situation requires careful handling and diplomacy.

- The expatriate manager cannot simply be expected to behave according to Indian custom either, as his/her culture must also be taken into account.

The scenario can be used as a springboard for a discussion of how "in-groups" form in different cultures.

Chapter 6 Experiential Exercises

Self-assessment 6.1: Identifying your in-group and out-group

This exercise looks at LMX and the impact of in-groups and out-groups from the leader's point of view. Whereas exercise 6.2 is appropriate for students with different levels of work experience, this self-assessment tends to be more appropriate and effective for students who have managed subordinates. For those students, this self-assessment can be a helpful developmental tool to use to understand the extent to which they use in- and out-groups and their potential impact on their followers and coworkers.

As is the case with Exercise 6.2, this assessment should be completed after students have a good understanding of the LMX concept.

Overall: Students tend to find this assessment to be very informative. Although most have in and out-groups, few are aware of their impact or even think much about how membership is determined.

 Course Assignment

> This exercise can be used as an assignment for the course. The students would be asked to record their in-group and out-group as described by the exercise and provide a written analysis of the benefits and disadvantages along with a plan for future action.

Self-assessment 6.2: Leadership substitutes

The self-assessment is based on the leadership substitutes concept and allows students to identify leadership neutralizers and substitutes for leader consideration and structuring behaviors. It is most useful for students who have managerial experience, although the term "subordinates" can be replaced with "people I work with" to make it applicable to non-work situations or to people who are not in leadership situations.

The assessment can be used as a basis for discussion during the class on leadership substitutes or to as one of the tools to be used to evaluate whether a group is ready for operating as a self-managed team (topics presented in chapter 7).

It is helpful to point out to students that, although traditional views of leadership may make the presence of substitutes undesirable, more current views of a leader as a facilitator and coach would actually require increasing the number of substitutes in order to remove the leader from the team.

 Course Assignment

> This exercise can be used as an individual assignment for the course for students who are in leadership/ supervisory positions. The work group can be evaluated in terms of the presence of substitutes and the analysis used as the basis for action recommendations.

Exercise 6.1: Removing obstacles

The exercise is based on the path-goal theory. It is designed to allow students to identify the task that their followers are performing, evaluate their need for autonomy, and use the propositions of path-goal to determine the appropriate leadership behaviors. The exercise is most effective if used after students have read chapter 6 and/or after class presentation of path-goal concepts. In addition to potential developmental use by the students, the exercise can be used as a check on their understanding of the model.

 Course Assignment

> This exercise can be used as an assignment for the course. The students can be asked to describe the team, department or organization they are evaluating, use the items in the exercise to analyze the situation and to develop a series of alternative courses of action for the leader to follow.

Exercise 6.2: In-group/out-group

This exercise is a very engaging and effective way to help students understand and experience the impact of in- and out-groups in organizations as described by the LMX model. It works well for students with all levels of work experience as in- and out-groups exist in all organizations, not only work settings.

The exercise is a collaborative-learning group activity.

Total time: Minimum depends on number of groups in class (10 minutes group preparation)

Materials needed: Paper and pencil; use of flip chart or board

The instructor needs to form groups of 3-6 students (the number of students is not very important). If there are existing groups in class, this is good opportunity for them to interact and work together. More than 8 groups in one class tend to be difficult to manage and make the exercise unnecessarily redundant.

Half of groups can be assigned Step 1 (being in the in-group), the other half can be assigned Step 2 (being in the out-group). Allow the groups 10 minutes to answer the four questions in the exercise.

Going from group to group in a round robin-fashion, ask each group to provide you with answers to each question. Start with either in- or out-group and record their answers on separate parts of the board.

Once all information from all groups is recorded, the discussion should focus on the difference between in- and out-groups and its impact on motivation and performance.

Overall: This is a very engaging and very simple exercise that generates a lot of discussion. Students from all levels can identify with the issues well and therefore provide a lot interesting examples and input.

Leadership in Action

The Caring Navy Commander

Case summary

Michael Abrashoff is the commander of the USS Benfold. The U.S. Navy ship has been ranked as one of the best of the fleet in a number of different areas. Abrashoff violates many of the stereotypical expectations of a military officer. He focuses on performance rather than obedience and discipline. The hallmark of his leadership style is listening to his crew and actively changing the things that makes them unhappy and block their performance. His has created a climate where the lowest crewmember is important. Replacing metal ship parts with stainless steel ones to reduce the much hated chipping and painting chores, providing SAT testing for his crew, improving the food on board, and disregarding strict military policies in favor of more liberal shore leave regulations are some of the actions Abrashoff has taken to increase his crew's satisfaction. His efforts have been rewarded with focus on the task, outstanding performance, and considerable admiration and affection of the leader.

1. What are the elements of Abrashoff's leadership?

   Abrashoff prides himself on his ability to get know all members of his ship and listening to them. His focus is on performance rather than military rules and obedience. He has developed personal relationships with his crew members. He uses the information he acquires through listening to his crew to implement needed changes that allow them to perform their job well.

2. What factors contribute to his effectiveness?

   The development and management of the relationships with his sailors is key to Abrashoff's success and effectiveness as a leader. Abrashoff removes obstacles for his crew, thereby increasing their satisfaction and allowing them to do their job. His style is unexpected in a military organization where discipline and obedience tend to be primary. However, because of the personal relationships he has developed, he has considerable referent power, as well as the other traditional sources of power. His crew's personal relationship and admiration allow him to maintain the discipline necessary for military operations.

3. What models can be used to explain his performance?

   Abrashoff's performance can be analyzed using any of the contingency models of leadership. Each model allows for consideration of slightly different aspects of his style and effectiveness. Fiedler's model, the path-goal theory, and substitutes for leadership are particularly enlightening.

   Based on Fiedler's Contingency Model, Abrashoff is likely to be a task-motivated leader. While he has excellent interpersonal skills, he is focused on performance and getting things done. He faces a high control situation since he has excellent leader-member relations, high task structure, and high position power. He is therefore in match and, as predicted by the model, is effective.

   Abrashoff's performance can be easily understood using the Path-Goal Theory. By listening to his crewmembers and addressing their needs, he removes obstacles to allow them be motivated and perform well. His actions provide structure, change the task, or show concern for his crew. For example, he removed a source of dissatisfaction and made his crew's job less tedious and more interesting by replacing metal ship parts with stainless steel ones.

Bending the shore leave rules is another example of addressing crew satisfaction. In other cases, he provided resources, such as SAT testing or AOL On-Line connection, to address their needs. In all cases his structuring or consideration behaviors removed obstacles for his followers.

Abrashoff appears to create appropriate substitutes for leadership thereby empowering his crewmembers to do their job better. He uses his crew's experience and professionalism to replace his direct orders. By allowing more autonomy, he provides his crew with more challenging tasks and substitutes for the need to be considerate and supportive.

In addition to using contingency models, Abrashoff's style can be viewed in light of the participative and empowerment models of management that are discussed in the next chapter or the change-oriented leadership models presented in Chapter 8.

For more information about Michael Abrashoff see:

For a web cast of Commander Abrashoff: http://www.grassrootsleadership.com/new/ (then select videos under CLIENT RELATIONS)

Abrashoff, D. Michael. 2002. It's Your Ship: Management Techniques from the Best Damn Ship in the Navy. Warner Books.

Abrashoff, D. Michael. Retention Through Redemption (HBR OnPoint Enhanced Edition) [DOWNLOAD: PDF] (Digital)

http://www.signonsandiego.com/news/business/kinsman/20020526-9999_1b26kinsman.html

PART THREE

CURRENT DEVELOPMENTS AND APPLICATIONS

CHAPTER 7

PARTICIPATIVE MANAGEMENT AND TEAMS

Chapter Overview

The chapter tracks the evolution of participation in leadership by presenting the situations that make participation desirable and outlining the benefits and disadvantages of employee participation. Delegation is discussed as an application of participation concepts. The benefits and steps to proper delegation are presented. The chapter ends with a focus on the current use of teams in organizations and its effect on leadership roles. The concepts of self-managed teams and super-leadership are presented as current forms of formalized participation in organization. The chapter has a strong cross-cultural focus since the success of participative management depends to a great extent on cultural values of collectivism and power distance.

Chapter Objectives

OBJECTIVES	THROUGH BASIC TEXT	THROUGH TABLES AND BOXES	THROUGH EXERCISES
Understand when and why participation should be used to improve leadership effectiveness	✓	Figure 7.1 (p. 200) Ford Motor Company (p. 200-201) Royal Philips Electronics (p. 201) Genencor (p. 201 Table 7.1 (p. 202) Kiwi Airlines (p. 203) Leadership on the cutting edge (p. 198)	

Explain the role of culture in the use and success of participative leadership	✓	Mexico, Dominican Republic, Sweden France, U.S., Australia, Afghanistan, Germany, Sweden, Israel (p. 204) Leadership on the cutting edge (p. 206)	
Specify the elements of effective delegation	✓	Table 7.2 (p. 207) Table 7.3 (p. 208)	Exercise 7.1 (p. 220-221) Self-assessment 7.1 (p. 225)
Clarify the role of leadership in self-managed teams	✓	Table 7.4 (p. 209) Rackspace (p. 209 Figure 7.2 (p. 211) Effective leadership from the grassroots (p. 212) Leading change (p. 215) Figure 7.3 (p. 216)	Self-assessment 7.2 (p. 226)
Explain the principles of super- and self-leadership	✓		Exercise 7.2 (p. 22-224)

Chapter Outline

1. When should participation be used?

    a. Criteria for participation

    This section presents the various factors that affect the use of participation by the leader and the types of participative management and teams used in different organizations (Figure 7.1; Table 7.1). Task complexity, employee commitment, organization readiness, and task characteristics are some of the relevant factors.

    b. Role of culture

    The key role of culture in the use and success of participative management is discussed while pointing out that high power distance and collectivism have a great impact on the leaders' use of participation as a management tool.

2. The issue of delegation

    This section provides a detailed description of the advantages and disadvantages of delegation as a leadership tool.

    a. Benefits of delegation

The benefits of delegation include: Freeing up the leader's time, providing employees with growth opportunities, allowing them to be involved in tasks, providing the leader with opportunities to observe employees, and increasing employee motivation and satisfaction.

b. Guidelines for good delegation

The steps to proper delegation are presented (Table 7.2).

Leadership on the Cutting Edge presents Van de Vliert and Smith's (2004) research about he impact of economic development climate on participation in organizations. The researchers found that leaders rely less on subordinates in less developed countries with harsh climes. Moderate participation occurs in temperate climates and the highest level of participation occurs in the most developed countries with harsh climates.

c. Why do leaders fail to delegate?

The factors that cause many leaders to fail to delegate tasks and responsibilities to their followers are presented (Table 7.3).

3. Evolution of participative management: Use of teams and superleadership

The use of teams as a formal structure to encourage participation in decision making is discussed.

a. Characteristics of teams

Table 7.4 summarizes the difference between groups and teams. Commitment to common goals and procedures, shared responsibility and leadership, and synergy are key elements of teams.

b. Self-managed teams

Elements of self-managed teams are presented. These include: the power to manage their own work, not having an outside manager, coordination and cooperation with other teams, and internal leadership based on facilitation.

Effective leadership from the grassroots presents practical tips based on sports team for making work teams in effective.

The importance of building trust and the elements that lead to trust in teams are presented (Figure 7.2)

c. Helping teams become effective

Teams require special training to become effective. The training should include: team building, cross training, coordination training, self-guided correction, and assertiveness.

d. Super- and self-leadership

Super and self-leadership are presented as one of the applications of participative management in organizations. In team environment, the need for leadership is reduced. Therefore all team members should be encouraged to become self-leaders. Superleadership includes the following elements: developing positive and motivating thought patterns, personal goal setting, observation and self-evaluation, and self-reinforcement.

Strategies for the development of self-leaders include: listening, asking questions, sharing information, encouraging independence, encouraging creativity.

5. Role of leaders in a team environment

The new roles of leaders in a team environment are presented (Figure 7.3) and the stresses and obstacles associated with the new roles are discussed. A cultural analysis of teams is presented by focusing on the U.S. and Australian individualism cultural value as the basis for the new concept of *collaborative individualism* that is suggested to replace the eastern-based concept of cooperative and harmonious teams.

Leading Change describes how Dr. Nancy Hutson, VP of Global R&D at Pfizer keeps her team members motivated in the face of recurring failure in drug development. She focuses on paying attention to people first, being supportive, actively mentoring employees, and celebrating all victories.

e.   Summary and conclusion

Searching the Web

Delegation

www.ittoolkit.com/articles/projects/ease_delegation.htm

This site contains a plethora of information regarding how to get comfortable delegating, when to delegate, and an assortment of links, role-playing exercises. Helpful resources focus on using delegation to deliver project success - both in process and outcome, and a how to model to do so. Plenty of extras.

www.mindtools.com/tmdelegt.html

Site features further info on the art of delegation including topics like what should or shouldn't be delegated, and why people fail to delegate. The how-to section offers a simple outline that is easy to understand. Lots of links here to explore as well.

www.psconsult.de/scripts/English/doc/MgmtDelegation.pdf

This article is another helpful delegation article featuring a helpful 5 step implementation section.

Team building

www.teamtechnology.co.uk/tt/h-articl/tb-basic.htm

This page gives a basic overview to team building including a look at the stages involved include clarifying the goal, identifying the inhibitors and removing them. Covers terms often used in a team building context, charts common goals of team building, and offers several helpful links.

Being an effective team member

www.mgmt.utoronto.ca/~baum/mgt2005/valuable.html

The article "Being a Valuable Team Member" covers how all team members are responsible for their team's success and how to get past prior experience simply being a member of a work group. Details how to approach one-on-one relationships, meetings, and goal setting in order to change to a team model.

Leading informal groups

www.accel-team.com/work_groups/informal_grps_02.html

Web article that deals with managing the norms of informal groups in the work place. Covers communication, cohesion, and norms, change informal group norms, and how leader perceptions influence performance and the self-fulfilling prophesy. Within the study is a great list of prevalent and important definitions and ten pre-determined dimensions of norms.

Different types of teams and managing team performance

www-hr.ucsd.edu/~staffeducation/guide/teamdef.html

The Guide to Performance Management is a great resource for managing team performance definitions from the HR department website of University California, San Diego. Definitions and practical explanations for concepts like Natural Work Group, Cross-functional Team, and Self-directed Work Team among others.

Whole Foods

www.wholefoodsmarket.com/company/philosophy.html

Whole Foods Market is a dynamic leader in the quality food business. Their website outlines their philosophy, their mission statement, and notably their Declaration of Interdependence which highlights their belief that their success hinges and depends on the positive relationships between the company, its employees, and its customers.

The Leadership Challenge: Who Gets the Project?

Students are asked to make a delegation decision while considering the issue of in- and out-group. Factors that they must consider include:

- How was the original in-group formed and how can followers become part of the leader's in-group.

- Reviewing the rules of delegation and objectively identifying candidates without the issue of in-group. In the U.S. and many other Western cultures, the expectation is that the best person for the project should be selected based on objective criteria.

- The information regarding a potential complaint should not interfere with the current decision. However, the information is useful feedback for the leader to review his/her action and consider the potential for bias. The potential complaint provides an opportunity for review and self-analysis.

Chapter 7 Experiential Exercises

Self-assessment 7.1: Delegation scale

This self-assessment is based on the typical myths about delegation and allows students to evaluate their level of comfort and inclination towards delegation. It should be assigned as a homework assignment prior to class discussion on delegation and used as a tool to encourage student participation in such discussion.

Self-assessment 7.2: Are you a team leader?

This self-assessment is based on the team leader roles presented in the chapter. It allows students to evaluate their general ability and level of comfort with the team leadership roles. It can be completed either before or after the discussion of team leadership.

Exercise 7.1: To delegate or not to delegate?

This exercise is a role play that demonstrates the elements of good delegation by providing students with various delegation options and requiring them to make a decision regarding which one of the subordinates should be delegated a task.

The role play situation requires no prior preparation from the instructor or the students. Having students read the basic scenario prior to coming to class can help save some in-class time. The role play works best after class discussion of delegation in order to allow students to apply the knowledge they acquire through the text and the class.

Total time: Minimum 45 minutes in class (10-15 minutes preparation; 25 minutes role play; 10 minutes debriefing)

Materials needed: Enough room for several groups to role play

Role Play (35 minutes minimum; includes preparation)

Instructions for each role and manager and observer worksheets are included at the end of this chapter.

The class should be divided in groups of five students each (one manager and four subordinates). All the names used in the role play are androgynous allowing for roles to be assigned to either male or female students. Students assigned to role play managers can use their own names.

Review the general scenario with the whole class reminding them of the role-play rules (used in Narian Bridges):

- Stay in the general guidelines provided by your role

- Improvise as needed while keeping goal in mind

- Practice role for a few minutes alone or with your team

- Provide rich role play so that others can respond to you

- Be as creative as you feel comfortable; some of you will play your role more intensely than others; differences are normal

The instructor then needs to review each role with students playing that role (i.e., all managers, all Frans, all Gerrys, etc.).

The role play takes place in two stages.

Stage 1: In the first stage the manager meets with the four subordinates to describe the new client and ask for ideas and input from the group. This provides an opportunity for team members to reveal as much or as little as they want about their role and their motivation and for the manager to have more information to make a decision on who gets the new account. This stage should last no longer than 10 minutes.

Stage 2: In the second stage the manager makes a selection alone, and prepares for the meeting with the selected employee using the manager's worksheet in the textbook (5-10 minutes). He/she then meets with the selected employee to hand-off the account (5-10 minutes).

The other three employees will serve as observers in the meeting between the manager and the selected employee using the observer worksheet to evaluate the process. The selected employee should also complete the worksheet at the end of the meeting. Remind students that they will have to share their comments with the manager and the employee and that therefore they need to:

- Focus on specific behavior

- Be critical but constructive

- Be professional (stay away from personal comments)

Debriefing (10 minutes)

The debriefing can be done either within the groups only or both in the groups and with the whole class. Students are often interested in other managers' choices and their reasons. The instructor may want to put the choices and the justifications on the board. Although the choices are often similar, depending on how each student has played a role, there may be interesting differences.

The evaluation of the delegation should be done in each group with the instructor's help.

Overall: I have a used this role-play a number of times in my classes. It works well and provides students with an experience with the nuts and bolts of delegation. As with many other role-plays, students with some work experience handle the task better, although the setting provides a nice opportunity for practice for more traditional and younger students with limited or no managerial experience. The only drawback of the exercise is its length.

Exercise 7.2: Strategies for becoming a superleader?

This exercise is based on the steps to superleadership described in the chapter. It is designed as a developmental tool for students. It is most effective if students have a good understanding of superleadership concept, so it should be completed after the class presentation on the topic.

 Course Assignment

The exercise works very well as a homework/journal-type assignment requiring students to track their own behaviors and to perform basic goal-setting in regard to areas that they would like to change.

Leadership in Action

Whole Foods

Case summary

The case describes John Mackey, the CEO of Whole Foods and the company he has created. Whole Foods is changing the grocery business with its focus on nature foods, bright, well-decorated facilities, and outstanding customer service. Mackey founded the company in 1980 and has created a culture that reflects his own values of democracy and equality. A vegan, he emphasizes healthy foods, stays involved in his business, and practices a frugal lifestyle in spite of the considerable success of his company. Teams are the basis of all decision-making at Whole Foods; they decided whom to hire, what products to carry, and even how to allocate raises. The company prides itself on its "Declaration of Interdependence" which affirms the important of employees, customers, community, and all other stakeholders. Whole Foods implements John Mackey's democratic ideals by sharing decision-making, sharing profits with employees, making employee fun and happiness a priority, continuously training employees, and promoting from within to encourage and develop talent. The team-based, employee focused culture and structure have allowed the company to thrive and grow.

1. What are the elements of John Mackey's leadership?

   John Mackey has stayed true to his roots as, what one person describes an anarchist. His focus on democracy, healthy foods, and the building of community permeates his company. Even with considerable financial success, he remains accessible and involved in his business. His deep-seated beliefs in equality and democracy have been translated into team-based approach to management. While he remains involved in the company, the decisions are made by teams at all levels. With a focus on employee empowerment and development, John Mackey appears to have instituted a sense of super and self-leadership at Whole Foods.

2. What makes the teams at Whole Foods effective?

   The teams at Whole Foods are an integral part of the culture and structure of the company. They are not an afterthought; they are the company. They complete involvement at all levels of decision making makes them central to the organization and allows them to be effective. The focus on interdependence among employees, customers, and other stakeholders further emphasizes the importance of cooperation and working together, further reinforcing the role of the teams.

   Overall, the teams at whole work well because their task is complex, the employees are committed and highly competent, and the leader and the organization are ready for empowerment.

To Delegate or Not to Delegate

Instructions for the Team Manager

You come to Sunshine with an MBA from a major state institution. Your undergraduate background is also in general business. After your B.S., you started working for a major hotel firm and, as a result of several mergers they experienced, you have worked in different aspects of the hospitality industry for the past nine years. You managed to quit to go back for your MBA which you finished just over a year ago. Sunshine offered you a great opportunity just before you finished, and you joined the organization 18 months ago. You have really enjoyed your job, although it is the first time you are actually managing people. You are responsible for their growth and development, a responsibility you take very seriously. Your boss is only interested in results. Like many others in the industry, Sunshine has been slow at adopting new management techniques. Many of its employees move up through the ranks without major formal training. You are actually one of the few outside managers but your career track is very attractive and you know that the only way to move up is to deliver results without problems. Your boss leaves you alone and expects no requests for help.

Your employees

Fran Smith has been with Sunshine for 8 years and has been a strong performer. S/he is one of your trusted employees.

Gerry Narden has been with Sunshine for 5 years moving up through the ranks. S/he is very eager but makes mistakes.

Terry Chan has a 9-year tenure at Sunshine. S/he is a high performer and seems to like to doing her/his own thing with personal contacts.

J.P. Ricci is the youngest member of the team with barely one year at Sunshine. S/he is very bright but not always very motivated.

To Delegate or not to Delegate

For Managers: Decision and Meeting Worksheet

Who are you selecting? What are your reasons?

Plan the meeting during which you will delegate the task. What do you need to say? What areas do you need to cover? How are you addressing your employees' needs? etc.

To Delegate or not to Delegate

Instructions for Fran Smith

You have enjoyed working at Sunshine for 8 years now, but you are getting bored with the job. You have plans to go graduate school, but except for your current boss, not too many managers of the organization have higher-level degrees, so you are not sure that the organization would value it. You also have recently taken on several projects in your community that you are enjoying, and you have, as a result, started to reduce your involvement with Sunshine. You would like to talk to your boss about your loss of interest, but are afraid that it may affect your relationship.

Instructions for Gerry Narden

You consider yourself one of Sunshine's most dedicated employees. The organization has been very good to you since you joined 5 years ago, and you love your job. The career progression has been great, and you have dreams of some day running this place! You are eager to learn and not afraid to make mistakes. You have made some mistakes in your new job but are now getting the hang of it, and you are feeling very good about your performance and looking for new challenges.

Instructions for Terry Chan

You have been a loyal Sunshine employee and a successful performer for 9 years. You were looking forward to becoming the manager of the team before they brought in the new boss, and you have had trouble getting over the resentment. By all accounts, you should have had the job! You have your own sources and your own clients, and you particularly are plugged into several major corporations that just bring you their business. You are not planning to help the new boss look good yet, but you are taking a wait-and-see position for now.

Instructions for J.P. Ricci

You are still looking for something that would really turn you on, career-wise. You know you can do the job at Sunshine with your hands tied behind your back, and you have for the past year, but you have not found the right challenge yet. Things just have not been interesting enough. You really like the job and your colleagues, but you are just not sure that this is the right thing.

For employees: Observer Worksheet

What does the selected employee need to do a good job?

Evaluate the manager based on:

1. Clarity of information about the task:

2. Clarity of expectations regarding the task:

3. What are the manager's strengths?

4. What could have been done better?

CHAPTER 8

CHANGE-ORIENTED LEADERSHIP

Chapter Overview

The theories of charismatic, transformational, exemplary, and visionary leadership are presented as the major models focused on how leaders enact change in organizations. Charismatic leadership is defined as an intense emotional relationship between leaders and followers where leader, follower, and situational characteristics all play key roles. Transformational leadership, which uses charisma as one of its elements and is focused on large-scale change in organizations, is discussed and contrasted with transactional leadership, which is primarily concerned with exchange between leaders and followers. The key role of credibility in change-oriented and exemplary leadership is also presented.

Chapter Objectives

OBJECTIVES	THROUGH BASIC TEXT	THROUGH FEATURES, TABLES, FIGURES, AND EXAMPLES	THROUGH EXERCISES
Describe the various leader, follower, cultural, and situational characteristics that contribute to charismatic leadership	✓	Michael Saylor, Howard Charney (p. 231) Table 8.1 (p. 225) Martin Luther King, Ghandi (p 231) Steve Case, Aung San Suu Kyi; Fidel Castro, Gamal Abdul Nasser, Nelson Mandela (p. 232) Hatin Tyabji, Cheong Choong Kong, Bill George, John F. Kennedy (p. 233) Table 8.2 (p.234); Table 8.3 (p. 235) Cross-cultural attributes of leadership; Table 8.4 (p. 236) Leadership on the cutting edge (p. 239)	Exercise 8.1 (p 252-253) Exercise 8.2 (p. 254)

Explain the positive and negative impact of charismatic leadership on organizations	✓		
Distinguish between transactional and transformational leadership	✓	Mark Wallace, Jack Welch, Andy Grove (p. 241-242)	
Understand the key role of contingency reward and the impact of management by exception	✓	Rocky Flats nuclear site (p. 241)	
Present the elements of transformational leadership and their impact on followers and organizations	✓	Figure 8.1 (p. 242)	
Describe the role of visionary and exemplary leadership in bringing about change in organizations	✓	Leading change (p. 245) Patrick Kelley (p. 246); Figure 8.2 (p. 247) Rob Waldron (p. 247) Effective leadership form the grassroots (p. 249) Kathy Taggares (p. 241)	Self-assessment 8.1 (p. 255)

Chapter Outline

1. A brief history of charismatic and transformational leadership and its impact

    The relatively brief history of the charismatic/transformational leadership research is presented and its current impact on the field of leadership is discussed.

2. Charismatic leadership: A relationship between leaders and followers

    Charismatic leadership is defined as a relationship between leaders and followers rather than a simple collection of leader traits and behaviors.

    a. Characteristics of charismatic leaders

        The personality and behavioral characteristics of charismatic leaders are presented (Table 8.1) along with several U.S. and international examples of charismatic leaders. High self-confidence and excellent articulation skills are central (Table 8.1)

    b. Characteristics of followers

        The personality and behavioral characteristics of followers of charismatic leaders are discussed (Table 8.2). Loyalty to and obedience of leader are essential elements.

    c. The charismatic situation

        Since charismatic leadership is defined as a relationship between leaders and followers, the elements of a charismatic relationship and the situation in which it occurs are key

External crisis and turbulence is key to the emergence of charismatic leaders (Table 8.3). . Whether real or perceived, a sense of crisis and ability for the leader to articulate his/her vision to resolve the crisis are important.

Internal organizational conditions include: the organizational life cycle, the type of task, and the organizational culture and structure. The more uncertainty, the more likely that a charismatic leader will emerge.

Role of culture. The role of culture in charismatic leadership is explored. Some research suggests that cultures with a strong prophetic salvation are more likely to give rise to charismatic leaders than those without such views. These cultures include many with a Judeo-Christian tradition (Table 8.4).

    d.   The dark side of charisma

This section discusses the characteristics of unethical charismatic leaders who use their relationship with followers to pursue their personal goals and agenda. Negative charismatic leaders may also present a flawed vision that is self-serving or unrealistic.

    d.   Evaluation and application

The section ends with an evaluation of charismatic leadership concepts. A number of different interpretations of charismatic leadership have been proposed. The concepts have a strong appeal although charismatic leadership should not be viewed as a cure-all.

Leadership on the cutting edge presents research about the link between charisma and corporate corruption. Researchers deCelles and Pfarrer (2004) proposes that pressure from stakeholders directly influences the extent of corruption. Additionally, they suggest that environmental uncertainty and leader charisma also create the context in which corruption is more likely to occur.

3.   Transactional and transformational leadership

The concepts of transformational and transactional leadership are presented. Whereas transformational leadership is focused on large-scale change in organizations, transactional leadership focuses on basic exchanges between leaders and followers.

    a.   Transactional leadership

Contingency reward. Transactional leadership is based on the concept that the leader provides followers with resources and rewards in exchange for motivation and productivity. When well implemented, this exchange is at the heart of motivation and can lead to highly desirable results.

Management by exception (MBE). MBE is another type of transactional leadership where the leader only intervenes when things go wrong, relying on discipline and punishment. MBE is usually associated with follower dissatisfaction and poor performance.

    b.   Transformational leadership

Transformational leadership is concerned with inspiring followers to enable them to enact revolutionary change in their organization. The components are presented in Figure 8.1.

Charisma and inspiration. The first component of transformational leadership is the creation of an intense emotional bond between leaders and followers through charismatic leadership.

Intellectual stimulation. The second component of transformational leadership is the leader's ability to challenge followers intellectually to solve problems through new and creative means.

Individual consideration. The third component of transformational leadership is establishment of personal relationships with each follower.

The three components combine to allow leaders to transform organizations.

a. Evaluation and application

There are many studies of transformational leadership from those testing the basic hypothesis to several others looking at the concepts across culture and gender. Although the model has been generally supported, further research is needed in regards to the measurement of the concepts. Several recommendations for application include: Projecting confidence, providing a clear vision, encouraging creativity, setting high expectations, and establishing personal relationships with followers.

4. Change-oriented visionary leadership concepts

Leading change presents the case of Sir Richard Branson, the founder and CEO of the Virgin Group, a family of companies headquartered in London. Branson is a self-made entrepreneur with a flare for outrageous marketing stunts. He has also built his company on the philosophy that leaders must like people and focus on bringing out the best in every employee.

The concepts related to change-oriented leadership include: the importance of having a clear vision, empowerment and confidence in followers, flexibility and change, and teamwork and cooperation.

A model proposed by Kouzes and Posner is presented with focus on development of credibility at the heart of leadership (Figure 8.2). The continuous questioning of old beliefs and assumptions is also key.

Effective leadership from the grassroots outlines key factors for rewarding and encouraging followers to motivate and inspire them. The guidelines are based on research by Kouzes and Posner.

a. Evaluation and application

Change-oriented models have considerable popular appeal. They tend to propose a "one best way" rather than a contingency view of effective leadership style. There is also limited empirical research about the models. The models provide useful guideline for leaders; these guidelines include: having passion, developing credibility, clarifying vision and values, including followers in decisions, and role modeling.

5. Summary and conclusion

Searching the Web

Charismatic leader

http://psychology.about.com/library/weekly/aa012500a.htm

An interesting site and article detailing different elements of what it is to be a charismatic leader. Definitions and links supply readers with ample information regarding the Charisma Theory of Leadership and phenomena surrounding charismatic leadership.

http://web.cba.neu.edu/~ewertheim/leader/charisma.htm

This website features an interesting article examining if Charisma really matters. Questions like where to find charismatic leaders and facts that show that charisma doesn't always equate to success pepper this article that aims to consider Charismatic leadership from an academic perspective.

www.breakoutofthebox.com/charismatic.htm

A conversational article that comes from a column that featured a series of interviews aimed to investigate the pros and cons of charismatic leadership. Discusses what a charismatic evokes from employees, and how therefore employees and peers motivations and reactions derive from the leader's symbolic status.

www.strategosinc.com/what_leaders_do.htm

This website covers what charismatic leaders do like challenging the status quo, creating a compelling vision, enabling others to act, and encouraging the heart of followers and peers. Other resources on similar subjects under links.

Leading Change

http://drucker.org/leaderbooks/L2L/summer99/kanter.html

A compelling article on enduring skills of change leaders, this page offers an in depth look at how leaders affect change in their current situations. The article features a number of specific points like Keys to mastering change, a 7 point list of classic skills for leaders, and Being a Force of Change. The hosting website features a variety of resources.

www.advantagepoint.com/articles/change/art7.html

This article offers a 5 point lesson plan for implementing change and creating the future in a company or association through the exciting work of strategic planning. The articles section of this website also boasts a wide variety of articles dealing with change management like "Managing in Times of Unrest, Uncertainty, and Change", "Inside the Box Creative Decision Making" and "People Leave Managers, Not Companies: How to Increase Employee Retention."

www.sba.gov/managing/leadership/changemanagement.html

This article from the Small Business Administration covers how to implement change management from the top down with an assortment of helpful tips and tools. Also offers a insight into reducing the frustration of the change process with six key phases people go through whenever they are experiencing any type of change, be it personal or professional.

www.esi-intl.com/public/publications/22002changemanagement.asp

This site features a great article detailing Leading Change throughout history from ancient Greece to today. Suggestions include a detailed look at a three step process American social psychologist Kurt Lewin observed during the 1940s and described as defending the status quo, taking actions that bring about change, and anchoring the changes in the corporate culture.

The Leadership Challenge: Standing Up to a Charismatic but Unethical Leader

Students are presented with the difficult situation of how to handle a potentially unethical and abusive leader. Issues of unethical charisma as well as "evil managers" (presented in chapter 4 Cutting Edge) are key. Issues students should consider are:

- What is objective data as compared to subjective information? Does the follower have enough objective information?

- Personal values and priorities including the importance of career progress and the potential negative consequences of standing up to the leader. Students' personalities (for example their Mach score) and personal values are key in this analysis.

- How to deal with abusive bosses including careful documentation, awareness of legal rights, knowledge of company policy as well as company culture.

The answer to this challenge is highly personal and individual. There clearly is no best or correct course of action, except for careful documentation. Students differ considerable in their choice of course of action. The case provides a good opportunity to discuss employee rights, organizational politics, and career management.

Chapter 8 Experiential Exercises

Self-assessment 8.1: Building credibility

Having credibility is suggested to be one of the central factors in effective change-oriented leadership. This self-assessment is designed to allow students to evaluate their credibility and identify areas where their actions may be jeopardizing their credibility.

The first part includes a questionnaire based on elements of credibility identified by Kouzes and Posner. The second part requires students to identify areas where they may be weak and develop an action plan to enhance their credibility. Students should be encouraged to develop their action plan following the principles of good goal setting. The goals should be: behavioral, specific, measurable, achievable and reasonable, and have a clear timeline.

This is a very effective developmental exercise particularly for students who have some work experience.

 Course Assignment

This exercise can be used as an assignment for the course by asking students to analyze the elements of their credibility and present an action plan to improve it.

Exercise 8.1: Do you know a charismatic leader?

This exercise is based on the concepts of charismatic leadership. It is designed to allow students to evaluate leaders they know and consider effective in terms of charismatic leadership. It can be used either as an opening or as a conclusion to the topic of charismatic leadership.

Option: Step 4 can be used to make the exercise a group activity. Each group could then select one of its members as leader, analyze his/her behavior, followers' behavior, and the situational elements that allow for the emergence and effectiveness of charismatic leadership.

 Course Assignment

This exercise can be used as an assignment for the course by asking students to describe and analyze a charismatic leader, his/her followers, and the leadership situation.

Exercise 8.2: Charismatic speech

This exercise focuses on the articulation skills of charismatic leaders. One of the major characteristics of charismatic leaders is their ability to articulate their vision clearly and to inspire their followers through their message. Although such skills often take much practice to develop, there are several specific aspects of charismatic speech that can be identified and practiced. This exercise provides students with a list of the major elements of charismatic speech and with an opportunity to practice those skills. It is most effective when assigned after the discussion on charismatic leadership.

Because of the time required to complete this exercise, the groups should be required to do their preparation outside of class after having been provided with the necessary information.

Total time: Minimum 50 minutes preparation (15 with the instructor; 35 in the group); 5 minutes per group presentation.

Materials needed: Paper and pencil; use of board or flip chart.

Step 1: Preparation

Students should be assigned to groups of 3 to 5. Existing groups can be used.

- Each group must select a topic for a 5-minute speech. The topics should have the potential to inspire and motivate. Good options are company or school mission statements. Other examples are the introduction of a new product or service to a sales group, the presentation of a major strategic change to a department or team, or the introduction (self or by someone else) of a new leader.

- Each group needs to select the target audience for their speech. All presentations will be made to the class after informing them of the target audience. The intended audience will affect the speech and therefore needs to be identified.

Following are definitions and examples of framing and rhetorical techniques to help the groups prepare for their speeches (for more details see Conger 1989 and 1991).

Framing involves selecting a framework for the message around certain goals. For example, the two statements "our company goal is to build communication devices," and "our company goal is to connect human beings to one another" deliver the same basic message with very different frames. Some methods for framing are:

- **Amplify values and beliefs**: Select values and stories that illustrate the core higher values that appeal to the audience.

- **Bring out the importance of the mission**: Emphasize and exaggerate the need for change and the attractiveness of the solution.

- **Clarify the need to accomplish the mission**: Focus on the "good" of the mission and the dangers of not accomplishing it.

- **Focus on the efficacy of the mission**: Provide examples of how the mission will work in order to build the audience's confidence in the correctness of the selected path.

All the above techniques are designed to provide the audience of followers with a reason for accepting the proposed change or idea.

Rhetorical techniques are used to further emphasize the message. These include:

- Use of **metaphors, analogies, and brief stories** to make the mission and goals concrete, set them apart for undesirable things or events that the audience is likely to know, and create the needed emotional reactions in followers.

- **Use of language that the audience will understand** is key to an effective message.

- **Repetition** of the key message through various means and media emphasizes its importance

- **Alliteration** is the repetition of initial consonants sounds (e.g., mighty mountains of Montana) which provide a pleasing rhythm to the speech.

- **Nonverbal messages** need to be consistent and support the spoken words. For example, the style of dress, clear and confident voice, and lack of hesitation can all be used to further send a message of confidence

Overall: This exercise is often difficult for students, but it can be very effective. The ability to develop a well crafted message is often closer than most students think and even partially succeeding in that task demonstrates one of the major behavioral components of charismatic leadership. The fact that some students are more comfortable with this exercise than others can also be used to point to the effect of personality on one's ability to practice and learn new behaviors.

 ### Course Assignment

This exercise can be used as an assignment for an oral presentation in the course. Because of its difficulty, it may not be appropriate for a large percentage. I have used it as an alternative or addition to class participation grade.

Leadership in Action

Andrea Jung Orchestrates Avon's Makeover

Case summary

Andrea Jung, Avon's first female CEO, is in the process of reinventing the 120 year-old company to succeed in the 21st century. In spite strong sales, Avon is struggling with the introduction of internet and retail sales while maintaining the loyalty of its traditional sales force, 3.4 million the Avon ladies. Jung is knows for her drive, enthusiasm, and passion for the company. She also has a strong focus on internal and external communication to build and share a vision of the company she is leading.

1. What are the key elements of Andrea Jung's leadership style?

    A passion for her organization, a need for consensus building, high enthusiasm, and a focus on communication are key to Jung's leadership effectiveness. Her extensive experience in retail and tenure with Avon provide her with the credibility she needs to run her organization. Her insistence on developing a shared vision that fully includes the traditional backbone of the company – the Avon ladies – is evidence of her awareness of the importance of forging a new organizational culture based on the successful elements of the existing one.

2. How closely does she match elements of charismatic and transformational leadership?

    A strong conviction and enthusiasm about Avon, high energy and enthusiasm, strong communication skills, and active image building (such as leadership in charities focused on benefiting women) are all elements of charismatic leaders that are present in Jung. Because of some decline in sales and threats from new retail outlets such as the internet, a sense of urgency and crisis is present. Not as evident is the strong follower emotional reaction to Jung's leadership.

    In terms of transformational leadership, Jung has demonstrated her ability to intellectually stimulate her followers by allowing and encouraging active participation and ownership of changes implemented in the company. Her high enthusiasm and relentless confidence in the company, along with her consensus building, further help her followers overcome resistance to change.

    The most apparent elements of visionary leadership are enthusiasm, collaboration in the development of a vision, and her focus on people.

The case shows a leader with considerable passion and enthusiasm for her organization, its vision, and its employees. The focus on inclusion and consensus building while communicating the vision for Avon, are hallmarks of Jung's style. Jung's style is more stereotypically female when contrasted with Darla Moore (Case in Chapter 4). However, like Moore, and other successful leaders, Jung's extensive knowledge of her industry is one of the key factors in her success.

CHAPTER 9

THE UPPER-ECHELON VIEW:

STRATEGIC LEADERSHIP

Chapter Overview

This chapter focuses on leadership at upper levels of organizations. While the models presented throughout the book tend to be concerned with micro leadership (small groups and departments), upper-echelon leadership is focused on macro levels. The differences between the two levels are presented and the processes of strategic leadership are outlined. An integrated view of upper-echelon leadership, which considers the leader to be both the creator and the implementor of culture and strategy, is proposed, and the moderators that limit the impact of the leader on the organization are discussed and the individual characteristics of strategic leadership and the processes through which they impact their organization are outlined.

Chapter Objectives

OBJECTIVES	THROUGH BASIC TEXT	THROUGH FEATURES, TABLES, FIGURES, AND EXAMPLES	THROUGH EXERCISES
Differentiate between micro and upper echelon leadership	✓	Table 9.1 (p. 260) Effective leadership from the grassroots (p. 261)	
Describe the domain and roles of strategic leaders in the management of an organization	✓	Figure 9.1 (p. 261); Figure 9.2 (p. 262) Paula and Margaret Quenomoen (p. 262) Leading change (p. 263)	Exercise 9.1 (p. 284-285)

Identify the external and internal factors that impact strategic leaders' discretion	✓	Table 9.2 (p. 264) Charlie Feld (p. 253-264) U.S. Postal Service, Carly Fiorina (p. 265) Mickey Drexler (p. 266) Carl Vogel, Carly Fiorina (p. 266) Mercedes Benz, Dick Grasso, Tyco (p. 266) Leadership on the cutting edge (p. 267)	
List the individual characteristics of strategic leaders and their impact on their style	✓	Richard Branson (p. 268) David Rockwell, Monica Luechtefeld (p. 269) A.G. Lafley, Mickey Drexler (p. 269) Herb Stokes (p. 270)	
Contrast the four strategic leadership types and discuss the role of culture and gender in strategic leadership	✓	Figure 9.3 (p. 270) Mickey Drexler, Janie and Victor Tsao, Ellen and Melvin Gordon (p. 271) Table 9.3 (p. 272) Ricardo Semler; Roy Wetterstrom (p. 273) Jon Brock (p. 273-274) Gerstner (p. 274) Leading change (p. 266) Multicultural organizations, French executives (p. 275) Linda Hoffman (p. 275) Shelly Lazarus, Meg Whitman, Shelly Lansing; Gail McGovern (p. 276)	Self-assessment 9.1 (p. 289-290)
Explain the processes through which strategic leaders manage their organization	✓	Figure 9.4 (p. 277) Jeff Bezos (p. 277); Fergal Quinn, Stan Shih, A.G. Lafley (p. 278)	Exercise 9.2 (p. 286) Exercise 9.3 (p. 287-288)
Review issues of executive compensation and accountability	✓	U.S. executive salaries; Jill Barad; Carly Fiorina, Michael Capellas, Michael	

		Eisner, Christopher Galvin (p. 279)	
		Table 9.4 (p. 280)	
		Exxon, Union Carbide (p. 280)	

Chapter Outline

1. Differences between micro and upper-echelon leadership

   The major differences between micro and upper-echelon leadership are presented (Table 9.1). These are scope, focus, effectiveness criteria, and level of decision-making.

   The new strategic focus for leaders at all levels is discussed.

   Effective leadership from the grassroots provides guidelines for successful transition to upper management.

1. The domain and impact of strategic leadership

   The six strategic forces of environment, technology, strategy, culture, structure, and leadership are proposed as the domain of strategic leaders (Figure 9.1). Leaders in the upper echelon of organizations juggle these six forces to help organizations reach their goals.

   a. The role of leadership in strategic management

      An integrated view of the role of leadership in strategic management is presented whereby the leader is assumed to play a central role in the creation of the culture and strategy of an organization. Additionally, when the organization is well established, the leader plays a role in the implementation of strategy (Figure 9.2).

   a. Executive discretion: Moderating factors of the role of leaders

      The external and internal factors that moderate the power and influence of upper-echelon leaders on organizations are discussed (Table 9.2). These factors either limit the power and discretion of the leader or limit the impact of the leader's actions and decisions.

   Leading change presents the case of Anne Mulcahy, CEO of Xerox who has been task with reviving the almost dying company after a series of scandals in early 2000. An insider to the company, Mulcahy is passionate about Xerox, and has focused on modeling the dedication and hard work that the company needs. *External factors* include: environmental uncertainty, type of industry, market growth, and legal constraints.

   Internal factors include: Organizational stability, size and structure, culture, stage of organizational development, and the presence, power, and makeup of a Top Management Team (TMT).

   Leadership on the Cutting Edge presents research about CEO succession. Researchers Zhang and Rajagopalan studied 204 CEO successions in 164 firms and concluded that having more internal candidates reduces the change of relay succession (insider groomed for the position), while relay succession improves the firms' performance particularly in times of instability. Researchers suggest that, contrary to popular belief, insiders may be better able to change strategic directions.

2. Characteristics of upper-echelon leaders

The research on the impact of upper-echelon's individual characteristic on their leadership style and their organization is reviewed. Four strategic leadership types are proposed.

a.   Demographic and personality traits

After a review of various individual characteristics of strategic leaders, two common themes that run through the research emerge. These are the degree of the leader's challenge seeking and his or her need for control.

Challenge-seeking: The degree to which a leader seeks challenge, is a risk taker, and is open to change and innovation is one of the key characteristics of upper-echelon leaders. This characteristic has the most impact on the way a leader formulates the strategy of his/her organization. At one end are leaders who seek challenge and are innovative, at the other end are leaders who are risk averse and uncomfortable with change.

Need for control: Need for control is the second characteristic of upper-echelon leaders and includes degree of delegation, participative leadership, and encouragement of and tolerance for diversity of form and opinions. This characteristic has the most impact on the internal culture and structure of an organization. High-control leaders push for uniformity and control, while low-control leaders allow flexibility and openness.

b.   Strategic leadership types

The combination of challenge-seeking and need for control yields four strategic leadership types (Figure 9.3). The type of leadership that is effective is contingent upon an organization's environment, culture, strategy, and structure. Additionally, each type of leader is likely to create a different type of organization.

Strategic leadership types and their impact on organizations (Table 9.3).

High-control innovator (HCI): HCIs are challenge-seekers who have a high need for control. They select high-risk, innovative strategies while creating centralized structures with strong cultures.

Status quo guardian (SQG): SQGs are challenge-averse and need high control. They select strategies that are tried and true and maintain high control over their organizations.

Participative innovators (PI): PIs seek challenge and innovation in their strategies while creating a loose, open, and participative culture and structure inside their organizations.

Process manager (PM): PMs allow for openness of culture and structure while avoiding risky and innovative strategies.

c.   Strategic leadership: Culture and gender

The effect of culture: Culture may have an impact on strategic leadership type. Using Trompenaars dimensions an analysis of the potential impact of culture using the example of French top executives is presented. Hierarchy, elitism, and focus on intellectual achievement are partly attributed to the French cultural value of high power distance.

The effect of gender: Although there is limited empirical research regarding the effect of gender, anecdotal and case studies of female executives are discussed pointing to many female executives using a more participative style.

3.   How do executives affect their organization?

The processes used by upper echelon leaders to affect their organization are discussed (Figure 9.4)

120

a. Direct decisions

Direct decisions regarding all organizational factors including strategy, mission, culture, and structure is one of the most obvious ways in which upper-echelon leaders impact their organizations.

b. Allocation of resources and control over the reward system

Control over resources and rewards provide upper-echelon leaders with considerable opportunities to shape their organizations.

c. Setting the norms and modeling

Setting decision standards and behavioral norms and modeling of certain styles and actions are indirect but still powerful means for upper echelon leaders to impact the organization.

5. Strategic leaders' accountability

The responsibilities of upper echelon leaders are discussed with a focus on the need to match the considerable power assigned to them with accountability for their own and their organizations' actions (Table 9.4).

6. Summary and conclusion

Searching the Web

Executive compensation

www.aflcio.org/corporateamerica/paywatch/index.cfm

Article listing the top 10 highest paid CEO's and their wage form the American Federation of Labor and Congress of Industrial Organizations (AFL CIO) website. Site includes a long list of articles that examine executive pay like "2004 trends in CEO pay" and "What is wrong with CEO pay and what can be done to fix it?"

www.bls.gov/oco/ocos012.htm

This article details the nature of work, responsibilities, and compensation for executives. Other details that reveal the inner workings of the executive role and lifestyle include employment information, how one goes about training, and what other qualifications lead to positions and advancements. The hosting site, the US Department of Labor, Bureau of Labor Statistics, offers a variety of other resources.

Example of highest paid executives salaries

www.chron.com/content/chronicle/business/chron100/00/00executives.html

This page offers the top 100 highest paid executives a glimpse. Details include a numeric breakdown of annual salaries, cash bonuses, other payments, and perks.

Information about strategic management and strategic leadership

http://knowledge.wharton.upenn.edu/
http://knowledge.wharton.upenn.edu/index.cfm?fa=viewArticle&id=1193

This page offers summaries that link to a number of articles that outline details about strategic management and strategic leadership. Topics include the featured piece entitled "Leadership by the Numbers? It's One Part of Todd Thomson's Management Strategy at Citigroup," which is an interview between Todd S. Thompson, Citigroup's CFO and Chief Strategist and Wharton's Michael Useem. During the interview Thompson discussed the importance of focusing on facts, motivating employees, and treating shareholders as customers, among other topics.

Procter & Gamble: Company values

www.pg.com/company/who_we_are/index.jhtml

The Who We Are section of Proctor and Gamble shows off the leadership and organizational structure and style behind their powerful presence in their field after more then 165 years of business. The site features their philosophy and discusses in detail their winning ways.

The Leadership Challenge: BOD and CEOs

This brief challenge presents the highly complex issue of the relationship between the board of directors and company CEOs. The issue of corporate governance is one that students are likely to have, or will encounter when they take a strategic management class. The focus is on CEO accountability. Many current business examples (e.g., Enron and Xerox) can be used to illustrate the complexity of these concepts. Issues students should consider include:

- The importance of a cooperation and collaboration between the board and the CEO. This need for harmony and collaboration has prompted CEO involvement in the selection of the board.

- The need to balance the board with members nominated by different constituents including the upper management of the company.

- The fiduciary duty of the board and the CEO towards stockholders in the case of public corporation.

- The lack of ideal solution and the importance of reaching a workable balance and constant reevaluation and renegotiation.

Chapter 9 Experiential Exercises

Self-assessment 9.1: What is your strategic leadership type?

This exercise is a self-rating based on the four strategic leadership types presented in the chapter. Students can also use the scale to rate their organizational leaders. The quadrants are used to place students in one of the four categories.

Exercise 9.1: Understanding the strategic forces

This exercise is designed to help students understand the role of leaders in managing the six strategic forces of environment, strategy, culture, structure, technology, and leadership presented in the chapter. The choices upper-echelon leaders make regarding which of the six to emphasize and how to manage each depend to a great extent on the leaders' personality and background. The leaders' choices, on the other hand, have a profound impact on organizations.

Total time: Minimum 30 minutes preparation; 5 minutes per group presentation.

Materials needed: Paper and pencil; use of board or flip chart.

After reading the scenario, assign students to groups of 3-5 to complete the worksheet and make a recommendation regarding their choice of new principal.

Worksheet Sample

Strategic Forces	J.B. Davison	Jerry Popovich
Environment	Defined primarily as school board and parents	Defined broadly to include community
Strategy	Focus on basics (reading, writing, math and discipline)	Focus on community partnerships including parents and businesses
Culture	Tight controls, paternalistic	Open
Structure	Centralized, formalized	Fluid/organic
Technology	Likely not major focus	Major focus
Leadership	Authoritarian; control-oriented	Participative

Discussion items

1. How are the two candidates different?

   Davison's orientation to education is traditional with an emphasis on the basics and on discipline. His education and background are also traditional. Popovich's approach is more focused on community and is likely to be more creative. Her background with computers and industry is less typical of a school principal. They are both well qualified for the job.

2. What explains the differences between them?

    The factors that explain the differences are:

    - their age: Davison is 15 years older than Popovich and almost from a different generation

    - their educational background; Davison is more traditional

    - their gender; Popovich seems to practice the interactive leadership often attributed to female leaders

3. The choice

    Both candidates are good choices for the job. It is important for students to understand that there is no right choice. Whom each group picks depends on how they view the situation at the school. Each candidate brings a unique and different set of skills. Their approaches are very different. Davison's may have a quicker response while Popovich's approach is likely to be more long-term. The quick response from Davison's approach may not provide long-term solutions, while Popovich's approach may not have a chance to work without quick solutions.

Overall: The brief scenario provides a good mechanism for students to analyze the impact of upper echelon leaders. The major theme for this exercise is to realize that there is no right answer and to understand the consequences of the choice that is made.

 Course Assignment

This exercise can be used as an assignment for the course. The mini-case can be analyzed and students can be asked to present their recommendations and justifications.

Exercise 9.2: Your organization

This exercise is designed to draw the students' attention to the result of an upper echelon leader's influence. When using the vignettes presented at the end of the chapter, it is most effective if students rate the organization prior to the discussion of strategic leadership types. The discussion and predictions regarding the leader's strategic type should take place after coverage of the topic in class.

Option 1: Ask students to rate their own organization, department, or team. This option is most effective with students with work experience.

Option 2: Provide students with the cases at the end of this chapter and ask them to rate the organization and leaders described in the cases. This option is most effective with students with limited work experience, or as a practice for rating their own organization.

Total time: Minimum 15 minutes for Option 1 (5 minutes for rating, 10 minutes for discussion); minimum 25 minutes for Option 2 (15 minutes for rating, 10 minutes for discussion).

Materials needed: Paper and pencil

In-class discussion: Option 1

If students have rated their own organization, their ratings and their predictions regarding the leader's strategic type can be used as a basis of discussion of the chapter.

Students can also be assigned to small groups of 2-3 to predict one another's leader's style based on the organization rating.

Case solutions for option 2

	Culture	Structure	Leadership
Southern State University	Loose and fluid Many sub-cultures co-exist	Decentralized	Process manager Low need for control and challenge averse
Chip Factory	Tight controls; no tolerance for differences; one way of doing things	Centralized; formalized; high control	High-control innovator High need for control and innovative
Northern Lights	Tight controls; no tolerance for differences; one way of doing things	Centralized; formalized; high control	Status quo guardians High need for control and challenge averse
D.C. Medical	Loose and fluid Many sub-cultures co-exist	Decentralized	Participative innovator Low need for control and innovative

 Course Assignment

This exercise can be used as an assignment for the course. Students can be asked to either provide a description of their own organization or use one or more of the cases at the end of the chapter to do a case analysis of the organization, its culture, structure, and leadership.

Exercise 9.3: Influence processes

This exercise is designed to help students identify the processes that upper echelon leaders use to impact their organization and most particularly its culture. The three vignettes provide simple case studies of the different processes used. The exercise should be used after discussion of the processes described in Chapter 10; it can be used as either a group or as an individual exercise.

Total time: Minimum 15 minutes per case

Materials needed: Paper and pencil

Case solutions

	J.C. Green	Leslie Marks	Joseph Hadad
Direct decisions	Selection of replacement	Work assignments and location her own office	Compensation system
Allocation of resources			Based on performance
Reward system	Reward for intelligence, wit and analytical skills		New compensation and benefit system
Selection of other leaders	Choice of Stanley Wang	Focus on internal promotions	Based on performance
Role modeling	Running	Open door; office moved to first floor; informal dress	Focus on financial factors

Course Assignment

This exercise can be used as an assignment for the course. Students can be asked to analyze, compare, and contrast the influence processes used by the three leaders.

Leadership in Action

A.G. Lafley Reinvents Procter & Gamble

Case summary

A.G. Lafley replaced Durk Jager as CEO of P&G in 2000 and started a major transformation of the venerable, but stogy and under-performing company. His efforts have paid off as P&G is once again successful and growing. Lafley's quiet determination, soft-spoken style, and focus on the customer and the product are responsible for the dramatic turnaround. His messages are simple and repetitive making sure everyone understand the importance of the customer. He used several dramatic symbols, such as transforming the executive top floor to a training center and moving managers to the same floor as their employees, to signal the changes that he wanted to see. Lafley emphasizes collaboration and consensus-building. He is a careful listener who believes in using teams while also able to be decisive. Employee development and mentoring are assuring that the culture that Lafley has created will take hold.

1. What strategic forces impact P&G?

   All the strategic forces presented in Figure 9.1 impact P&G. Particularly, the changing environment and competition, and new technology have forced the company to look for new products and new markets. Internally, the culture of the company played a significant negative role in preventing the necessary changes. However, the new culture, with more openness and focus on the customer is supporting the strategies that Lafley has put in place. Changes in the structure, towards teams and decentralization, have further supported the new strategies. Leadership has played a key role; under Jager the company was shaken at its core and unable to perform. Lafley's leadership has brought stability and hope.

2. How would you describe Lafley's strategic leadership style?

   Lafley is known for understated and quiet determination. He is not flashy; rather he is a careful listener. He has encouraged use of teams, decentralized decision-making, and allowed with increased participation. Furthermore, under his leadership, P&G has added many new products either through internal development or acquisitions. Lafley show the low control and high innovation typical of Participative Innovator (PI).

3. What are the factors that contributed to his success at P&G?

   The fact that he was an insider with a long-standing stake and interest in the company provided Lafley with the credibility and capital he needed to be able to change the culture. His success provides support for the research presented in "Leadership from the cutting edge." He is the insider who, because he knows the company well, is able to move it in the right direction.

   Lafley's understated and quiet style and his passion for focusing on the customer have further served as a role model for others in the company. His message is simple; he uses dramatic symbols to make his point; he is a careful listener; and he has provided a clear focus. All these factors have contributed to his success.

   While P&G had a long history of success, it found itself slowly deteriorating and unable to compete. The leadership of Lafley re-energized the company and brought it back beyond its past successes. Although he has changed the culture, his style matches the culture and he has been able to earn the trust needed to make those drastic changes.

Your Organization: Cases

Southern State University

The College of Foreign Languages at Southern State University has 15 full-time faculty and 4 support staff. The College offers courses in French, Italian, Spanish, German, Japanese and Mandarin Chinese. Many of the faculty teach in more than one language program, and they are not divided into the typical departments. Over half the faculty are tenured. The rest are at various career stages. The atmosphere is generally collegial. The faculty associate with those who teach similar classes, and it appears that everyone is left alone to do their "own thing" as long as the students are taken care of and the quality of instructions stays high.

Most decisions are made by faculty committees, and the dean, Robert Hunt, is very supportive of shared governance. He has been dean for seven years and is well-liked. For the past three years, there has been much debate among the faculty regarding computerized language instruction. Several faculty have been very vocal in asking the dean's support to write grants to obtain the necessary equipment and training. Although the dean has not voiced his disagreement, he appears to be siding with several of the more senior faculty who are strong proponents of traditional language instruction and appear to be "computer phobic." Several other issues regarding changes in tenure and promotion procedures and criteria and curricular changes have also been at the dean's desk for over a year after having been approved by faculty committees.

The Chip Factory

The Chip Factory is an entrepreneurial success story. The small company has become famous throughout its Northwestern home state for the high quality cookies and cakes and the growth in sales has been phenomenal. Since its creation four years ago, the one Chip Factory store has grown to 28 throughout the state, and there is much talk about franchising the operation to support the growth. The stores are very cheap to operate. Each needs three to five low-skill employees, and two supervisors who are trained for one week at the mother store by the owner and her husband for one week. They are taught everything they need to know, from how to dress (they all wear uniforms), to how to clean the stores, how to talk to customers, how to arrange the display...etc. The cookie and cake secret dough and ingredients are shipped three times a week to all stores and require simple mixing and baking.

Almost every month, the stores offer new flavors and new goodies ranging from special seasonal items to novelty containers and gourmet coffees. Most of the new items are very successful, and they are regularly replaced. All employees receive thorough training on how to prepare and present the new items, and very strict quality control is maintained through regular spot inspections, and a variety of awards are handed down by the owners. The employees are generally high-school students who are attracted to the flexible hours and the better than average pay.

Michelle Gerard and her husband, Alberto, are sole owners of all the Chip Factory stores. Michelle is responsible for all the recipes and the training. Alberto runs the other business aspects including managing the 3 quality-control inspectors.

Northern Lights

Northern Lights utilities is one of two major utility companies in a three-state region in the midwest. In spite of the changes in the industry and the increasing competition as a result of new deregulation, the publicly owned company continues to be successful as it has been for the past 35 years. The company is known for its performance-based incentive system that focuses entirely on monetary rewards for employees and managers. The system has been in place for almost the life of the company and has been very effective. The turnover rate is considerably below industry averages. As a result, the average tenure of employees and managers is over 10 years. All of the managers are promoted from within, and most have come up through the ranks with company- supported education. Productivity is high, and profits have been good.

The organization has a strong family atmosphere. In spite of its size, most people know one another and family members by name. The president, Thomas Wysocki, has also come through the ranks. He is a "company man," and both his sons also work for Northern Lights. Whereas many of the company's competitors have ventured into acquiring other companies and new industries, Northern Lights has stuck to its core business. Their growth has been through the growth of their region.

D.C. Medical

As a result of the major changes in the health-care industry, D.C. Medical was divested by a major hospital that owned this out-patient clinic. Instead of risking shut-down, the employees and managers of the clinic decided to buy their own organization. Three years after the buy-out, the employee-owned clinic is thriving. Its 20 physicians, and 42 staff are known for quality, low-cost health-care. Quality and concern for their patients are the common threads for all the employee-owners who are managing the clinic with the help of their administrator, Amy Hidalgo, one of the few people who is not an owner.

The employees have organized themselves into cross-functional teams that run the different departments and report to Hidalgo. The employees see Hidalgo as the "obstacle remover." Her role is to obtain resources and facilitate providing quality health-care. She has focused much of her attention on external relations and marketing, which are her strong points. She has developed a number of very successful P.R. campaigns and has established partnership with several businesses. The various teams have been very successful in running the facility. Each department has come up with many new procedures to address their clients needs leading to considerable success for the clinic.

PART FOUR

LOOKING TOWARD THE FUTURE

CHAPTER 10

WHAT WILL WE BE WHEN WE GROW UP?

Chapter Overview

This chapter focuses on leadership at upper levels of organizations. While the models presented throughout the book tend to be concerned with micro leadership (small groups and departments), upper-echelon leadership is focused on macro levels. The differences between the two levels are presented and the processes of strategic leadership are outlined. An integrated view of upper-echelon leadership, which considers the leader to be both the creator and the implementor of culture and strategy, is proposed, and the moderators that limit the impact of the leader on the organization are discussed and the individual characteristics of strategic leadership and the processes through which they impact their organization are outlined.

Chapter Objectives

OBJECTIVES	THROUGH BASIC TEXT	THROUGH FEATURES, TABLES, FIGURES, AND EXAMPLES
Summarize the information and knowledge that you acquired from this book and outline areas in need of further clarification	✓	
Explain the changes in the leadership context	✓	Table 10.1 (p. 299) Rosenbluth International (p. 299) Wipro and AES (p. 300-301)
Distinguish between previous and current definitions of leadership	✓	
Understand the challenges that leaders face in the future	✓	MBARI (p. 302) Table 10.2 (p. 301)

Chapter Outline

1. What we know and what we don't know

   a. What do we know?

   A brief summary of our knowledge about leadership based on information provided in the text is presented.

   b. What don't we know?

   Areas that need further research and clarification include: The role of traits, the importance of the organizational context, and the cross-cultural differences in leadership.

2. Changes in the leadership context and its consequences

   a. Changing context

   The various changes in organizations and the leadership context are presented (Table 10.1). These include: structural changes, changing demographics, globalization, changing work ethics, the need to learn and increasing knowledge, changing technology, and the need for flexibility and change.

   b. Changing leadership

   The consequences of the changing context are presented through the example of Wipro and AES corporation and their effort to implement its innovative management methods world-wide. Table 10.2 summarizes the changes and their consequences for leadership in the twenty first century.

3. Looking to the future

   The final section presents themes that are predicted to impact leadership in the future.

   a. What's on the research horizon?

   New areas of leadership research include: spiritual leadership, authentic leadership, role of emotions, and continued research on cross-cultural aspects.

   b. What's a leader to do?

   To address the changes leaders must: Understand themselves, adopt a service mentality, have a global perspective, understand organizations, be flexible and open, commit to learning, and achieve balance between their life and their jobs.

Searching the Web

www.tgci.com/magazine/98fall/mission.asp

This page features "How to Write a Mission Statement", a great hands on tool for professional mission building. Readers may test their skills and see how well they express an organization's purpose in a way that inspires support and ongoing commitment from those connected to the organization.

<u>www.franklincovey.com/missionbuilder/</u>

The Franklin Covey Personal Mission Builder enables readers to create their own personal mission statement. The site offers a step-by-step program called the Mission Wizard that will assist in creating a unique, personalized Mission Statement to guide your life.

Chapter 10 Experiential Exercises

Self-assessment 10.1: My Personal Mission Statement

This exercise provides students with the opportunity of self-reflection and a start at developing a personal mission statement that can guide their career and their development as a leader. This is an individual exercise that can used as a concluding exercise or even as an on-going exercise throughout the semester. The various self-assessments throughout the book, especially Self-assessment 3.1 can be used as supporting information to allow students to understand themselves, and their values.

Total time: Minimum 30 minutes and up to 2 hours depending on level of student involvement

Materials needed: Paper and pencil

Step 1: What I want to be when I grow up

This step is a self-exploration. Encourage students to answer the questions honestly and to take their time doing so. Remind them that there are no right or wrong answers and that this is a personal discovery.

Step 2: My personal mission statement

Using the answers that students have developed in the first step, they should write their own mission statement. An excellent step-by-step process is presented in the web site www.franklincovey.com/mission builder/ (computer must allow pop-ups).

 Course Assignment

This exercise can be used as an assignment for the course. It can be used either as a concluding exercise or as a staged exercise that students revise several times during the semester. Grading this assignment cannot be based on the content of the mission statement, rather students should be evaluated on how thoroughly they complete the process. Preferably, a pass/fail grade should be assigned.

SECTION THREE

VIDEO GUIDES

Japan-Based Nidek Responds to the Challenges of Globalization

Synopsis

Surrounded by scenic Mikawa Bay, Gamagori, Japan is the home of Nidek, the world's leading supplier of surgical and diagnostic products for vision care. In 1971, Hideo Ozawa founded Nidek to help doctors protect against vision loss and improve quality of life for their patients. Today Nidek is developing a vision prosthesis to restore vision to the blind. This "artificial eye" could be ready for use within the next 10 years. A leader in innovation, Nidek is firmly established in over 90 countries worldwide, with branch offices in the United States, France, Italy, Germany, Australia, and China.

On the company's 25th Anniversary, Nidek announced its entrance into the new business domain of eye and health care. Hiroshi Okada, Executive Vice President and General Manager of Nidek, U.S.A. is excited about the new product line geared to baby boomers like himself. "They are able to spend more money to look better or younger," he says. Laser type dermatological equipment is used for skin rejuvenation or hair removal. Hideo Ozawa's move to diversify his product offerings, underscores his keen understanding of the need for corporate agility in today's rapidly changing marketplace.

Nidek has long been a respected presence in the global business community, gaining international recognition in 2001 for its company-wide quality control system.[1] "Nidek is truly a quality driven company. ...It has been Mr. Ozawa's wish from the very beginning. Quality products are the bedrock of Nidek," says Kuntal Joshi, Director of Marketing and Business Development, Nidek U.S.A.

Despite its considerable business acumen, management at Nidek, U.S.A. was recently faced with unprecedented high turnover rates in its sales force. "Our competitors were stealing our sales people...They were offering more money than I could offer," David Yeh, Director of Sales explains.

At Nidek Co., Ltd. in Japan, sales people are paid the same amount biweekly regardless of performance. This system works well in Japan; a traditional country, where one's work is an extension of one's identity. Life long loyalty to the company is expected. According to Joshi Kuntal, "Japanese employees are very hard working, they have a sense of pride, a sense of belonging to the company." By contrast, tenure in America ranges from three to five years. People are more than likely to leave a job for a salary increase or a career opportunity. Aware of the differences between the national cultures of Japan and America, Nidek U.S.A. had already implemented a performance based pay check, but even that wasn't enough to hold American sales people.

Ultimately the crisis presented an opportunity for David Yeh and his management team to restructure the jobs of the entire sales force, as well as their bonus plans. After careful analysis, David Yeh utilized Nidek's vast line of product offerings to resolve the situation. He realized that the competition allowed sales people to sell only one product, basing their earnings on sales of that item alone. By training sales people at Nidek to sell a vast array of products, they could make substantially more money. For now, the sales effort at Nidek U.S.A. is back in gear and the discrepancies between Japanese style management practices and American culture have been resolved.

Discussion Questions

As you watch the video, consider the value of the study of Organizational Behavior in today's dynamic marketplace. Appraise how it might be used to effectively manage a competitive workforce in a foreign culture.

Specifically, answer the following questions.
1. Do you think a firm grasp of organizational behavior might have helped David Yeh to avoid high turnover rates among his sales people? If so, explain how. If not, explain why not. You may want to include an intuitive guess at his people skills in your answer.

---

[1] ISO 9001 Quality Systems Model in design, development, production and customer service., www.nidek.com

OB concepts may have helped David Yeh to gain a deeper understanding of American culture and how it has shaped his employees. Most importantly he might have been able to better adapt his management style to prevent this situation from escalating. Additionally, stronger people skills might have helped him to predict this behavior and saved Nidek the cost of high turnover among sales team members in both financial and human terms. Some students may argue that David Yeh could not have foreseen the use of such aggressive tactics by his competitors.

2. Do you agree with David Yeh's assessment that salesmanship is an innate personality trait? Why or why not? Which individual level variables, ie.biographical characteristics, abilities, values, attitudes and personality type, would you look for in a potential sales person for Nidek? Explain how your criteria would ensure satisfied employees and organizational productivity.

Opinions may vary as to whether salesmanship is a natural talent or an acquired skill. Regardless, students might look for the following variables when filling a sales position at Nidek, U.S.A.: A background in science or engineering would be desirable for in-depth understanding of surgical and dermatological equipment; excellent communication skills would indicate an ability to deal effectively with doctors, suppliers, and fellow sales people. Someone who is ethical, ambitious, extroverted, and open to new ideas and learning would do well at Nidek where sound business principles and innovation go hand in hand.

3. What could management at Nidek U.S.A. do *now* in order to forestall the problems of a 2006 labor shortage?

By implementing sophisticated recruitment and retention strategies now, Nidek might be able to minimize the effects of the impending labor shortage. Hypothetical strategies would include use of in-house training and development programs to groom employees for assignments abroad; design of highly motivating jobs to attract the largest talent pool possible; and modification of hiring practices in each branch to reflect culture-based norms. Finally, a concerted effort should be made to continue to build Nidek's reputation not only as a leader in its field, but as a great place to work, as well.

4. What work/life conflicts might employees at Nidek USA encounter as a result of both the company's Japanese roots and the company's global presence? Explain.

Judging from the video, the dominant culture among management at Nidek is Japanese. It is based on a tradition of employee loyalty and dedication to work. Employees in America may experience difficulty in balancing a lifestyle that is predicated on leisure and family time with high corporate expectations at work. For those married to a working spouse and juggling parental responsibilities, the demands may be quite stressful. Additional sources of conflict would stem from the travel requirements that often accompany jobs in global companies like Nidek. The need to consult with colleagues or customers around the world, across time zones, may force employees to work at all hours, interfering with a harmonious home life.

Note: For anecdotal material on the topic of global Japanese corporations and American business people see James Brooks, Learning to Avoid a Deal-Killing Faux Pas in Japan, The New York Times, Sept. 17, 2002, pp. C10

Flying High: JetBlue

Learning Objectives
The purpose of this video is to help you:

1. Understand the value of the contingency approach to a start-up enterprise in a highly competitive arena such as the airline industry.
2. Identify the areas of planning and control that would benefit from using the quantitative approach to decision making.
3. Discuss the necessity of creating learning capabilities throughout an organization in order to achieve better performance.

Synopsis.

Launched in February 2000, with an unprecedented $130 million investment from Weston Presidio Capital, J.P. Morgan Partners, and Soros Private Equity Partners, [1] JetBlue<www.jetblue.com> is the brainchild of Chairman and CEO David Neeleman. In 1981, at the age of 21, Mr. Neeleman started a Salt Lake City travel agency. He partnered with travel agent June Morris three years later to found Morris Air, a small discount airline, where he developed the first ticketless system. In 1983 he left to help start Canadian airline West Jet, and then headed Open Skies, a company that created touch-screen electronic reservations and check-in systems. [2] JetBlue is a low-cost, low-fare airline featuring leather seats equipped with free live satellite television. The airline has remained profitable despite the adversities of 9/11 and the Iraq War by flying into airports where the landing slots cost less, turning planes around quickly, and keeping maintenance to a minimum by using only new aircrafts. The company continues to take delivery of a new Airbus A320 jet every 5 weeks. Currently serving 22 destinations in the U.S. and Puerto Rico, JetBlue plans to expand to Canada and the Caribbean.

Discussion Questions

1. *For analysis:* What effect might Mr. Neeleman's prior experience in aviation have had on his business model for JetBlue? As an entrepreneur how does this venture differ from his previous endeavors?

No doubt, his 20 years in the field helped Mr. Neeleman to convince investors to give him $130 million in seed money. His intimate knowledge of the players in the industry and the competition allowed him to put together a star management team for JetBlue. His familiarity with low-cost carrier routes and equipment enabled him to make solid decisions in order to maximize ridership, minimize turn around time, and choose the best headquarters for his new company. Unlike his earlier ventures, this is a long term commitment with a business model projecting 5 or 10 years into the future characterized by global thinking.

2. *For analysis:* How would you say the quantitative approach has helped Mr. Neeleman to formulate a strategy for JetBlue? Do you think it will continue to be useful to him in the future? Explain.

Statistical methods and quantitative models are essential to JetBlue's outstanding performance. Management's calculations of operating budgets for all areas of the company including purchase of new planes and hiring of personnel. The ability to measure cost per available seat mile, on-time performance percentages and to monitor customer satisfaction surveys all contribute to the health of the business. Quantitative analysis will become increasingly important in the face of more competition from small carriers and the financial burden of new security measures.

---

[1] Eryn Brown," A Smokeless Herb," *Fortune Magazine*, May 28, 2001, 78-79.
[2] www.fsb.com/fortunesb/articles/02227,1416000.html

3. *For application:* In order to adopt a contingency approach at JetBlue, which variables would you advise Mr. Neeleman to take into account? Explain.

Environmental uncertainty is a given in our post 9/11 world. Unpredictable terrorist attacks and the aftermath of decline in travel will continue to challenge JetBlue's original plans. JetBlue should also allow for potentially aggressive tactics by competing carriers. (American Airline's recently offered free tickets to passengers who might otherwise fly JetBlue.)[3] The organization's growth will change the efficient flow of communication that exists between management, staff, and customers. Future globalization, an increasingly diverse workforce, and an inevitable increase in maintenance jobs and costs are all situations that will impact on Jet Blue's management team.

4. *For application:* What steps might Mr. Neeleman take in order to ensure that JetBlue remains a learning organization as he pursues a growth strategy?

As JetBlue takes on more destinations, staff and crew members will come from an increasingly diverse pool of talent. Mr. Neeleman's ubiquitous presence will be more difficult to maintain. In an open letter to shareholders posted on the Web site, he writes:"...great People drive solid operating Performance which yields continued Prosperity." The company values "safety, caring, integrity, fun and passion." Customer satisfaction and safety depend on open communication among all JetBlue employees, and the willingness to constantly reinvent themselves in order to get things done in the most efficient way possible. Mr. Neeleman's hiring practices and training methods must become a vital part of the organization so that everyone continues to give 100%. As human resources moves to hire from different cultures the company will have to be sensitive to varied needs. Relocation may become an issue as will revamping the intranet so that customer's receive seamless service both on-line and in person.

5. *For Debate:* Do you agree with Mr. Neeleman's decision to buy new A320s manufactured in France by the European consortium Airbus, rather than one of the popular Boeing models made in America? Support your opinion.

Students may agree that the superior quality and 5 year warranty of the new planes are central to Jet Blue's ability to keep costs as low as possible, translating into lower fares for customers and fewer mechanical problems. The willingness to partner with a European company may be interpreted as a gesture of good will and foresight towards the establishment of a truly global economy. Some students may wish to argue that dependence on a manufacturer who is outside the country may cause problems later on, when parts need to be shipped and warranties have expired. Other students may prefer a corporate image of "buying American" at a time when we are engaged in an unpopular war in Iraq and young American lives are on the line. Other students may feel the source of the aircraft makes little difference as long as it is good for the bottom line.

Online Exploration
Browse JetBlue's home page www.jetblue.com. Explore the corporate job listings, culture, benefits and diversity pages. Look at the Annual Report and read Mr. Neeleman's letter to shareholders. Note the uniformly open, copy. What does this tell you about JetBlue? Does it make you feel welcome as a customer? a potential employee? an investor? How important is this aspect of JetBlue's Web site to organizational goals? Why would a company that uses the Web for e-commerce, notably ticket sales and flight information also have such an extensive selection of information available to site visitors? Explain your response.
Recent corporate scandals have served to erode public confidence and inspired a movement toward transparency on the part of the business community. JetBlue's customer oriented philosophy is a natural springboard for creating and maintaining consumer trust. The Web site reflects a positive corporate image.

---

[3] *Fast Company,* March 2004, 31.

In September 2003 JetBlue was the target of two inquiries by federal agencies in response to the airline's admission that it had provided travel records on more than a million passengers to a Pentagon contractor for use in identifying terrorists, violating its own privacy rules. JetBlue had originally cooperated with the Department of Defense in the wake of the Sept. 11 attacks, out of patriotism. David Neeleman apologized personally to the public via e-mail. He is one of many executives who have recently used the corporate Web site as a venue for repairing a damaged public image.

Note: The text of the message appeared in <u>The New York Times</u>, Saturday, September 20, 2003.

Impact of Culture on Business: Spotlight on Latin America

Learning Objectives
The purpose of this video is to help you:
1. Realize the culture impacts all the communications and interactions of international business
2. Realize that economic conditions vary from country to country.
3. Recognize that business culture differs throughout the region of Latin America.

Background Information
Whether a business is truly multinational or sells to only a few foreign markets, several factors will affect its international operations. Its success in foreign markets is largely determined by the ways in which it respond to social, economic, political, and other cultural barriers to international trade. Companies must recognize and respect the many cultural differences the distinguish people in one country from people in another. Such differences can lead to misunderstandings in international business relationships and communication barriers, particularly if language differences also exist.

Synopsis
The video suggests that culture impacts all human interactions, including business. Businesses are owned and operated by people who sell to and buy from people. In an effort to demonstrate how culture impacts international business communications and operations, the video takes a close look at Latin America and examines the impact culture has on development and business as well as discussing the outlook for change in the region.

Discussion Questions
1. List some aspects of Latin American culture and indicate the influences on their development. Be sure to address communication issues in your response.

   ➢ *Geography – national and regional*
   ➢ *History – impact of colonization and Spanish conquest*
   ➢ *Language – primarily Spanish, but Portuguese culture and language is a major influence in Brazil, which constitutes half of the population of South America*
   ➢ *Influences of indigenous cultures and immigrants from Africa, Japanese, Italy, Germany, and East India*
   ➢ *Economy and wealth- economic challenges exist but Latin America remains a region with huge potential*

2. What current factors might cause cultural change to occur in Latin America? What are the likely changes?

   ➢ *Political – restoration of democratic rule*
   ➢ *Economic – wealth redistribution and move to new industries like high-tech while maintaining traditional industries like agriculture*
   ➢ *Foreign influences of products and services*

3. As discussed in the video, several common themes permeate Latin American business culture. Discuss each of these and their ability to ensure effective communication if an organization wishes to engage in international business with Latin America.

   ➢ *Latin American businesses typically are hierarchical in their structure, with decisions made from the top down. This is important to know, as it may be best for a company wishing to engage in international business with a Latin American company to talk directly with top management to avoid wasted time.*
   ➢ *Developing trust and gaining respect in the business environment oft Latin America is all about forming and maintaining good relationships. This often includes quite a bit of socializing. This is important to know, as it may be best for a company wishing to engage in*

international business with a Latin American company to make a considerable effort to develop personal relationships, focus on gaining respect, and practice patience in their business dealings with the individuals in this culture.

4.   In most Latin American countries, do they prefer formal or informal business communications and interpersonal relationships? Explain you answer.

> *In most Latin American countries, Old World manners are still the rule, and an air of formality is expected in most business interactions and interpersonal relationships, especially when people are not well acquainted with one another.*
> *People in business are expected to dress conservatively, and professionally, and to be polite at all times.*

5.   List several examples of acceptable forms of nonverbal communication in Latin America.

> *Latin Americans are generally very physical and outgoing in their expressions and body language.*
> *They frequently stand closer to one another when talking than in many other cultures.*
> *They often touch, usually an arm, and even kiss women's cheeks on a first meeting.*

Follow-Up Assignment
The Internet provides access to information about other countries and cultures. The world is "figuratively" shrinking in terms of exposure to other cultures. How can you use the Internet to learn more about other cultures? Furthermore, assume you are an executive that is sent on a global assignment. Will the Internet provide opportunities for communication with corporate and personal contacts? What other ways will the Internet be used to effectively communicating with suppliers, contacts, or customers across borders?

For Further Exploration
Do research to determine the major elements of the business culture of the regions of the United States and Canada. Define some parameters about the way people communicate, how business is organized in terms of hierarchy, and attitudes toward work in general. After obtaining this information, explain how U.S. and Canadian business culture differ from the business culture of Latin America.

Creativity & Innovation and Communication: Second City Communications

Learning Objectives
The purpose of this video is to help you:
1. Understand the functions of interpersonal communication in the workplace.
2. Identify the ways to overcome barriers to effective communication.
3. Discuss the importance of active listening both socially and professionally.

Synopsis
Now the world's greatest comedy theatre, Chicago's Second City Improv <www.secondcity.com>, is bringing much more than its famous brand of humor to corporate giants like Coca-Cola, Motorola, and Microsoft. With over 40 years of experience in corporate services, Second City's teachers give business professionals the communication skills they never learned in school: like taking risks and thinking on their feet. Business Communications Training is Second City's fastest growing practice, fueled by the demands of over 200 Fortune 500 companies for solutions. Workshops are tailored to client's needs including: improved listening and presentation skills, collaborative leadership and team skills, interview skills, breaking down barriers to successful communication, and the uses of humor to convey important messages. The next time you sit back and watch Saturday Night Live, ask yourself how a lesson in the art of improvisation might give your career and your social life a boost.

Discussion Questions
1. *For analysis:* How do the exercises featured in this video clip address the contrasting needs of the trial lawyer, the divorce lawyer, and the media buyer?

All of the exercises address the seven elements of the communication process. Each of these students is learning about their own skills and attitudes as they encode messages and receive messages. However they are facing different barriers to communication. For example students may include any of the following in their responses: the trial lawyer needs to improve his skills in watching and using nonverbal cues; the divorce lawyer needs to accurately assess feedback that may be colored by extreme emotions; the media buyer needs to gain confidence.

2. *For analysis:* Would ABC's talkative guest Kay Jarman, the 47-year-old award winning salesperson, be a good candidate for Second City's training workshop?

All the exercises featured in the workshop including the "and that's all " exercise alluded to, would help Kay to "dialogue" rather than to "monologue," to focus on others rather than on herself and to listen. However, some students may feel that her pronounced lack of self-awareness may be a liability in the social context of a group workshop, making her a better candidate for private coaching.

3. *For application:* What other workshops might Tom Yorton want to offer companies in response to our current economic and political climate?

Suggestions might include workshops to raise the level of communication skills among employees who must face constant security threats (travel industry), or participate in the rebuilding of a company after an unforeseeable disaster (such as 9/11) or an unplanned corporate crisis (such as that suffered by Martha Stewart Living Omnimedia as a result of Martha Stewarts indictment; or who face the challenge of a corporate merger; or who will be managing or working with diverse populations. Students will have additional ideas.

4. *For application:* How might the" yes and rule of improvisation" be used to train customer service representatives at an L.L. Bean or a Dell computer call center? Without physical cues, such as facial expression and body language, is the "yes and rule" still effective?

Today customer service requires representatives to have all pertinent information available and that they are able to respond quickly and effectively to customer needs; regardless of the channel of communication. The yes and rule of improvisation would work well as a training tool in both cases even without nonverbal cues. Some students may feel that diversity and language differences may be a stumbling block in the case of Dell, where much of the call center business is outsourced to India.

5. *For debate:* According to President and Managing Director, Second City Communications, Tom Yorton: "Y`u have to be willing to fail to be able to get the results you want...to connect with an audience." Do you agree that this is as true in business as it is in comedy? Support your chosen position.

Students who agree may follow an entrepreneurial path, where risk taking is necessary in order to succeed; or they may believe that adversity can be a valuable teacher; or that in order to make business connections we must constantly risk failure. Other students may argue that avoiding failure can be a successful business strategy, as well.

Online Exploration

Enjoy Second City Communication's Web site www.secondcity.com. If you are a loyal fan, you might want to check out the book titles offered, and read more about the group's history. Now explore Second City's Corporate Services: scan their client roster, read the testimonials, and then select a case study you find compelling. If you are currently employed, which workshop would be most beneficial to you and to your work team? Explain. If you are currently a student, how might you and your fellow business students benefit from a Second City workshop? Which workshop would you most like to participate in? Explain how you think it might help you in terms of your social life, your career planning, and your interviewing skills.

Student responses will differ, depending on the variety of professions and the age groups represented in each class. If students are serving in internships, they may have specific challenges in downward, upward, lateral, and diagonal communication. Regardless of current career status, there is no one who cannot benefit from practicing public speaking and learning to listen actively. Students who belong to on or off campus organizations may want to hone leadership skills in order to gain more prominence or to boost self-confidence.

Starbucks

Synopsis

Starbucks' strategy is based on four pillars: 1) Providing the best coffee, 2) Offering the finest products associated with coffee, 3) Creating an environment that is inviting, and 4) Being socially responsible. The phenomenal growth of this Seattle-based company can be found through the implementation of these pillars by its "partners" or employees. The result is a company that is passionate about creating a coffeehouse experience. Connecting with the customers through its partners and listening to their suggestions for innovation is how Starbucks will remain locally relevant and not become a faceless logo. As the company expands globally, its challenge is to stay locally relevant, but keep the experience consistent. Starbucks intends to achieve this through its partners. The company spends more money on taking care of its employees through training and benefits than it does on marketing. As the company sees it, if it takes care of the employees, they will take care of the customers.

Employees are the driving force behind creating the Starbucks' experience and, along with the product, are a firm specific advantage that is part of the brand. The essence of the brand lives in the company's caring and passionate partners. Additionally, consistency in communication is key as the company expands internationally and into new partnerships. It is important to have one voice in all growth activities. The primary marketing vehicle driving this growth has been word of mouth about up and coming stores and the success of the stores themselves. The company has leveraged this success to expand. With growth through product extensions such as bean sales in grocery stores and partnerships with airlines, the focus is on keeping the brand pure and making it sustainable. A sustainable global brand is one that is based on emotional bonding with the customer because the brand lives with the customer, not with the company.

Discussion Questions

1. **Starbucks' strategy is based on four pillars. Identify these pillars.**

   - providing the best coffee
   - offering the finest products associated with coffee
   - creating an environment that is warm, welcoming, and inviting
   - being socially responsible and being involved in the fabric of the community

2. **How is growing the Starbucks' brand oversees different from Starbuck's home market?**

The difference relates to the development stage. While the Starbucks' brand was introduced in North America in 1971, it was not introduced on an international level until approximately 10 years ago. The Starbucks' experience is well-known and understood in North America; however, the Starbucks' brand oversees is at a different development stage. The focus in international markets is on establishing the brand and allowing consumers to discover what the Starbucks' experience is all about.

3. **How does Starbucks stay "locally relevant" as they become global? Is this important to the success of Starbucks' as they expand into global markets?**

Starbucks can stay locally relevant by maintaining tight connections with their partners (employees) in the stores and partners then maintain those connections with the customers. The goal is to make certain that the essence of the brand and the experience of the brand is consistent and relevant to the local culture.

Remaining locally relevant is extremely important to the success of Starbucks internationally. Respecting differences in cultures abroad shows the commitment Starbucks' has to "knowing its' customers" and to providing an experience that is suitable for each market. The company realizes that a sustainable global brand is one that is based on emotional bonding with the customer because the brand lives with the customer, not with the company.

4. **What are the key successes of Starbucks' branding?**

Starbucks offers more than just a product, it is about the experience. The essence of the brand lives in the company's caring and passionate partners. Employees are the driving force behind creating Starbucks' experience and, along with the product, are a firm specific advantage that is part of the brand. This is how they influence and touch the consumers. Additionally, consistency in communication is key as the company expands internationally and into new partnerships.

5. **Describe Starbucks' people-to-people business philosophy? How has this led to Starbuck's success?**

Starbucks is interested in influencing and touching consumers. Starbucks' brand was built on word of mouth, not extensive and broad advertising campaigns. The key to the success of the Starbucks' expansion program was investment in generating extensive word-of mouth publicity campaigns. In addition, consumers touch and influence the corporation by offering suggestions.. The local connection and the brand building it has created has led Starbuck's to move into other success venues such as bean sales in grocery stores and partnerships with airlines. Furthermore, Starbucks has moved the brand successfully and extensively into different regions like Asia and Europe.

Leading with Integrity and Compassion at Quova: How One Silicon Valley CEO Inspires People to Succeed

Synopsis

Marie Alexander, President and CEO of Quova,Inc., comes by her leadership style naturally. She has always believed that one's work should enrich one's life, not just one's bank account. Before entering the field of business information systems, she earned a degree in music therapy, ran an amusement park, and worked in a mental institution. Each of these experiences has contributed to her behavioral approach to leadership and to her conviction that people need to know that it is okay to fail sometimes.

Founded in January 2000,Quova, a small Mountain View, CA start-up finds itself thriving in the aftermath of the information technology boom. As the frontrunner in geo-location, Quova is literally mapping uncharted territory. Quova's GeoPoint service pinpoints the location of Web site visitors in real time, giving customers around the world a competitive edge without violating the privacy of internet users.

For the first time, retailers can easily target their online marketing campaigns and detect fraud. Using Quova's systems bookmakers, casinos and lottery operators can ensure that all bets placed are legal. Hollywood film companies can use Quova's technology to customize content for use on movie Web sites around the globe. Quova's clients include Amazon.com, Visa International, and E-Gaming.

But the creativity and teamwork it took to bring groundbreaking software to the marketplace didn't happen overnight. In the crowded field of Information Technology, leadership can make all the difference. Comfortable with herself and at ease with her employees, Marie Alexander attributes Quova's success to a "hands-under" leadership style. She believes in catching people if they fall and helping them to achieve their personal goals, as well as the company's goals. Again and again she has set the bar higher and her employees have stretched themselves to meet the challenge. Alexander clearly thrives on the idea of building a business, but she does not lose sight of her deeply held conviction that is the human beings involved in this enterprise that matter most.

This confident, young CEO has never considered being a woman an obstacle in her professional life. To the contrary, she feels that being a woman probably makes it easier for her to be nurturing, open, and compassionate in the workplace. She makes a continuous effort to listen, motivate and provide support to her subordinates, the gender specific traits attributed to contemporary leaders scoring high in Emotional Intelligence.[1] Alexander views conflict as a necessary part of organizational growth and she is not shy about stepping in to help find a resolution. Nor is she stymied by the responsibilities of her executive office when it comes to making tough decisions like firing people.

Marie Alexander is striving to build a sound, resilient business that will be able to surmount the political and economic upheavals of our global community. In a down market, when public trust has been further eroded by the recent Enron debacle, it is likely that we will see the emergence of a more moral leadership style. Marie Alexander's unique blend of integrity and compassion should help Quova stay a winner.

Discussion Questions

As you watch the interview with Marie Alexander, keep in mind that Quova is currently weathering the aftermath of the technology industry implosion and the effects of the Sept. 11th terrorist attack. This means that many businesses around them have folded, the energy in Silicon Valley is no longer as frenetic, and corporations are not buying technology as easily as they were in the boom years. Specifically, answer the following questions:

---

[1] Chapter 12,*Myth or Science*, Men Make Better Leaders Than Women

1. Which aspects of the behavioral based Ohio State Studies pertain to Marie Alexander's leadership style? Which aspects of the contingency based Path-Goal Theory would best define Marie Alexander's leadership style?

According to the Ohio State Studies, Marie Alexander would rate high in consideration behavior. Her leadership style is based on nurturing people and helping them to achieve both personal and organizational goals. She also expects high standards of performance and inspires the excitement necessary to create innovative technology. Therefore it is likely that she would be considered "high in initiating structure", as well. Following the Ohio State Studies criteria her leadership style would probably be defined as "high-high."

The Path-Goal theory is similar to Marie Alexander's own brand of "hands under" leadership, and is in keeping with her commitment to be supportive of her employees while never losing sight of what is necessary to build the company. The video confirms that Alexander is both a supportive an achievement oriented leader. While it is not certain that she is participative or directive, it can be inferred that she may display all four of House's behaviors as the situation requires.

2. Do you think it is truly feasible or desirable to *choose* a leadership style? Do you think Marie Alexander consciously chose her leadership style or do you think it evolved as a result of her career choices? Support your opinion based on the video you have just seen.

Some students may feel it is advantageous to choose a leadership style in order to promote one's own career growth and improve one's own effectiveness as a leader. Others may feel that ultimately leadership style springs from the roots of one's personality and cannot truly be learned (or taught).

Student opinions will vary concerning Marie Alexander, but answers should address the influence of her background running an amusement park, earning a degree in music therapy and working with people in mental institutions. Her own desire to achieve and to help others achieve; her view of success as something more than monetary wealth and her innate honesty may all be perceived as contributing to her leadership style.

3. In what ways does Marie Alexander embody the qualities needed by contemporary leaders in order to cope with change? Do you agree with her assessment that being a woman may be helpful in this regard?

At Quova, Alexander has proven her flexibility. She is passionate about her people and her business. She knows how to listen, motivate and provide support wherever and whenever it is needed. These are all traits of Emotional Intelligence (EI) that women score higher on than men. EI involves teamwork, trust, and information sharing that is necessary in today's corporations. She exhibits compassion, calmness and openness. Her optimism and her dedication to building this company give her the strength to fire someone when she has to. It seems that she feels supported by the organizational culture that she has been so instrumental in shaping. As a woman she has been able to remain a nurturer and a non-nonsense CEO at the same time.

4. Do you think deterrence-based trust, knowledge-based trust or identification-based trust is most likely to be operant at Quova? Why?

Although all three types of trust may be operant at some level inside Quova, knowledge-based trust is most likely to be prevalent. The work environment at Quova is both open and supportive allowing for emotional expression and creativity. In order to sustain Quova's success in the marketplace cooperation and trust among teams must remain high. Since the business is small it may be inferred that identification-based trust may exist as well.

5. Would you characterize Marie Alexander as a transactional leader or a transformational leader? Why?

Marie Alexander is likely to be perceived by employees as a transformational leader who communicates high expectations, promotes intelligence, rationality, and careful problem solving, and gives individual consideration. It will be interesting to see whether students perceive her as someone who is charismatic.

6. Which view of conflict would Marie Alexander be most likely to embrace? How is this congruent with her personal philosophy?

According to Alexander, conflict is a good thing. She wholeheartedly espouses coming to a resolution through open discussion. This is an expression of the interactionist approach that views organizational stasis as unresponsive to needs for change and innovation. Her personal philosophy of leading a rich, open, honest life in which people are paramount is in keeping with the human relations position.

Corporate Coaching International

Discussion Questions

1. What techniques of effective group behavior does Frankel use herself, and which does she advocate for the group? How will participants try to change their behavior as a result?

Lois Frankel uses good communication skills and good listening skills. She acts as a facilitator, of course, and she is careful to treat everyone in the group in the same way regardless of their position in the organization. She advocates the same techniques for the group as well as constructive (functional) conflict and problem solving, leadership, group maintenance and mutual encouragement, gate-keeping, and the establishment of clear roles. Her hope for changed behavior, as she expresses it herself, is that the group will learn how to create an action plan for future tasks.

2. Do you think the group's body language conveys the same message as their words? If not, point out inconsistencies.

Allowing for their occasional self-consciousness, the members of the group seem generally consistent in their spoken language and body language.

3. Is there a group leader (not Lois Frankel)? Who is it, and what is the basis of his or her leadership?

Various members play leadership roles at different points in the session. Sometimes these are formal, such as when individuals act as facilitators or recorders for discussions, and sometimes they are informal, such as when individuals direct group discussion by being particularly vocal or emphatic.

4. Can you discern any conflict within the group? What kind of conflict do you think it is—task, relationship, process? Do you think it can be turned into functional conflict? If so, how?

Most of the conflict within the group appears to be task conflict. Some of this is apparent in group discussions and some is generated by the nature of the group assignments members are given, such as the desert survival and boat-drawing exercises. There are some references to process or perhaps relationship conflicts in the past that appear to have been resolved. The type of task conflict shown in the video appears to be capable of being turned into functional conflict as the group completes its assignments.

Is This Any Way to Run a Business? SAS Institute

Learning Objectives
The purpose of this video is to help you:
1. Understand the impact of an organization's structure and design on its workforce.
2. Identify the positive influence corporate culture can have on employee retention.
3. Discuss the advantages and disadvantages of a flat management structure.

Synopsis
Headquartered just outside Raleigh, North Carolina, SAS Institute Inc <www.sas.com> is the world's largest privately owned maker of statistical analysis software. Its corporate campus resembles a magical kingdom; replete with private office space for every employee, state of the art technology, two basketball courts, pool tables, a yoga room, workout areas, an on-site day care facility, family friendly dining, and unlimited M&M's every Wednesday. According to CEO and co-founder Jim Goodnight, this is part of a retention strategy based on his vision of a workplace that encourages creativity in a stress-free environment. The company's hierarchy is so flat that people move in and out of management routinely and the CEO has 22 direct reports. Since its inception in 1976, the company has built a client base of 40,000 customer sites worldwide including many of the top Fortune Global 500 and employs nearly 10,000 people in over 200 locations.

Discussion Questions

1. *For analysis*: What are the advantages and the disadvantages of the flat hierarchy at SAS?

Among the advantages are the direct communication between people at all levels, the atmosphere of mutual trust and respect, a shared passion for writing code, and the gift of being able to achieve work/life balance without being judged. Disadvantages might come about when people are in need of more direction or if they become disenchanted with the ubiquitous presence of their CEO, or unhappy with their lack of status and income, compared to colleagues in other software corporations in their Research Triangle neighborhood like Cisco, IBM, and Sprint. Students will have additional ideas.

2. *For analysis:* How does SAS's stress-free culture serve as a retention strategy for the company?

When people have access to everything they need in order to do a good job and fulfill their roles outside the workplace, as well, there is no reason to leave. They have the luxury of being physically and spiritually nurtured. By saving money on the cost of recruiting, hiring and relocating new employees, the company channels funds into the company for better research & development and employee benefits, like free health care.

3. *For application*: Can you suggest any instances in which a more vertical management structure might be useful at SAS? Explain.

Among the sales force or within a marketing group, where the company must present a corporate image to Fortune 500 clients, a more clearly delineated hierarchy might work better. As the two co-founders grow older, they may want to set up a more vertical hierarchy in preparation for the company's future. For the duration of a particularly challenging project, employees may be more comfortable operating within the bounds of formal roles. Students will have a variety of ideas.

4. *For application:* What problems might SAS face if Jim Goodnight were to go public and sell shares in the company?

SAS would be subject to investor pressure on various issues. There would be an extra layer of bureaucracy created by news hungry Board of Directors and the CEO would have less discretionary spending power. He may be forced to lay off employees during lean times rather than accept a loss in profits, as he has chosen to do before.

5. *For debate*: According to David Russo, Human Resources, "Jim's idea is that if you hire adults and treat them like adults, they they'll behave like adults." Would you agree or disagree with this statement? Support your chosen position.

Students may agree that generally the higher your expectations of people, the greater the likelihood that they will live up to them. When people are accorded respect, they feel good about making an effort for the company in return. In light of the recent corporate scandals where people behaved without regard for others; it might be interesting to discuss how the corporate culture truly affects employee behavior and just how difficult it is to remain ethical in a corrupt environment. Students who disagree with the statement may argue that employees could easily be tempted to take advantage of the "relaxed" atmosphere.

Online Exploration

Browse SAS's homepage www.sas.com and read through the statistics, the history, awards and recognition, press center and worldwide offices. You will be amazed at the variety of uses for SAS software from Major League Baseball to healthcare to government and banking. Take note of what appeals to you and what does not. After assessing what you have seen in the video clip and on the company's Web site, would you pursue a career here? Assume that you are planning a managerial career in the software industry, would the SAS's middle management track be right for you? Are you interested in playing a leadership role to your direct reports? Are you passionate about writing code? Are you desirous of status and stock options? Consider your preferences and explain why this would or would not be an ideal place for you to work.

Student responses should reflect an honest appraisal of their individual likes and dislikes. This is an ideal place for a highly intelligent and intense worker, who is community or family oriented. It might not suit a swinging young single in search of a glitzy lifestyle.

BusNow: Sytel: A CEO Who Makes Things Happen

Synopsis

"When you hire Sytel, you get the entire company including the CEO," says Jeannette Lee White. White founded Sytel in 1987 after becoming frustrated with the sluggish bureaucracy that bogged down her analytic work at government and nonprofit organizations "Everything was just so slow-paced…I knew that it could be done better and that there was a big market for what I wanted to do." [1] By 1991 she had maxed out 16 credit cards to keep Sytel going. She felt it was more important to protect the company than to protect her own credit rating.

Today this small, agile e-Business solutions firm with a staff of 275 is in a much better position with annual revenues of $40 million in 2002[2]. Sytel's partner list includes industry giants Dell, Compaq, and Oracle. White attributes the company's success to an effective set of internal checks and balances, a short term focus, and the ability to draw top talent who can deliver *fast*.

White is a hands-on leader. She came to America from South Korea as a shy 12 year old girl who wanted to become a nun. But years of helping out at her father's Maryland convenience store helped her develop her outgoing personality and a capacity for hard work. She understands that clients like the U.S. Air force and National Institutes of Health work in an unforgiving environment where there is no allowance for errors. Sytel's history of meeting customer demands with a blend of creativity, accuracy and speed have earned it accolades in both the government and the private sector. Sytel has made the Inc. 500 list several times. In 2,000 White won a national entrepreneur award from Working Woman magazine One of her proudest accomplishments, she feels, is the Web portal designed to help the Air Force improve its mission performance, and to provide employees with access to information in just seconds, a task that used to take days or weeks.

In the late 1990's Sytel took 2 years off, but the company's growth slowed down and she reclaimed her position as CEO. Experience has taught her to delegate the technical work to the IT people and concentrate on the big picture. With her eye on the future, Jeannette Lee White is planning to lead Sytel into the wireless technology market and through the changes that lie beyond.

Discussion Questions
1. Would you say Jeannette Lee White has succeeded in creating a culture of trust at Sytel? Explain why or why not.

Judging from her ability to attract top talent while keeping the company small; as well as the strength of Sytel's reputation for reliability among government clients, it appears that Jeannette Lee White has built a culture of trust.

2. Your text describes e-business leaders as sprinters and leaders in traditional businesses as long-distance runners. Using this analogy, how would you characterize Jeannette Lee White?

As Founder and CEO of an e-based business, who claims that maintaining a short term focus with lots of attention to detail is the key to her company's success, Jeannette Lee White is a sprinter. However, her perseverance over the course of 15 years, through economically challenging periods, is evidence of her ability to work towards organizational goals with the planning and foresight that might be attributed to the long-distance runner.

---

[1] Ellen McCarthy, *Master of Change and Challenge*, washingtonpost.com
[2] www.washingtonpost.com/

3. Which of the cutting-edge approaches to leadership best describes Jeannette Lee White? Explain.

Students will be able to substantiate an answer of transformational, transactional, charismatic, or visionary leadership. Individual student choices should draw on the history of the company and clues to Jeannette Lee White's personality exhibited in the video and the video case.

4. As a woman competing in a male dominated sector, do you think Jeannette Lee White's leadership is in any way affected by the gender differences discussed in your text? Support your opinion.

Some students will argue that as a woman, Jeannette Lee White may be more naturally attuned to the flexibility, teamwork and partnering, trust and information sharing needed to operate in the fast-paced IT sector than her male counterparts. Others may feel that the influence of a male dominated norm may make gender differences irrelevant.

Feeling Like Part of the Family: Kingston Technology

Learning Objectives
The purpose of this video is to help you:
1. Understand the importance of motivating employees.
2. Consider how financial and non-financial rewards can motivate employees.
3. Explain how high morale can affect organizational performance.

Synopsis
Kingston Technology, based in California, is the world's largest independent manufacturer of computer memory products. Founded by John Tu and David Sun, Kingston employs more than 1,500 people but makes each employee feel like part of the family. The company returns 10 percent of its company profits to employees every year through a profit-sharing program. Just as important, it fosters mutual trust and respect between employees and management. Senior managers stay in touch with employees at all levels and conduct surveys to obtain employee feedback. For their part, employees report high job satisfaction and develop both personal and professional connections with their colleagues—boosting morale and motivation.

Discussion Questions
1. *For analysis:* After the sale to Softbank, employees learned from news reports that Kingston's $100 million profit-sharing distribution was one of the largest in U.S. history. What was the likely effect of this publicity on employee morale?

Employees were probably very proud to be part of one of the largest profit-sharing distributions in U.S. history. This milestone proved that the company's values could be translated into action to motivate employees and generate profits for everyone in the organization.

2. *For application:* What kinds of questions should Kingston ask to gauge satisfaction and morale through employee surveys?

Students may suggest a variety of questions to gauge employee satisfaction and morale. Some examples are: How satisfied are you with the working conditions at Kingston? How satisfied are you with opportunities for increased responsibility and challenge? Do you believe that company policies are fair and equitable?

3. *For debate:* Do you agree with Kingston's policy of giving new employees profit-sharing bonuses even when they join the company just one week before profits are distributed? Support your position.

Students who agree may say that this policy is an excellent motivational tool and shows new employees that the company backs up its words with actions. Those who disagree may say that long-time employees might resent sharing profits with employees who did not contribute to the company's performance during the previous profit-sharing period. Ask students to put themselves in the place of a new and an existing employee when debating this policy, so they can consider the issue from both sides.

Online Exploration

Visit Kingston Technology's website <www.kingston.com> and follow the link to browse company information and read about its awards. From the company information page, follow the link to learn about the organization's values. How do these values support the founders' intention to create a family feeling within the company? How do they support employees' achievement of higher-level needs? Why would Kingston post this listing of milestones on its website, starting with the company's founding and continuing with honors bestowed by *Fortune* and others?

Showcasing these values on the website implies management's highly public commitment to fostering a family atmosphere through good teamwork, respect, fairness, fun, and the other items mentioned in the list. Higher-level needs such as esteem and self-actualization can be realized when employees have the opportunity to learn, are encouraged to achieve high quality standards, and gain the flexibility and adaptability to respond to customers' needs. Posting corporate milestones on the website helps build employees' pride in the company and enhances their status as an employee of an award-winning firm. It also brings the company's accomplishments to the attention of customers, prospective customers, suppliers, and other stakeholders.

SECTION FOUR

TEST BANK

Chapter 1

<u>Multiple Choice Questions</u>

1. Various definitions of leadership include all <u>but one</u> of the following: (p. 4)
   a.   influence process
   b.   goal achievement
   c.   group phenomenon
   d.   control*

2. Which one of the following is <u>not</u> part of a general definition of leadership? (p. 4)
   a.   exercise of control*
   b.   group
   c.   influence
   d.   hierarchy

3. The definition of leadership has how many key elements? (p. 4)
   a.   one
   b.   two
   c.   three*
   d.   four

4. Lorraine Monroe, director of the School of Leadership Academy considers which of the following to be key to leadership? (p. 4)
   a.   setting goals
   b.   articulating a vision*
   c.   taking care of followers
   d.   addressing the needs of stakeholders

5. Mary Sammons, president of Rite Aid believes that _____ is/are the key to leadership. (p. 4)
   a.   followers*
   b.   inspiration
   c.   goal setting
   d.   control

6. Mitt Romney, the Governor of Massachusetts and Joyce Wycoff the founder of Innovation Network both agree both agree that: (p. 4)
   a.   a leader must guide the group in reaching its goals
   b.   followers are key to good leadership*
   c.   the key to leadership is intelligence
   d.   leadership is a myth

7. Which of the following factors are <u>not</u> part of the definitions of leadership effectiveness? (p. 5)
   a.   achieving goals
   b.   follower satisfaction
   c.   implementation of change
   d.   maintaining control*

8. Chick-fil-A, the chicken fast food company focuses on _____ as the key element in leadership effectiveness. (p. 5)
   a.   employee empowerment
   b.   goal achievement
   c.   customer satisfaction*
   d.   increase in stock price

161

9. According the Fred Luthans, effective managers focus on _____ while successful managers focus on _____ . (p. 5)
   a.   stakeholders/goal achievement
   b.   employee satisfaction/quick promotions*
   c.   goal achievement/stock prices
   d.   change management/employee satisfaction

10. According the Fred Luthans, <u>effective</u> managers are those who: (p. 5)
   a.   take care of their own careers
   b.   take care of their employees*
   c.   worry about all stakeholders
   d.   maintain control through a crisis

11. According the Fred Luthans, <u>successful</u> managers are those who: (p. 5)
   a.   take care of their own careers*
   b.   take care of their employees
   c.   worry about all stakeholders
   d.   maintain control through a crisis

12. Based on Fred Luthans' research, what percentage of managers are both effective and successful? (p. 5)
   a.   10%*
   b.   30%
   c.   50%
   d.   over 60%

13. Which of the following statements is true about the definition of leadership effectiveness? (p. 6)
   a.   Leadership effectiveness depends on the goals of the organization*
   b.   Leadership effectiveness must take into account the personality of the leader
   c.   Leadership effectiveness is the same regardless of the organization
   d.   Leadership effectiveness is always based on performance

14. The case of the New York Times newspaper is an example of: (p. 6)
   a.   the importance of stakeholders in defining effectiveness
   b.   the role of national culture
   c.   generational differences
   d.   the complexity of defining effectiveness*

15. Which one of the following factors is the key element of most definitions of leadership effectiveness? (p. 6)
   a.   employee satisfaction
   b.   stakeholder needs
   c.   focus on outcome*
   d.   financial measures

16. While _____ is an important aspect of leadership effectiveness, the key element is _____ . (p. 6)
   a.   leader style/providing direction
   b.   process/outcome*
   c.   goal achievement/stakeholder satisfaction
   d.   empowerment/participation

17. Which one of the following is <u>not</u> an element of the definition of leadership effectiveness? (p. 6)
    a.   goal achievement
    b.   smooth internal functioning
    c.   external adaptability
    d.   efficiency*

18. The three key elements of leadership effectiveness are: (p. 6)
    a.   goal achievement, smooth internal processes, external adaptability*
    b.   follower satisfaction, leader control, empowerment
    c.   goal achievement, stock prices, customer satisfaction
    d.   flexibility, follower satisfaction, stakeholder satisfaction

19. Which of the following is <u>not</u> part of the mission of Small Dog Electronics? (p. 7)
    a.   commitment to employees
    b.   customer service
    c.   maximum profit*
    d.   creating a family culture

20. The leaders at Small Dog Electronics are effective because: (p. 7)
    a.   they focus on the financial bottom line
    b.   they have put their customers ahead of their employees
    c.   have created a company based on their own values*
    d.   they provide clear goals for their employees

21. Culture is important because: (p. 8)
    a.   some cultures are more powerful than others
    b.   culture guides people's assumptions and behaviors*
    c.   culture can be changed to match the organization
    d.   Leaders must learn to ignore culture

22. Which of the following best defines culture? (p. 8)
    a.   Culture is the traditions, living style, and art of a group of people
    b.   Culture is what people believe
    c.   Culture is the combination of religion and beliefs
    d.   Culture is the commonly held values of a group of people*

23. How many levels does culture have? (p. 8-9)
    a.   two
    b.   three*
    c.   four
    d.   five

24. The three levels of culture are: (p. 8)
    a.   personal, group, and organizational*
    b.   national, ethnic, and organizational
    c.   art, religion, and traditions
    d.   individual, group, and organizational

25. Gender belongs in the _____ level of culture. (p 8-9)
    a.   first
    b.   second
    c.   third*
    d.   fourth

163

26. Male traits of _____ and _____ are often associated with leadership in many cultures. (p. 9)
    a.   aggression/independence*
    b.   intelligence/goal orientation
    c.   cognitive skills/ruthlessness
    d.   individualism/competition

27. The problems faced by the New York Times newspaper have been attributed to: (p. 9)
    a.   Jason Blair's unethical behavior
    b.   the culture of the organization*
    c.   the lack of challenging performance expectations
    d.   the national culture

28. The leadership at the New York Times newspaper created culture that focused on (p. 9)
    a.   the well being of employees
    b.   attention to ethical standards
    c.   careful promotion based on seniority
    d.   performance at all costs*

29. David Peterson, CEO of North Highland created an organizational culture that: (p. 9)
    a.   took into consideration the employees' personal life*
    b.   separated personal and organizational goals
    c.   allowed for excellent financial performance
    d.   rewarded top financial performance

30. The examples of North Highland and Atlantic Group Furniture are similar in that in both cases: (p. 9)
    a.   employees came first
    b.   financial performance came first
    c.   the leaders shaped the culture*
    d.   national culture influenced organizational culture

31. As opposed to people in the U.S., people in many cultures expect their leaders to _____. (p. 10)
    a.   be infallible*
    b.   be people oriented
    c.   take charge
    d.   be action oriented

32. The example of President Vincente Fox of Mexico stating: "I believe there are no mistakes" illustrates: (p. 10)
    a.   his leadership style
    b.   the influence of the Mexican culture on leadership*
    c.   the economic and political situation in Mexico
    d.   the impact of organizational factors on leadership

33. National organizational heritage refers to: (p. 10)
    a.   the wealth of each organization
    b.   the culture of different organizations
    c.   the management styles based on national cultures*
    d.   organizational events that shape national culture

34. The fact that the cultures of French companies tend to generally be more similar to one another than to organizational cultures in the U.S. is an example of: (p. 10)
    a.   the strength of the French culture
    b.   the differences between France and the U.S.
    c.   the cultural characteristics of each national culture
    d.   the national organizational heritage*

35. The High and Low Context model of culture was developed by: (p. 10)
    a.   Hall*
    b.   Trompenaars
    c.   Hosftede
    d.   GLOBE

36. The High and Low Context model of culture addresses: (p. 10-11)
    a.   different cultural values
    b.   differences in communication styles*
    c.   differences in leadership patterns
    d.   the organizational cultural context

37. People from high context cultures typically: (p. 10-11)
    a.   rely on non-verbal cues and situational factors to communicate*
    b.   rely on the written word and clearly stated statement to communicate
    c.   value leaders who take care of people
    d.   value leaders who focus on the task

38. People from low context cultures typically: (p. 10-11)
    a.   rely on non-verbal cues and situational factors to communicate
    b.   rely on the written word and clearly stated statement to communicate*
    c.   value leaders who take care of people
    d.   value leaders who focus on the task

39. The fact that the Vietnamese and Italians pay attention to a leader's title and do not always rely on written contracts can be partially attributed to: (p. 10-11)
    a.   the two cultures being relaxed
    b.   the two cultures being people oriented
    c.   the two culture being high-context*
    d.   the two cultures being collectivist

40. A U.S. manager who is negotiating in China has difficulty getting his Chinese counterparts to agree to put the details of their new contract on paper. At the same time, the Chinese managers are frustrated at the U.S. manager's insistence to clarify every detail. This conflict is can be partially attributed to: (p. 10-11)
    a.   the U.S. superiority in business interactions
    b.   the Chinese not trusting the U.S. manager
    c.   the difference in how the two culture use context*
    d.   the differences in the two countries political systems

41. A Mexican manager is upset at the fact that his German colleague jumps right into business without taking the time to get to know him and establish a relationship. The German manager is frustrated at how long it takes to get anything done and is pushing for quicker decision making. This cultural conflict can be partially explained by: (p. 10-11)
    a.   the typical impatience of the Germans
    b.   the Mexican's longer time orientation
    c.   the fact that Mexico is high context and Germany is low context*
    d.   the typical cultural differences between Western Europe and Latin America

165

42. Which one of the following is <u>not</u> one of Hofstede's cultural dimensions? (p. 11)
   - a.   time orientation
   - b.   power distance
   - c.   uncertainty avoidance
   - d.   egalitarianism*

43. Geert Hofstede developed his cultural values model based on surveys of: (p. 11)
   - a.   managers in the European Union
   - b.   IBM employees in 40 countries*
   - c.   North American and Canadian managers
   - d.   Students in introductory psychology classes

44. Hofstede's model includes how many cultural dimensions? (p. 11)
   - a.   two
   - b.   four
   - c.   five*
   - d.   seven

45. Power distance refers to: (p. 11-12)
   - a.   how much power managers have
   - b.   the extent to which people accept unequal power*
   - c.   the power of the leaders to make changes without consulting followers
   - d.   how paternalistic and male dominated a society is

46. French employees typically do not expect to participate in decision making to the same extent as U.S. or Swedish employees. This may be partially because: (p. 11-12)
   - a.   France is a high power distance culture*
   - b.   U.S. and Swedish employees are often better trained
   - c.   France is less collectivistic that the U.S. or Sweden
   - d.   the French are not comfortable with uncertainty

47. Tolerance of uncertainty refers to: (p. 11-12)
   - a.   how much uncertainty exists in the political system
   - b.   how quickly managers make decisions
   - c.   the extent to which employees rely on their manager for decision making
   - d.   how comfortable people are with ambiguity*

48. When a culture is high in uncertainty avoidance, people are likely to: (p. 11-12)
   - a.   search for absolute truths*
   - b.   expect their leaders to allow participation
   - c.   rely on their community for information
   - d.   have a short term orientation

49. Individualism/collectivism refers to: (p. 11-12)
   - a.   the extent to which leaders have power
   - b.   the degree to which groups and social structures are the basis of society*
   - c.   how much power individuals have in the political system
   - d.   how assertive people are when working with their group

50. Individualistic cultures tend to: (p. 11-12)
   - a.   expect people to conform to social norms before they become independent
   - b.   emphasize performance over social support
   - c.   focus on individual achievement*
   - d.   value material goods

51. Although many companies in the U.S. have adopted team-based management that are very successful in Japan, U.S. managers and employees often have a difficulty working in teams. This may be because: (p. 12)
     a.   Japanese managers are generally superior in motivating their employees
     b.   the U.S. employees are not comfortable with uncertainty
     c.   the Japanese have lower power distance and are more egalitarian
     d.   the U.S. employees are more individualistic*

52. Based on Hofstede's model, which of the following best describes the culture of the U.S.? (p. 12)
     a.   The U.S. is an individualistic culture where people are long-term oriented, value achievement and are highly competitive.
     b.   The U.S. culture places a high value on individuals and achievement and tends to be egalitarian and short-term orientated with low power distance.*
     c.   The U.S. is highly competitive, power oriented, and focused on improving social justice
     d.   The U.S. culture is high on context, power, achievement, and competitiveness

53. Harry Triandis proposes that the concept of uncertainty avoidance can be further refined by: (p. 12)
     a.   adding the concept of time orientation to tolerance for uncertainty.
     b.   looking at how uncertainty avoidance is different in vertical and horizontal cultures.
     c.   introducing the concept of tight and loose cultures to uncertainty avoidance.*
     d.   combining context and individuality to explain uncertainty avoidance.

54. In _____ cultures such as Japan, people follow rules, norms, and standards closely. (p. 12)
     a.   power oriented
     b.   collectivistic
     c.   long-term oriented
     d.   tight*

55. In Thailand, there is much tolerance for behaviors that are considered acceptable and violation of rules is often overlooked. This can partly be explained because: (p. 12)
     a.   Thailand has a loose culture.*
     b.   Thailand is collectivistic.
     c.   Thailand emphasizes consideration for individual rights
     d.   Thailand is a low power distance culture.

56. Mehran has grown up in a culture where breaking rules and norms of behavior is considered to be serious. Her parents and teachers often reminded her that rules are to be obeyed and that she risked serious consequences if she did not conform. Based on this information, one could deduce that Mehran's culture is: (p. 12)
     a.   very harsh.
     b.   high power distance.
     c.   a tight culture.*
     d.   ascriptive and collectivistic.

57. The concept of individualism/collectivism can be further refined by considering: (p. 12)
     a.   whether leaders have power and how they use power.
     b.   how tight or loose the culture is.
     c.   whether followers make decisions on their own.
     d.   whether the culture focuses on hierarchy or equality.*

58. _____ cultures focus on hierarchy; while _____ cultures focus on equality. (p. 12)
   a. Vertical/horizontal*
   b. Tight/loose
   c. Ascriptive/prescriptive
   d. Collectivistic/individualistic

59. In vertical individualistic cultures: (p. 12)
   a. all members of the groups are seen as equal.
   b. the individual is seen as unique and superior to others.*
   c. individuals must sacrifice themselves for the group.
   d. the individual is unique but equal to others.

60. In horizontal individualist cultures: (p. 12)
   a. all members of the groups are seen as equal.
   b. the individual is seen as unique and superior to others.
   c. individuals must sacrifice themselves for the group.
   d. the individual is unique but equal to others.*

61. In horizontal collectivistic cultures: (p. 12)
   a. all members of the groups are seen as equal.*
   b. the individual is seen as unique and superior to others.
   c. individuals must sacrifice themselves for the group.
   d. the individual is unique but equal to others.

62. In vertical collectivistic cultures: (p. 12)
   a. all members of the groups are seen as equal.
   b. the individual is seen as unique and superior to others.
   c. individuals must sacrifice themselves for the group.*
   d. the individual is unique but equal to others.

63. Japan and Korea are examples of _____. (p. 12)
   a. loose cultures
   b. individualistic cultures
   c. vertical collectivistic cultures*
   d. cultures that are comfortable with uncertainty

64. Vertical/horizontal dimension impacts leadership because: (p. 12)
   a. it deals with people
   b. it relates to how rules are used
   c. it focuses on how leaders use participation in their culture
   d. it affects views of hierarchy and equality*

65. As opposed to Hofstede who considers general cultural dimensions and values, Trompenaars and his colleagues have developed model that: (p. 12)
   a. looks at power relationships inside of organizations
   b. focuses on how national culture affects corporate cultures*
   c. allows managers to understand the motivation of their followers
   d. considers the communication context within organizations

66. The two dimensions used by Trompenaars to classify cross-cultural organizational cultures include: (p. 13)
   a. egalitarian-hierarchical and person-task*
   b. tight-loose and vertical-horizontal
   c. proactive and reactive
   d. high context and low context

67. Which one of the following is <u>not</u> one of Trompenaars cross-cultural organizational cultures? (p. 13)
   a.   incubator
   b.   guided missile
   c.   community*
   d.   Eiffel tower

68. According to Trompenaars, incubators are: (p. 13)
   a.   egalitarian and focused on taking care of individual needs.*
   b.   egalitarian and focused on the task.
   c.   hierarchical and focused on taking care of people.
   d.   hierarchical and driven to accomplish tasks.

69. According to Trompenaars, Eiffel towers are: (p. 13)
   a.   egalitarian and focused on taking care of individual needs.
   b.   egalitarian and focused on the task.
   c.   hierarchical and focused on taking care of people.
   d.   hierarchical and driven to accomplish tasks.*

70. According to Trompenaars, families are: (p. 13)
   a.   egalitarian and focused on taking care of individual needs.
   b.   egalitarian and focused on the task.
   c.   hierarchical and focused on taking care of people.*
   d.   hierarchical and driven to accomplish tasks.

71. According to Trompenaars, guided missiles are: (p. 13)
   a.   egalitarian and focused on taking care of individual needs.
   b.   egalitarian and focused on the task.*
   c.   hierarchical and focused on taking care of people.
   d.   hierarchical and driven to accomplish tasks.

72. Jerry is working in an organization where people are very relaxed and there are few rules and hierarchy. However, getting the task done is everyone's primary concern. The cross-cultural organizational culture of Jerry's company can be best classified as: (p. 13)
   a.   guided missile*
   b.   individualistic and task oriented
   c.   organic
   d.   family style

73. French organizations often fall in the Eiffel tower category. They are characterized by: (p. 13)
   a.   individualistic and highly competitive organizations.
   b.   stable rigid organization focused on rules and performance.*
   c.   leadership based on expertise and expectations for follower participation.
   d.   family-oriented organizations where the leader has absolute power.

74. Nigel has a new job and during orientation he is told that the organization treats employees as professionals and gives them considerable latitude. He is also told that leadership is based on competence and expertise. Based on this description, Nigel is most likely working for which type of organization? (p. 13)
   a.   guided missile
   b.   incubator*
   c.   Eiffel tower
   d.   Family

75. The GLOBE project includes information about cross-cultural difference from how many cultures? (p. 14)
    a.   close to 300
    b.   over 100
    c.   around 60*
    d.   about 20

76. Based on GLOBE findings the U.S. is among the highest on: (p. 14-15)
    a.   power distance and tolerance ambiguity
    b.   humane orientation and performance
    c.   gender egalitarianism and individuality
    d.   assertiveness and performance*

77. Which one of the following is <u>not</u> one of the GLOBE dimensions? (p. 15)
    a.   collectivism
    b.   assertiveness
    c.   emotionality*
    d.   future orientation

78. Based on GLOBE dimensions a culture that values fairness, generosity, caring and kindness is likely to be high on which dimension? (p. 15)
    a.   human orientation*
    b.   gender egalitarianism
    c.   collectivism
    d.   future orientation

79. The difference between Collectivism I and Collectivism II in the GLOBE cultural dimensions is related to: (p. 15)
    a.   focus on people or social systems
    b.   the degree of assertiveness of the individual versus the group
    c.   the degree to which performance is based on the group or the organization
    d.   focus on social institutions or family and organizations*

80. One of the contributions of the GLOBE research has been: (p. 14-15)
    a.   more dimensions to explain culture
    b.   identification of universal and culturally contingent leader behaviors*
    c.   the clarification of the dimensions presented by other researchers such as Hofstede and Trompenaars
    d.   to recognize autonomy and assertiveness as key universal leadership styles

81. According to the GLOBE findings _____ is generally valued in most cultures. (p. 14-15)
    a.   team-based leadership*
    b.   directive leadership
    c.   self-protective leadership
    d.   active and assertive leadership

82. Research presented in the "Cutting Edge" suggest that: (p. 16)
    a.   GLOBE has considerably increased our understanding of culture.
    b.   Culture is a stable system of beliefs that must be understood to prevent shock.
    c.   Culture is highly dynamic and continuously changes as a result of interaction of national and corporate cultures.*
    d.   Individuals rather than groups create culture and leadership tends to be based on individual cultures.

83. Which one of the following is <u>not</u> one of the obstacle to effective leadership? (p. 16-17)
    a.   Uncertainty that creates pressure for quick responses
    b.   Vague definition of leadership*
    c.   Rigid and short-term oriented organizations
    d.   Inaccessible academic research

84. While managers focus on _____, leadership is aimed at _____. (p. 17-18)
    a.   getting power/here and now
    b.   getting follower motivated/sharing values
    c.   order/change*
    d.   personal relationships/political networks

85. Leadership and management become more closely similar when considering the issue of: (p. 17-18)
    a.   effectiveness and competence*
    b.   national and organizational culture
    c.   individual traits
    d.   organizational performance

86. Which of the following is <u>not</u> one the managerial roles proposed by Mintzberg? (p. 19)
    a.   figurehead
    b.   leader
    c.   conflict manager*
    d.   resource allocator

87. According to research by Mintzberg, the job a of a manager is characterized by: (p. 19)
    a.   many cultural encounters
    b.   wide variety of tasks and many interruptions*
    c.   a series of well defined activities that start with planning and end in controlling
    d.   political activities that are essential to being effective

88. Helgesen's research about gender differences in management found that: (p. 19-20)
    a.   women are better managers
    b.   women preferred face-to-face communication*
    c.   women managers often have to focus on their job at the expense of personal life
    d.   women are more isolated then men

89. Helgesen called the "female" style of management _____. (p. 19)
    a.   the web*
    b.   participative management
    c.   interconnected management
    d.   non-hierarchical charisma

90. Meg Whitman, CEO of eBay believes that: (p. 20)
    a.   the exercise of power is essential to leadership
    b.   women often have less power than men
    c.   there are no differences between men and women in how they use power
    d.   having power means being willing not to have any*

91. The example of Ben and Jerry gourmet ice cream illustrates: (p. 21)
    a.   the importance of social responsibility
    b.   how founders can impact an organization*
    c.   the importance of quality in the mission of an organization
    d.   how men and women both practice participative management

92. Leaders are often role models for their followers. Recent research suggests that leaders must also pay attention to: (p. 22)
   a.   sexual harassment and its negative impact
   b.   the use of power
   c.   how outsiders impact their followers
   d.   their own emotional reactions*

93. Leaders shape the culture of their organization through <u>all but one</u> of the following: (p. 21-22)
   a.   role modeling
   b.   the reward system
   c.   establishing personal relationships with followers*
   d.   hiring decisions related to employees and other managers and leaders

94. The key argument against the impact of leadership centers around the idea that: (p. 22-25)
   a.   most leaders are simply not effective
   b.   social and environmental factors affect organizations more than leaders*
   c.   culture and organizational rigidity does not allow leaders to make their mark
   d.   other managers impact organizations as much as leaders

95. A commonly accepted position regarding the significance of leadership in organizations states: (p. 22-25)
   a.   Leadership is a myth that plays an important role in followers' perception.
   b.   While leaders are important, environmental factors often impact the organization more.
   c.   In most organizations, leaders have some, but not much discretion to impact the organization.
   d.   Leadership is one of many important factors in organizations.*

96. Which of the following factors is key to JetBlue's flexibility? (p. 34-35)
   a.   The airline's growing size and importance in its industry.
   b.   The emphasis on teamwork.*
   c.   A powerful leadership team.
   d.   A centralized organization where all employee can stay in touch.

97. Which one of the following is <u>not</u> one of the factors in JetBlue's success? (p. 34-35)
   a.   David Neeleman
   b.   A decentralized structure
   c.   JetBlue's ability to copy other airlines*
   d.   Constant communication with employees

<u>True/False Questions</u>

98. There is one commonly accepted definition of leadership. (p. 4)
   a.   true
   b.   false*

99. A leader is defined as a person who influences individuals and groups, helps them in establishing goals, and guides them towards achievement of those goals. (p. 4)
   a.   true
   b.   false*

100. It is easy to define leadership. (p. 4)
   a.   true
   b.   false*

101. Researchers agree that a leader is effective when the group performs its task. (p. 5)
   a.   true
   b.   false*

102. The definition of leadership effectiveness often depends on the point of view of the person who is defining effectiveness. (p. 5)
   a.   true*
   b.   false

103. For Barbara Waugh, personnel manager of Hewlett-Packard Laboratories, effectiveness is communication, collaboration, and innovation. (p. 5)
   a.   true*
   b.   false

104. According to Fred Luthans, effective and successful managers engage in different types of activities. (p. 5)
   a.   true*
   b.   false

105. Fred Luthans found that the majority of managers are both effective and successful. (p. 5)
   a.   true
   b.   false*

106. Fred Luthans found that only 10% of managers are both effective and successful. (p. 5)
   a.   true*
   b.   false

107. Based on Luthans' research, in order for organizations to be effective they must reward effective managers and help them become successful. (p. 5)
   a.   true*
   b.   false

108. The definition of leadership effectiveness depends on the organization and the context. (p. 5-6)
   a.   true*
   b.   false

109. The common thread in many definitions of leadership effectiveness is the focus on outcomes. (p. 6)
   a.   true*
   b.   false

110. Leaders are effective when their followers achieve their goals, can function well together, and can adapt to the changing demands from external forces. (p. 6)
   a.   true*
   b.   false

111. The effectiveness of Small Dog Electronics is based on its ability to keep focused on many different stakeholders. (p. 7)
   a.   true*
   b.   false

112. Culture consists of the commonly held values of a group of people. (p. 8)
   a.   true*
   b.   false

113. National culture is the set of values and beliefs shared by people within a nation. (p. 8)
   a.   true*
   b.   false

114. People learn culture through both formal teaching and informal observation. (p. 8)
   a.   true*
   b.   false

115. Culture mostly affects people's personal life, rather than leadership. (p. 8)
   a.   true
   b.   false*

116. Organizational culture influences leadership to a greater extent than national culture. (p. 8-9)
   a.   true*
   b.   false

117. Ethnic or group culture is the set of values and beliefs shared by cultural within a nation. (p. 8)
   a.   true*
   b.   false

118. Organizational culture is the set of values and beliefs shared by members of an organization. (p. 8)
   a.   true*
   b.   false

119. While traditional male traits are often associated with leadership, this is changing because of new organizational models. (p. 9)
   a.   true
   b.   false*

120. Leaders and organizational founders play a key role in the development of the culture of an organization. (p. 9)
   a.   true*
   b.   false

121. The leadership at the New York Times newspaper focused on creating a culture that balanced employee needs and well being with organizational performance goals. (p. 9)
   a.   true
   b.   false*

122. At the North Highland company and Lander International, leaders placed particular attention to employee needs. (p. 9)
   a.   true*
   b.   false

123. North Highland, Lander International, and Atlantic Group Furniture define the leadership effectiveness in the same manner. (p. 8-9)
   a.   true
   b.   false*

124. Most cultures accept the fact that leaders are fallible and are likely to make mistakes. (p. 10)
   a.   true
   b.   false*

125. Whereas in the U.S., people accept the fact that leaders make mistakes, people in many other cultures except their leaders to be infallible. (p. 10)
    a.   true
    b.   false*

126. Different countries and regions in the world have developed particular organizational and management styles based on their national cultures. (p. 10)
    a.   true*
    b.   false

127. National organizational heritage refers to management styles based on national cultures. (p. 10)
    a.   true*
    b.   false

128. The High and Low Context model of culture addresses differences in communication styles among different cultures. (p. 10-11)
    a.   true*
    b.   false

129. You can usually understand a country's culture by using one of Hofstede's cultural dimensions. (p. 11-12)
    a.   true
    b.   false*

130. In high power distance cultures, there is a wider gap between the powerful and the powerless. (p. 11-12)
    a.   true*
    b.   false

131. In individualistic cultures, people rely on their group for guidance. (p. 11-12)
    a.   true
    b.   false*

132. The U.S. and Australia are among the most individualistic cultures in the world. (p. 11-12)
    a.   true*
    b.   false

133. In Japan, while collectivism is very high and people place value on consensus, there is also high power distance. (p. 11-12)
    a.   true*
    b.   false

134. Harry Triandis is the person who originally proposed the concept of uncertainty avoidance. (p. 11-12)
    a.   true*
    b.   false

135. While Sweden and the U.S. are both individualistic cultures, in Sweden individuals are seen as unique and superior to others, while in the U.S., equality is the norm. (p. 11-12)
    a.   true
    b.   false*

136. According to Trompenaars, family type organizations are found most often in countries such as Greece, Singapore, and Japan. (p. 12-13)
    a.   true*
    b.   false

137. The leader's role in an incubator cross-cultural organizational culture is to be the undisputed head and take full responsibility for all that occurs. (p. 12-13)
- a. true
- b. false*

138. The GLOBE cultural model uses nine dimensions to understand and explain culture. (p. 14-15)
- a. true*
- b. false

139. All the dimensions proposed by the GLOBE model are new and different from those presented by other researchers. (p. 14-15)
- a. true
- b. false*

140. In assertive cultures individuals are direct and confrontational. (p. 14-15)
- a. true*
- b. false

141. Future oriented cultures tend to take a long-term orientation that ties the present to the past and future. (p. 14-15)
- a. true
- b. false*

142. Based on research presented in the "Cutting Edge," comparison of national cultures based on the models presented in the chapter is narrow and flawed. (p. 16)
- a. true*
- b. false

143. The key to effective leadership is practice and learning from one's mistakes. (p. 16-17)
- a. true*
- b. false

144. Most researchers agree that leadership and management are basically the same concept. (p. 17-18)
- a. true
- b. false*

145. While leadership is an age-old concept, the idea of management was developed during the industrial revolution. (p. 17-18)
- a. true*
- b. false

146. Effective managers often have to perform roles and functions attributed to leaders. (p. 17-18)
- a. true*
- b. false

147. Research about the difference between male and female managers indicates that women are generally less effective leaders, but excellent managers. (p. 17-18)
- a. true
- b. false*

148. There is general agreement that there are fundamental differences between how men and women manage. (p. 17-18)
- a. true
- b. false*

149. One of the primary roles of leaders is to create and maintain the culture of their organizations. (p. 19-20)
  a.   true*
  b.   false

150. Recent research suggests that leaders must be able to manage their followers' emotional states. (p. 22)
  a.   true*
  b.   false

151. The only means leaders have to influence their followers is through role modeling. (p. 21-23)
  a.   true
  b.   false*

152. Research has clearly established that leadership has a key impact on organizations. (p. 23-25)
  a.   true
  b.   false*

153. There is considerable debate among leadership scholars regarding whether leadership actually impacts organizations. (p. 23-25)
  a.   true*
  b.   false

154. While the leader's impact on the organization may not always be tangible, leadership is significant in providing a vision and direction for followers. (p. 23-25)
  a.   true*
  b.   false

155. David Neeleman believes that the key to his airline's success is his own leadership style. (p. 34-35)
  a.   true
  b.   false*

Chapter 2

1. Prior to the industrial revolution, the study of leadership relied on: (p. 37)
    - a.   scientific studies
    - b.   intuition and description*
    - c.   case analyses
    - d.   the trait approach to understand leaders

2. The modern scientific study of leadership can be divided into three eras. These are: (p. 37)
    - a.   trait, behavior, contingency*
    - b.   charismatic, visionary, exemplary
    - c.   case studies, research, theory building
    - d.   personality, event-based, complex analysis

3. The belief that leaders are born rather than made is part of which approach to leadership? (p. 37)
    - a.   scientific
    - b.   contingency
    - c.   case study
    - d.   trait*

4. Philosophers such as Thomas Carlyle, William James, and Galton believed that: (p. 37)
    - a.   followers are not important
    - b.   leaders and managers are different people
    - c.   innate qualities shape behavior and personality*
    - d.   leaders are the result of their trait and their environment

5. The trait approach to leadership suggests that: (p. 37)
    - a.   leaders have special innate qualities*
    - b.   leadership traits are clearly visible
    - c.   traits are based on social class
    - d.   traits cannot be measured

6. During the Industrial Revolution and at the beginning of the 20th century, which factors contributed or reinforced the assumption that leaders are born? (p. 37)
    - a.   social science research findings
    - b.   military needs
    - c.   the availability of reliable trait measures
    - d.   existing social structures*

7. The 20th century social and historical context reinforced the trait approach by: (p. 37)
    - a.   encouraging good leadership
    - b.   involving traits in the selection of leaders
    - c.   limiting opportunities for common people*
    - d.   allowing the best leaders to rise to power

8. Which of the following factors helped in the development of the trait approach to leadership? (p. 37)
    - a.   the need to find leaders during World War II
    - b.   the development of personality testing*
    - c.   the use of behavioral surveys to measure traits
    - d.   access to military leaders

9. The method most often used by researchers using the trait approach to leadership involves: (p. 37)
   a.   situational analysis
   b.   use of detailed biographies of leaders
   c.   behaviorally anchored scales
   d.   comparison of leaders and followers*

10. The results of the trait approach to leadership have established that: (p. 37)
   a.   leaders are born not made
   b.   follower and leaders have different personality traits
   c.   few, if any traits define leaders*
   d.   being sociable and intelligent is a requirement for leadership

11. Which of the following is not one of the traits typically associated with leadership? (p. 37)
   a.   sociability
   b.   thoughtfulness*
   c.   sense of humor
   d.   originality

12. The results of the trait approach to leadership indicate that: (p. 38)
   a.   traits should not be used in leadership
   b.   leadership cannot be studied outside of the situation or context*
   c.   some traits are excellent predictors of leadership effectiveness
   d.   traits are unreliable and invalid measures

13. Bass' review of individual factors related to leadership indicates that they can be classified in
    _____ categories. (p. 38)
   a.   two
   b.   four
   c.   six*
   d.   eight

14. Research on traits indicates that: (p. 38)
   a.   traits don't impact leadership
   b.   traits may limit a person's behavioral range*
   c.   emotional intelligence determines who is an effective leader
   d.   cognitive rather than emotional components are important in leadership

15. Which one of the following is not one of the categories of individual factors related to leadership suggested by Bass? (p. 38)
   a.   dominance*
   b.   achievement
   c.   participation
   d.   status

16. Which of the following factors contributed to the development of the behavior approach to leadership? (p. 38)
   a.   the need to find leaders during World War II*
   b.   the development of personality testing
   c.   the use of behavioral surveys to measure traits
   d.   access to military leaders

17. Which of the following factors contributed to the development of the behavior approach to leadership? (p. 39)
   a. the improvement of survey research tools
   b. the dominance of behavioral theory*
   c. the complex situational factors
   d. the development of motivation theories based on human needs

18. Which one of the following is one of the benefits of the behavior approach to leadership? (p. 39)
   a. behaviors are more broadly defined that traits
   b. behaviors are stable and predictable
   c. behaviors can be measured and changed*
   d. behaviors are more interesting than traits

19. The behavior approach to leadership has several advantages. They include all <u>but one</u> of the following: (p. 39)
   a. behaviors can be observed more objectively than traits
   b. behaviors can be measured more precisely than traits
   c. behaviors can be taught, whereas traits are innate
   d. behaviors are richer and more complex than traits*

20. Many organizations, such as the military relied on the behavior rather than the trait approach primarily because: (p. 39)
   a. they could focus on training leaders*
   b. the use of traits presents cross-cultural challenges
   c. behaviors are universal
   d. they did not know how to measure traits

21. In the early work on leader behavior, Lewin and his associates relied on which of the following three leadership behaviors? (p. 39)
   a. charismatic, participative, directive
   b. accommodating, conflicting, compromising
   c. democratic, autocratic, laissez-faire*
   d. structuring, consideration, instrumental

22. The major shortcoming of Lewin's early research on leader behavior was: (p. 39)
   a. it was not clear which behavior was most effective*
   b. the behaviors were difficult to define clearly
   c. the researchers could not measure the leader behaviors consistently
   d. only task behavior was shown to improve performance

23. Based on the early behavior research conducted by Lewin and his associates, managers who provide information but little guidance to their followers are likely to have: (p. 39)
   a. the best level of performance
   b. frustrated and disorganized groups*
   c. highly empowered followers who can make their own decisions
   d. relaxed and cohesive groups

24. Sanjay makes decisions alone. According to Lewin's research, his followers are likely to: (p. 39)
   a. admire him for his decisiveness
   b. be frustrated
   c. be submissive*
   d. be relaxed since the leader knows what to do

25. Studies conducted at _____ are among the best-known behavioral approaches to leadership. (p. 39)
   a.   Harvard University
   b.   Ohio State University*
   c.   The Center for Creative Leadership
   d.   The military

26. The two primary leadership behaviors that are still in use are: (p. 39)
   a.   laissez-faire and charismatic motivation
   b.   autocratic and democratic
   c.   visionary and practical
   d.   consideration and initiation of structure*

27. The _____ is one of the primary measures of leader behavior. (p. 39)
   a.   Leader Behavior Description Questionnaire*
   b.   Behaviorally Anchored Scale
   c.   Leader Behavior Scale
   d.   Least Preferred Co-worker

28. The most commonly used tool for measuring leader behavior is: (p. 39)
   a.   a structured interview
   b.   the MBRS
   c.   the LBDQ*
   d.   observation and feedback

29. Terry is a manager who believes in treating employees as equals, is friendly and approachable, and puts the work group's ideas into operation. Terry is using which leadership behavior? (p. 39-40)
   a.   people management
   b.   consideration*
   c.   motivation
   d.   conflict resolution

30. Ragu makes sure that his work unit knows what is expected, schedules the work and sets deadlines, and assigns people to different tasks. Ragu is: (p. 39-40)
   a.   being autocratic
   b.   initiating structure*
   c.   preventing his employees from being independent
   d.   a manager but not a leader

31. If you most concerned about employee satisfaction and loyalty are related to: (p. 39-40)
   a.   good leadership
   b.   laissez-faire
   c.   empowerment
   d.   consideration*

32. Jose focuses on looking out for the personal welfare of his work unit and on creating a pleasant work environment. Based on research on the impact of leader behavior, the most likely outcome for Jose is: (p. 39-40)
   a.   follower satisfaction*
   b.   high performance
   c.   empowerment
   d.   development of a strong team spirit

33. Research strongly suggest that leader consideration behavior: (p. 40)
   a.   is associated with follower satisfaction*
   b.   is more effective than structuring behavior
   c.   leads to higher performance
   d.   has little impact except to make people feel good

34. One of the major contributions of the leader behavior research has been to: (p. 40)
   a.   move us away from use of traits
   b.   lead to careful selection of leaders
   c.   focus attention on leadership training*
   d.   remind researchers about the role of situational factors

35. Which one of the following is not a contribution of the behavior approach to leadership? (p. 40)
   a.   identification of leadership behaviors
   b.   focus on leadership training
   c.   providing strong measure of behavior
   d.   having cross-cultural application*

36. The primary shortcoming of the behavior approach to leadership is: (p. 40)
   a.   lack of scientific rigor
   b.   disregard of situational elements*
   c.   reliance on limited behaviors
   d.   ignoring the importance of personal traits

37. The contingency approach to understanding leadership started: (p. 41)
   a.   in the 1960s*
   b.   during the scientific revolution
   c.   during World War II
   d.   when the trait approach failed to yield results

38. The primary assumption of the contingency approach to leadership is: (p. 41)
   a.   leadership depends on culture
   b.   what works depends on the situation*
   c.   behavior of leaders is contingent on their personality
   d.   leadership effectiveness is contingent on the role of followers

39. Which one of the following is not one of the assumptions of the contingency approach to leadership? (p. 41)
   a.   Not everyone can learn to become an effective leader.*
   b.   There is no one best way to lead.
   c.   Leadership affects groups and organizations.
   d.   Both the leader and the situation are important.

40. Misha is has been effective because he is able to use different behaviors in different situations to motivate his followers and accomplish the tasks. Misha is relying on which leadership approach? (p. 41)
   a.   behavior approach
   b.   contingency approach*
   c.   change approach
   d.   individual approach

41. Recent reviews of the research about the role of traits in leadership shows all <u>but one</u> of the following traits play a role in leadership. (p. 42)
   a.   stamina
   b.   education
   c.   intelligence
   d.   dominance*

42. The recent approach considering leader individual characteristics identifies several key leadership traits. Which of the following is <u>not</u> one the key traits? (p. 43)
   a.   drive and energy
   b.   desire and motivation to lead
   c.   honesty and integrity
   d.   desire for dominance*

43. Lisa Harper, CEO of Gymboree demonstrates which of the key leadership traits? (p. 43)
   a.   drive and energy*
   b.   desire and motivation to lead
   c.   honesty and integrity
   d.   desire for dominance

44. Steve Jobs of Apple and Fumio Mitarai of Canon are famous for their _____. (p. 43)
   a.   drive and energy*
   b.   desire and motivation to lead
   c.   honesty and integrity
   d.   desire for dominance

45. Which trait(s) is/are often associated with Russian business leaders? (p. 43)
   a.   ambition and drive*
   b.   consideration and caring for followers
   c.   integrity
   d.   dominance

46. _____ is often cited as one of the primary reasons leaders fail. (p. 43)
   a.   lack of skills
   b.   lack of integrity*
   c.   inability to get along with followers
   d.   poor financial skills

47. The GLOBE researchers have found which of the key leadership traits to be culturally universal? (p. 43-44)
   a.   Drive and energy
   b.   Knowledge of industry
   c.   Honesty and integrity*
   d.   Assertiveness

48. The example of the Italian company Parmalat shows that _____ is a leadership trait that is valued around the world. (p. 44)
   a.   Drive and energy
   b.   Knowledge of industry
   c.   Honesty and integrity*
   d.   Assertiveness

49. The key leadership traits are not enough to make a leader effective. Other factors that are important include: (p. 44)
    a.   followers
    b.   experience and correct choices*
    c.   culture and organizational structure
    d.   leadership and cultural training

50. Michael Eisner of Disney is an example of a leader: (p. 44)
    a.   who is highly effective
    b.   who does not pay attention to culture
    c.   who does not know enough about the business
    d.   who has too much need for control*

51. The demographic characteristics of U.S. executives include all but one of the following. (p. 44)
    a.   The majority is first-born
    b.   The majority has attended exclusive private universities*
    c.   They are more educated than the average person
    d.   They are males

52. Research on the demographic characteristics of U.S executives shows that: (p. 44)
    a.   they are mostly from upper middle class backgrounds
    b.   they are highly educated
    c.   they are very similar to one another*
    d.   they are aging and retiring in record numbers

53. In which area is the number of women business leaders in the U.S. in growing? (p. 45)
    a.   high technology
    b.   banking
    c.   government
    d.   small business*

54. The United States leads the world in the percentage of women in _____. (p. 45)
    a.   decision-making positions
    b.   government
    c.   accounting and finance
    d.   company boards*

55. The homogeneity among managerial ranks in terms of demographic and personal characteristics: (p. 45)
    a.   can be an obstacle when innovation is needed*
    b.   leads to better decision making
    c.   allows for easier negotiation among business leaders
    d.   causes conflicts with followers

56. What percentage of U.S. companies have at least one woman on their board of directors? (p. 45)
    a.   10% or less
    b.   30%
    c.   50%
    d.   Over 70%*

57. Women in the U.S. constitute close to _____ percent of the managerial and professional ranks. (p. 45)
   a. 15
   b. 30
   c. 50*
   d. 75

58. Many of the Western leadership theories are based on the assumption that: (p. 45)
   a. leaders have to take charge*
   b. culture matters
   c. followers are key to leadership
   d. empowerment is essential to effective leadership

59. Many organizations are expecting employees and managers to share in _____ functions. (p. 45)
   a. consideration
   b. strategic thinking*
   c. vision
   d. support

60. The factors that are pushing for new roles for leaders include all but one of the following. (p. 46)
   a. push for quality
   b. use of teams
   c. changing hierarchies
   d. increased homogeneity*

61. In traditional organizations, employees are primarily responsible for _____ while leaders are responsible for _____. (p. 46)
   a. production/planning*
   b. planning/controlling
   c. preparing/implementing
   d. controlling/quality

62. Changes in many organizations are causing leaders to rely more on _____ and less on _____. (p. 46)
   a. consideration/task
   b. vision/consideration
   c. facilitation/structuring*
   d. planning/leading

63. Which one of the following is not one of the key factors that the Hay Group has identified to be one of the key elements of an effective corporate culture. (p. 47)
   a. control*
   b. teamwork
   c. customer focus
   d. innovation

64. Leaders such a Jane Cummins, CEO of Holladay Park Medical ,and Philip Diehl, director of the U.S. Mint, have made _____ one of their key activities. (p. 47)
   a. quality control
   b. providing a vision
   c. leading
   d. communicating*

65. Which one of the following is <u>not</u> one of the factors that is fueling the changes in leadership? (p. 47-48)
   a. increase in global competition
   b. political changes
   c. legal requirements*
   d. demographic and social changes

66. According the research by Mumford and Licuanan, one of the most important factors in helping groups be creative is: (p. 48)
   a. the structure of the organization
   b. the leader's flexibility*
   c. matching the leadership with the culture
   d. training followers to make decisions

67. The fastest growing segment of the U.S. population is currently: (p. 50)
   a. African Americans
   b. Asian Americans
   c. Hispanics*
   d. European

68. The younger employees who are joining the workforce typically expect to: (p. 50)
   a. become leaders very quickly
   b. have autonomy and participate in decisions*
   c. be promoted slower than previous generations
   d. stay with the same company for over ten years

69. The increased cultural diversity in organizations is: (p. 50)
   a. causing most leaders to become ineffective
   b. causing changes in organizational practices*
   c. creating considerable resentment among employees
   d. leading to conflict between leaders and followers

70. Leaders such as John Grundhofer – aka Jack the Ripper – continue to remain in leadership positions, primarily because: (p. 51)
   a. they are effective
   b. organizational face short-term financial pressures*
   c. they focus on stakeholders
   d. they are able to manage global cultures

71. _____ is one of the barriers to changes in organizations and leaders. (p. 51)
   a. Lack of teams in upper management*
   b. Open structures and ill defined goals
   c. Global cultural changes
   d. The focus on team rewards

72. The XYZ organization recruits leaders who are dominant and willing to take control over those who focus on team building. This is an example of: (p. 51)
   a. cultural insensitivity
   b. lingering images of traditional leadership*
   c. organizational stupidity
   d. poor decision making

73. Jack Hartnett, owner of D.L. Rogers Corp. is an example of a leader: (p. 59-60)
    a. with a successful laissez-faire style
    b. who is a team builder
    c. who empowers his followers
    d. whose style fits the situation*

True/False Questions

74. Real interest in leadership started with the industrial revolution. (p. 37)
    a. true
    b. false*

75. Prior to the industrial revolution, interest in leadership on intuition and a description of existing practice. (p. 37)
    a. true*
    b. false

76. The argument that leaders are born not made suggests that innate qualities shape human personality and behavior. (p. 37)
    a. true*
    b. false

77. The development of personality testing helped in the development of the trait approach to leadership. (p. 37)
    a. true*
    b. false

78. The social structures of the early 20th century reinforced the trait approach. (p. 37)
    a. true*
    b. false

79. Based on the results of the trait approach to leadership, there is evidence that leaders are born rather than made. (p. 37)
    a. true
    b. false*

80. Intelligence has been found to be the one required leadership trait. (p. 37)
    a. true
    b. false*

81. Leaders are often more sociable, lively, and popular that other group members. (p. 37)
    a. true*
    b. false

82. Traits do not guarantee that a person will become a leader, let alone an effective leader. (p. 37)
    a. true*
    b. false

83. While one trait does not explain leadership, a combination of traits can often predict who will become a leader. (p. 37)
    a. true
    b. false*

84. Recent research show that some traits limit a leader's behavioral range. (p. 38)
  a.   true*
  b.   false

85. According to Bass' research the individual factors related to leadership can be classified in two primary categories of task and relationship. (p. 38)
  a.   true
  b.   false*

86. Leader personality is not the only determinant of leadership effectiveness. (p. 38)
  a.   true*
  b.   false

87. One of the benefits of the behavioral approach to leadership over the trait approach is that behaviors can be measured better than traits. (p. 39)
  a.   true*
  b.   false

88. As opposed to traits, which are innate, behaviors can be taught. (p. 39)
  a.   true*
  b.   false

89. Leadership traits are easily observed whereas behaviors are more difficult to see. (p. 39)
  a.   true
  b.   false*

90. The early research of Lewin and his associates about leadership behaviors clearly identified three different types of leadership behaviors. (p. 39)
  a.   true*
  b.   false

91. The early research of Lewin and his associates about leadership behaviors clearly identified which leadership behavior is most effective. behaviors. (p. 39)
  a.   true*
  b.   false

92. Based on the early behavior research conducted by Lewin and his associates, managers who provide information but little guidance to their followers are likely to have frustrated and disorganized groups. (p. 39)
  a.   true*
  b.   false

93. Consideration behavior includes things such as looking out the welfare of team members and making expectations clear. (p. 39-40)
  a.   true
  b.   false*

94. The BARS continues to be used as a measure of leadership behaviors. (p. 39)
  a.   true
  b.   false*

95. Consideration and initiation of structure are the two primary leadership behaviors. (p. 39-40)
  a.   true*
  b.   false

96. The research on leadership behavior has been able to identify clearly which leadership behaviors are most effective. (p. 39-40)
    a.   true
    b.   false*

97. Leader consideration is generally associated with follower satisfaction. (p. 40)
    a.   true*
    b.   false

98. When the leader provides structure and guidance, followers tend to become highly loyal. (p. 40)
    a.   true
    b.   false*

99. The LBDQ is rarely used in current leadership research. (p. 40)
    a.   true
    b.   false*

100. The leader behaviors are generally the same across all cultures. (p. 40)
    a.   true
    b.   false*

101. One of the major contributions of the leadership behavior research has been the use of scientific methods. (p. 40)
    a.   true
    b.   false*

102. One of the major contributions of the leadership behavior research has been to focus attention on the importance of leadership training. (p. 40)
    a.   true*
    b.   false

103. Similar to the trait approach, the behavior approach was not highly successful because it was difficult to implement. (p. 40)
    a.   true
    b.   false*

104. The contingency approach to leadership was started in the 1960s. (p. 40)
    a.   true*
    b.   false

105. According the modern views of leadership, there is no best way to lead. (p. 40)
    a.   true*
    b.   false

106. Based on the contingency approach of leadership, some people can learn to be better leaders. (p. 40)
    a.   true
    b.   false*

107. According to the contingency approach to leadership, we need to understand both the leader's traits and the situation. (p. 41)
    a.   true*
    b.   false

108. According the contingency approach, the situational factors are more important than the leaders' style and behavior. (p. 41)
   a.   true
   b.   false*

109. The Normative Decision Model is the first theory to take a contingency approach to leadership. (p. 41)
   a.   true
   b.   false*

110. The contingency assumes that training leaders is too difficult, therefore we should select leaders based on their abilities. (p. 41)
   a.   true
   b.   false*

111. Some recent trait research has re-established the importance of including traits in leadership. (p. 42)
   a.   true*
   b.   false

112. The new research on leadership traits indicates that integrity may be one of the key factors in leadership. (p. 43)
   a.   true*
   b.   false

113. The key leadership traits identified by Kirkpatrick and Locke can be detrimental in some cases. (p. 43)
   a.   true*
   b.   false

114. The new approach to leadership traits indicates that a combination of traits lead to effectiveness as a leader. (p. 43)
   a.   true
   b.   false*

115. Demographic survey show that most U.S. CEOs have attended exclusive private colleges. (p. 44)
   a.   true
   b.   false*

116. The most striking result of the research about the demographic characteristics of U.S. executives is that they are very similar to one another. (p. 44)
   a.   true*
   b.   false

117. Knowledge of the business is often more important than confidence and energy when it comes to key leadership traits. (p. 44)
   a.   true
   b.   false*

118. Michael Eisner, CEO of Disney shows that high energy and motivation to lead can sometimes be detrimental to leaders. . (p. 44)
   a.   true*
   b.   false

119. Although women are not well represented in executive positions around the world, they are holding a majority of board memberships. (p. 45)
   a.   true
   b.   false*

120. Women hold about 50% of managerial and professional positions in the U.S. (p. 45)
   a.   true*
   b.   false

121. The homogeneity of managers in the U.S. is highly beneficial to creativity. (p. 45)
   a.   true
   b.   false*

122. Leadership in traditional organizations continues to include a desire for control and power. (p. 45)
   a.   true*
   b.   false

123. The focus on quality forces organization to expect leaders to be in charge and show dominance. (p. 46)
   a.   true
   b.   false*

124. Today's leaders need to improve their structuring skills. (p. 46)
   a.   true
   b.   false*

125. As the leader's roles are changing, employees are increasingly expected to understand strategic and financial issues. (p. 46)
   a.   true*
   b.   false

126. Planning and organizing is increasingly being done by followers instead of leaders alone. (p. 46)
   a.   true*
   b.   false

127. As the leader's roles are changing, employees are increasingly expected to understand strategic and financial issues. (p. 46)
   a.   true*
   b.   false

128. Because of many changes in organizations, leaders have to increasingly rely on structuring skills to be effective. (p. 46)
   a.   true
   b.   false*

129. Rick Sapio, CEO of Mutual.com, and Jeff Imelt, of GE both focus on listening to their employess. (p. 47)
   a.   true*
   b.   false

130. Based on research done by Mumford and Licuanan on role of leadership in innovation, a leader's flexibility may be the most important factor in the creativity of the group. (p. 48)
   a.   true*
   b.   false

131. The factors that are fueling leadership changes include legal pressures and requirements. (p. 48-49)
   a. true
   b. false*

132. The United States is one of the few countries that is experiencing increased diversity. (p. 49)
   a. true
   b. false*

133. Baby Boomer managers often see the Generation Xers as being detached and expecting participation. (p. 49)
   a. true*
   b. false

134. By 2050, the average U.S. resident will be from a non-European background. (p. 50)
   a. true*
   b. false

135. By 2050, the majority of new entrants in the U.S. labor force will be Hispanic. (p. 50)
   a. true
   b. false*

136. Ted Childs of IBM and Joe Watson of StrategicHire.com both consider diversity to be an essential part of the business. (p. 50)
   a. true*
   b. false

137. Financial pressures often force organizations to select ruthless leaders. (p. 51)
   a. true*
   b. false

138. One of the obstacles to effective leadership is the extensive use of teams in upper management. (p. 51)
   a. true
   b. false*

139. Male images of leadership which include dominance and control are no longer used in most organizations. (p. 51)
   a. true
   b. false*

140. Few organization take full advantage of their employees' ideas and potential. (p. 52)
   a. true*
   b. false

141. Rewards based on individual performance and employees' lack of willingness to accept responsibility are two of the obstacles to effective leadership. (p. 52)
   a. true*
   b. false

142. Jack Hartnett, owner of D.L. Rogers Corp., is an example of the contingency model of leadership. (p. 59-60)
   a. true*
   b. false

143. Jack Hartnett should change his style to be kinder and more participative. (p. 59-60)
    a.   true
    b.   false*

CHAPTER 3

<u>Multiple Choice</u>

1. Which one of the following is <u>not</u> part of what makes an individual unique? (p. 62-63)
    a.   heredity
    b.   genes
    c.   gender
    d.   geography*

2. The interactionist view of individual differences suggests: (p. 62-63)
    a.   the environment determines who we are
    b.   genes are the most important factor in making people who they are
    c.   heredity and the environment both influence individual differences*
    d.   culture is one of the key factor in determining how people behavior

3. Although female babies tend to develop language skills earlier than males, parents speak more to girls than boys and schools expect girls to be proficient in language. This is an example of: (p. 62-63)
    a.   the interactionist approach*
    b.   sexism in our society
    c.   typical problems boys face in their development
    d.   the importance of parental influence

4. The primary reason boys are more competitive and aggressive than girls is that: (p. 62-63)
    a.   boys are genetically more aggressive
    b.   boys watch more violent movies and play more video games
    c.   typical male genetic traits are reinforced by society*
    d.   parents spend less time with boys than with girls

5. Personality is best defined as: (p. 63)
    a.   a person's traits based on their genes
    b.   a set of traits that make a person unique*
    c.   how people behave based on their values
    d.   behaviors that make people different

6. Which of the following is <u>not</u> part of the definition of personality? (p. 63)
    a.   personality is stable
    b.   personality is a set of traits
    c.   personality determines what we do*
    d.   personality is influenced by genes and the environment

7. Jose believes in being honest in all situations. This is a reflection of Jose's _____.(p. 63)
    a.   values*
    b.   personal choice
    c.   culture
    d.   temperament

8. _____ are natural aptitudes, whereas _____ are acquired talents. (p. 64)
    a.   Personality traits/behaviors
    b.   Abilities/skills.*
    c.   Leadership skills/management skills
    d.   Values/cultural tendencies

9. Abilities tend to be: (p. 64)
   a.   stable over time*
   b.   related to culture
   c.   based on values
   d.   related to leadership

10. Individual difference characteristics affect a person's behavior most when: (p. 64)
   a.   the situation provides clear guidelines
   b.   the situation is loosely structured*
   c.   the person is strong willed
   d.   the person is flexible

11. Christie is a lively, informal, and outgoing person who just started a new job. She quickly realizes that her new company is formal and very subdued. Christie adjusts her behavior and tones down her natural enthusiasm to adopt a more quiet style. This is an example of: (p. 64)
   a.   weak personality
   b.   conformity pressure
   c.   the power of clear situational cues*
   d.   the impact of culture and socialization on new employees

12. The best way to describe the influence of individual difference characteristics on behavior is: (p. 64-65)
   a.   Individual difference characteristics determine how we behave
   b.   Individual difference characteristics have little influence on our behaviors
   c.   Individual difference characteristics provide a range of comfortable behaviors*
   d.   Individual difference characteristics encourage us to try out new behaviors

13. When people are encouraged to behave outside their zone of comfort, they are likely to: (p. 64-65)
   a.   learn and grow*
   b.   develop leadership skills
   c.   become frustrated
   d.   resist change

14. Which one of the following influences a person's value system? (p. 66)
   a.   abilities
   b.   skills
   c.   leadership
   d.   culture*

15. Which one of the following has been found to be relatively universal values? (p. 66)
   a.   Individuality and Individual dignity
   b.   Personal achievement and performance
   c.   Fairness and honesty*
   d.   Desire for recognition and rewards

16. Japanese managers are likely to reward team effort over individual achievement. This is because: (p. 66)
   a.   the Japanese culture values community*
   b.   individuals tend to perform less well in Japan
   c.   the Japanese are less competitive
   d.   individual achievement is only rewarded in special cases

17. Which of the following cultures value the leader's ability to conform to social order? (p. 66)
   a.   the United States
   b.   Germany
   c.   Japan*
   d.   The Philippines

18. One of your Navajo employees quits after you surprise him with having won the company's most visible employee performance award which is advertised on the company web site and newsletter. His quitting is likely to be due to: (p. 66)
   a.   his shyness and personal reserve
   b.   his culture's emphasis not standing out*
   c.   the lack of individual recognition
   d.   unknown factors that often influence a person's behavior

19. A Brazilian employee bends the truth to protect several of his co-workers, when asked to report a safety incident. His behavior can be partly explained by: (p. 66)
   a.   the low power distance in the Brazilian culture
   b.   the uncertainty avoidance in Brazil
   c.   the high-context Brazilian culture*
   d.   high machismo in the Brazilian culture

20. Hard work, patriotism and frugality are values typically held by people in which of the following age groups? (p. 67)
   a.   Those over 65*
   b.   Those from 50 to 65
   c.   Those 35 to 50
   d.   Those 25 to 35

21. Non-conformity, idealism, and distrust of the establishment are values typically held by people in which of the following age groups? (p. 67)
   a.   Those over 65
   b.   Those from 50 to 65*
   c.   Those 35 to 50
   d.   Those 25 to 35

22. Ambition, material comfort, and success are values typically held by people in which of the following age groups? (p. 67)
   a.   Those over 65
   b.   Those from 50 to 65
   c.   Those 35 to 50*
   d.   Those 25 to 35

23. Enjoyment of life, and desire for autonomy and flexibility are values typically held by people in which of the following age groups? (p. 67)
   a.   Those over 65
   b.   Those from 50 to 65*
   c.   Those 35 to 50
   d.   Those 25 to 35

24. _____ are found to be often close to their family. (p. 67)
   a.   The Baby Boomers
   b.   The Generation Xers
   c.   The Yuppies
   d.   The Millennials*

25. Andy, who is in his early forties cannot understand why Malcolm, his coworker is so distrustful of the manager and often defies her authority. Malcolm is likely to belong to which of the following generations? (p. 67)
   a.   the Baby Boomers*
   b.   the Generation Xers
   c.   the Yuppies
   d.   the Millennials

26. Older generations in Western Europe and the U.S. tend to _____ than younger generation. (p. 67)
   a.   be more suspicious of authority
   b.   have a stronger sense of cultural superiority*
   c.   be more independent
   d.   be more tied to their parents and family members

27. A _____ view of ethics suggests that what is right or wrong depends on the situation. (p. 68)
   a.   universalist
   b.   contingency
   c.   relativist*
   d.   cultural

28. United States laws forbid business people to bribe others even in cultures where bribery is expected or necessary. This approach to ethics reflects a _____ view of ethics. (p. 68)
   a.   universalist*
   b.   contingency
   c.   relativist
   d.   cultural

29. Which of the following countries has been rated as the least corrupt by Transparency International? (p. 68)
   a.   Paraguay
   b.   Singapore*
   c.   The United States
   d.   Canada

30. Cross-cultural research about deception shows that: (p. 68)
   a.   people in individualist cultures feel guilty about lying.
   b.   people in collectivist cultures use more deception.*
   c.   deception is a universal concept.
   d.   most people lie to protect themselves.

31. What can a Western manager negotiating in Japan or Korea expect? (p. 68)
   a.   Open and honest negotiation
   b.   Cooperation based on the need for collective harmony
   c.   Some deception followed by guilt*
   d.   Some deception, but only when negotiating with a group

32. Examples of people such as movie producer Scott Rudin show that _____ may be more important than _____. (p. 69)
   a.   ability to relate to others/intelligence*
   b.   consideration for people/focus on the task
   c.   cognitive ability/social skills
   d.   cultural knowledge/task skills

33. _____ is increasingly being suggested as being more important than _____. (p. 69)
    a.   Ability to relate to others/intelligence*
    b.   Consideration for people/focus on the task
    c.   Cognitive ability/social skills
    d.   Cultural knowledge/task skills.

34. Research by Judge, Colbert and Ilies about the link between intelligence and leadership suggests that: (p. 70)
    a.   there is no link between intelligence and leadership.
    b.   leadership is key in leadership effectiveness.
    c.   how intelligent we think a leader is, rather than actual intelligence, is related to leadership.*
    d.   objective measures of leadership intelligence such as the IQ test have relatively strong relationships to leadership abilities.

35. Based on research by Judge, Colbert and Ilies, a leader's intelligence has more impact in which situation? (p. 70)
    a.   When there are complex problems.
    b.   In less stressful situations.*
    c.   When a leader needs to show consideration
    d.   When the organization is performance orientated.

36. You are selecting a team leader to head a new team that is likely to face considerable stress. Which of the following leaders would be most appropriate? (p. 70)
    a.   a leader with above average
    b.   a leader with moderate intelligence*
    c.   a leader with both high cognitive and social intelligence
    d.   a leader selected by the team members

37. Which of the following is not a component of emotional intelligence? (p. 70-71)
    a.   self-awareness
    b.   self-regulation
    c.   sympathy*
    d.   optimism

38. _____ is the ability to read others and be able to put yourself in their place. (p. 70-71)
    a.   self-monitoring
    b.   empathy*
    c.   consideration
    d.   social skills

39. Leaders who are high on _____ are better able to guide their followers through challenging tasks because they can recognize patterns and coordinate group activities. (p. 70-71)
    a.   self-monitoring
    b.   empathy*
    c.   consideration
    d.   social skills

40. _____ is the ability to read others and be able to put yourself in their place. (p. 70-71)
    a.   self-monitoring
    b.   empathy*
    c.   consideration
    d.   social skills

41. Emotional intelligence is important in leadership because: (p. 70-71)
    a. caring about others is important
    b. good self-presentation is key to leadership
    c. emotional intelligence has been found to be related to cultural sensitivity
    d. the ability to harmonize with others plays a key role in leadership*

42. While addressing employees after 9/11, Ken Chenault the CEO of American Express, openly expressed his sorrow and embrace grief-stricken employees. His behavior is an example of: (p. 72)
    a. his ability to present the appropriate emotions when needed
    b. his high level of emotional intelligence*
    c. his excellent self-presentation skills
    d. his leadership skills

43. _____ and _____ are often terms used to describe creativity. (p. 73)
    a. Divergent/lateral thinking*
    b. Opportunistic/thrill seeking
    c. Bold/aggressive
    d. Strategic/forward looking

44. In addition to coming up with new ideas, creative leaders must also have: (p. 73)
    a. consideration for others
    b. technical expertise*
    c. strong task focus
    d. strong risk taking ability

45. Which one of the following is one of the characteristics of creative people? (p. 73)
    a. high risk-taking
    b. leadership skills
    c. tolerance for ambiguity*
    d. being able to give up quickly

46. Which of the following is not one of the characteristics of creative people? (p. 73)
    a. perseverance in the face of obstacle
    b. high risk-taking*
    c. openness to new ideas
    d. ability to tolerate lack of structure

47. According to Theresa Amabile, which of the following is required for people to be creative? (p. 73)
    a. high stress
    b. tight deadlines
    c. creative leaders
    d. experience*

48. Which one of the following is not one of the leadership skills? (p. 74)
    a. technical
    b. interpersonal
    c. conceptual
    d. organizational*

49. Marta has just been appointed to a top level executive position in her company. Which of the following leadership skills is she most likely to need and use? (p. 74)
- a. technical
- b. interpersonal
- c. conceptual*
- d. organizational

50. Most organizations provide skills training to their employees and leaders because: (p. 74)
- a. skills can be learned*
- b. new skills can quickly be translated into behaviors
- c. skills are not influenced by culture
- d. the same set of skills can be applied in all situations

51. Understanding personality traits can help leaders because: (p. 74)
- a. traits often predict who will be an effective leader
- b. traits determine how people behave
- c. some traits are consistently associated with leadership*
- d. traits are easier to learn than abilities or skills

52. Which of the following is not part of the Big Five personality dimensions? (p. 75-76)
- a. conscientiousness
- b. emotional intelligence*
- c. openness to experience
- d. agreeableness

53. _____ and _____ are both part of the Big Five personality dimensions. (p. 75-76)
- a. Locus of control/need for control
- b. Cognitive/emotional intelligence
- c. Emotional stability/consideration for others
- d. Extraversion/openness to experience*

54. Which of the Big Five personality dimensions is most strongly correlated to job performance? (p. 75-76)
- a. conscientiousness*
- b. emotional intelligence
- c. openness to experience
- d. agreeableness

55. _____ is the Big Five personality dimension that is important in jobs such as management that require social interaction. (p. 75-76)
- a. Emotional intelligence
- b. Extraversion*
- c. Openness to experience
- d. Agreeableness

56. The XYZ corporation is looking for leader who can develop high job commitment and create high job satisfaction. According to recent research on the Big Five personality dimensions, which characteristics should they look for in that leader? (p. 75-76)
   a.   high conscientiousness, open to experience, moderate emotional stability, and highly agreeable
   b.   high on emotional stability, extraversion, and agreeableness, and low on conscientiousness*
   c.   low on introversion, agreeableness, and emotional intelligence, and high on conscientiousness
   d.   high on control and high on consideration

57. Locus of control is an indicator of: (p. 76)
   a.   how much control a person needs
   b.   how much control a person feels she/he has*
   c.   the control level of leaders
   d.   control available in the situation

58. People with _____ believe that the events around them are the result of their actions. (p. 76-77)
   a.   type A personality
   b.   internal locus of control*
   c.   external locus of control
   d.   type B personality

59. Which of the following is not one of the characteristics of people with internal locus of control when compared to those with external locus of control? (p. 76-77)
   a.   Internals experience lower anxiety.
   b.   Internals set hard goals.
   c.   Internals conform more to authority*.
   d.   Internals are more task oriented.

60. Todd Smith is the CEO of Widget Corp. He tends to select risky and innovative strategies for his company and proactive in his planning. Based on this information, Todd is most likely: (p. 76-77)
   a.   a good manager.
   b.   a Type A who needs control.
   c.   a person with internal locus of control.*
   d.   a high self-monitor.

61. Sally Colbert is very energetic, focuses on deadlines, is highly ambitious and likes working alone. Based on this information, Sally is most likely: (p. 77-78)
   a.   a good manager.
   b.   a Type A who needs control.*
   c.   a person with internal locus of control.
   d.   a high self-monitor.

62. _____ is the underlying construct in Type A. (p. 77-78)
   a.   The need for control*
   b.   How well people read their environment
   c.   The need for power
   d.   How people make decisions

63. There are _____ characteristics that define in Type A. (p. 77-78)
    a.   two
    b.   three
    c.   four*
    d.   five

64. Which one of the following is one of the defining characteristics of Type As? (p. 77-78)
    a.   Relaxed approach to time
    b.   Very cooperative
    c.   Focus on one task at a time
    d.   Hostility*

65. Which of the following best describe Type As? (p. 77-78)
    a.   Type As are strategic thinkers who are proactive.
    b.   Type As try to do more in less time.*
    c.   Type As are willing to cut corners to achieve their goals.
    d.   Type As are good at persuading others.

66. _____ need and increasing amount of control while _____ feel that they have control over their environment. (p. 77-79)
    a.   Extroverts/high Machiavellians
    b.   Low self-monitors/high self-monitors
    c.   Type As/people with internal locus of control*
    d.   People who are sensing-feelers/those who are intuitive-thinkers

67. _____ is one of the major challenges Type A managers are likely to face. (p 79)
    a.   Worrying too much about time and deadlines
    b.   Inability to delegate tasks*
    c.   Setting goals that are not challenging
    d.   Inability to plan

68. Diego Vasquez is very good at reading different situations and behaving appropriately event in difficulty settings. Based on this information, Diego is most likely: (p. 79)
    a. a good manager.
    b. a Type A who needs control.
    c. a person with internal locus of control.
    d. a high self-monitor.*

69. High self-monitors may have an advantage in leadership because: (p. 79)
    a.   they are better planners
    b.   they set challenging goals
    c.   they are flexible*
    d.   they handle power well

70. You are trying to select a leader to head a team that will be negotiating a international deal for your company. Which one of the following individual difference characteristics may be useful to you in making that decision? (p. 79-80)
    a.   Locus of control
    b.   Type A
    c.   Self-monitoring*
    d.   Myers-Briggs

71. One of the primary uses of the MBTI has been (p. 81)
    a.   in leadership skill development
    b.   to select leaders
    c.   to identify who should be promoted
    d.   in team building*

72. MBTI is particularly applicable to upper echelon leadership because: (p. 81)
    a.   upper echelon leadership involves decision making*
    b.   upper echelon leaders work in teams
    c.   top management involves relationship management
    d.   executives need cross-cultural skills

73. _____ have personal charisma, are open to ideas, but burn out easily and have trouble implementing ideas. (p. 82)
    a.   Sensation thinkers
    b.   Sensation feelers
    c.   Intuitive thinkers
    d.   Intuitive feelers*

74. _____ establish rule, focus on facts and have realistic goals, but are impatient with delays and jump into action too quickly. (p. 82)
    a.   Sensation thinkers*
    b.   Sensation feelers
    c.   Intuitive thinkers
    d.   Intuitive feelers

75. _____ are architects of progress and change agents, but often unaware of others' feelings and judgmental. (p. 82)
    a.   Sensation thinkers
    b.   Sensation feelers
    c.   Intuitive thinkers*
    d.   Intuitive feelers

76. _____ are pragmatic and methodical and understand organizations well, but are often reluctant to change and focus too much on the present. (p. 82)
    a.   Sensation thinkers
    b.   Sensation feelers*
    c.   Intuitive thinkers
    d.   Intuitive feelers

77. _____ are cynical and manipulative while _____ are trusting and poor negotiators. (p. 83)
    a.   High self-monitors/low self-monitors
    b.   Type As/type Bs
    c.   Intuitive feelers/sensation thinkers
    d.   High machs/low machs*

78. The high Machiavellian leader is likely to be _____ but not necessarily _____. (p. 83-84)
    a.   considerate/task focused
    b.   successful/effective*
    c.   good planners/good implementers
    d.   task oriented/people oriented

79. You have been charged to select a leader to lead a negotiation with a client with whom you would like to establish long-term relationships. Which one of the following is likely to be your best choice? (p. 83-84)
- a.   A Type A leader with internal locus of control
- b.   An ST leader who is a low self-monitor
- c.   A moderate mach who is a high self-monitor*
- d.   An NF who is a high mach

80. People from Hong Kong and the People's Republic of China tend to score higher on the Machiavellian scale. This may be related to: (p. 83)
- a.   the higher power distance in the Chinese culture*
- b.   the higher level of collectivism
- c.   the low-context culture
- d.   the fact that the Chinese are ascriptive

81. Which of the following is one of the primary reasons leaders fail? (p. 84)
- a.   An authoritarian style
- b.   Intimidation and arrogance*
- c.   Too much focus on people
- d.   Financial focus

82. In addition to leader individual characteristics, which factor contributes to leadership failure? (p. 84)
- a.   organizational climate and culture*
- b.   other leaders
- c.   hiring practices
- d.   national cultural values

83. Steve Bennett of Intuit managed to revive the company by: (p. 85)
- a.   taking care of employees
- b.   strengthening the informal culture
- c.   focusing on the task
- d.   creating an employee-centered structure

84. The most appropriate use of individual difference characteristics, particularly personality traits, is: (p. 86)
- a.   in leader selection.
- b.   to help leaders increase their leadership skills.
- c.   to help leaders increase their self-awareness.*
- d.   in human resource decision regarding promotion and salary.

85. A method that is often used to give managers feedback about their behaviors and style from multiple perspectives and increase their self-awareness is called: (p. 86)
- a.   self-development
- b.   interpersonal skills development
- c.   executive development feedback
- d.   360-degree feedback*

86. One of the major strengths of Pernille Spiers-Lopez, the president of IKEA North America is: (p. 100-101)
- a.   her financial skills
- b.   her focus on employees*
- c.   her strategic outlook
- d.   her creative marketing abilities

87. Based on the description provided in the case, Pernille Spiers-Lopez is most likely: (p. 100-101)
    a.   a person with external locus of control
    b.   a Type A*
    c.   a high mach
    d.   a sensation-thinker

True/False Questions

88. There are a number of individual traits that are good predictors of who will be a leader. (p. 62)
    a.   true
    b.   false*

89. Traits alone do not define leaders. (p. 62)
    a.   true*
    b.   false

90. The primary reason boys are more competitive and aggressive than girls is that typical male genetic traits are reinforced by society. (p. 62-63)
    a.   true*
    b.   false

91. Values are the individual difference characteristic that has the most influence on leadership. (p. 63)
    a.   true
    b.   false*

92. Personality traits are stable and rigid. (p. 63)
    a.   true
    b.   false*

93. The impact of personality on individual behavior tends to be limited to personal aspects of life. (p. 63)
    a.   true
    b.   false*

94. Personality traits affect behaviors in many settings. (p. 63)
    a.   true*
    b.   false

95. Values are principles that a person believes. (p. 63)
    a.   true*
    b.   false

96. Honesty is the best policy is an example of a personality trait. (p. 63)
    a.   true
    b.   false*

97. You cannot train leaders to develop abilities, but you can train them in skills. (p. 64)
    a.   true*
    b.   false

98. Individual characteristics influence behavior most when the situation is clearly structured. (p. 64)
    a.   true
    b.   false*

99. When the situation provides strong cues as to how people are supposed to behave, their personality plays a lesser role. (p. 64)
   a.   true*
   b.   false

100. Personality and other individual characteristics dictate how people behave. (p. 64)
   a.   true
   b.   false*

101. Personality and other individual characteristics provide a range of behaviors that are comfortable for people. (p. 64-65)
   a.   true*
   b.   false

102. Most people have difficulty acting outside the zone of comfort that is determined by their individual difference characteristics. (p. 64-65)
   a.   true*
   b.   false

103. Most learning takes place when people behave according to their individual difference characteristics. (p. 64-65)
   a.   true
   b.   false*

104. Behaving outside their zone of comfort is one way people can learn and grow. (p. 64-65)
   a.   true*
   b.   false

105. Factors such as age and gender influence a person's value system. (p. 65)
   a.   true*
   b.   false

106. The primary influence on a person's value system is personality traits. (p. 65)
   a.   true
   b.   false*

107. Most cultures in the world value compassion and frugality. (p. 66)
   a.   true*
   b.   false

108. Individual dignity is valued mostly in Western cultures. (p. 66)
   a.   true*
   b.   false

109. Many general values about what is right or wrong are the same across the world. (p. 66)
   a.   true
   b.   false*

110. Hard work, frugality and patriotism are values typically held by the generation raised by parents who went through the depressions. (p. 67)
   a.   true*
   b.   false

111. Baby boomers typically value ambition and material comforts. (p. 67)
   a.   true
   b.   false*

112. Yuppies are often success-driven. (p. 67)
   a.   true*
   b.   false

113. Generation Xers value autonomy and flexibility. (p. 67)
   a.   true*
   b.   false

114. Those who belong to the Millennial generation tend to resent authority and are highly independent. (p. 67)
   a.   true
   b.   false*

115. The Generation Xers and Millenials are similar to each other in that both tend to have little loyalty to their jobs and companies. (p. 67)
   a.   true*
   b.   false

116. Generational value differences exist all over the world. (p. 67)
   a.   true
   b.   false*

117. Singapore has been rated as one of the most corrupt countries in the world. (p. 68)
   a.   true
   b.   false*

118. The relativist view of ethics suggests that what is right or wrong depends on the situation or culture. (p. 68)
   a.   true*
   b.   false

119. You take a universalist view of ethics when you believe that universal rules cannot apply to all. (p. 68)
   a.   true
   b.   false*

120. The Japanese and Koreans may use more deception, but they often experience considerable guilt. (p. 68)
   a.   true*
   b.   false

121. Several sets of abilities have clearly linked to leadership. (p. 69)
   a.   true
   b.   false*

122. Intelligence is not clearly related to leadership. (p. 70)
   a.   true*
   b.   false

123. Intelligence is not clearly related to leadership but is related to perceptions of leadership. (p. 69-70)
   a.   true*
   b.   false

124. Research by researchers Judge, Colbert and Ilies indicates that intelligence is related to emergence of leadership and perceptions of leadership effectiveness. (p. 70)
   a.   true*
   b.   false

125. Research shows that a more intelligent leader is able to succeed regardless of the situation. (p. 70)
   a.   true
   b.   false*

126. The most important component of emotional intelligence is sympathy for others. (p. 70-71)
   a.   true
   b.   false*

127. Emotional intelligence is important because caring for others always pays off. (p. 70-71)
   a.   true
   b.   false*

128. Emotional intelligence is key to leadership because leadership requires working with others. (p. 70-71)
   a.   true*
   b.   false

129. People who have high emotional intelligence often feel sympathy for others (p. 70-71)
   a.   true
   b.   false*

130. The way a leader delivers a message is sometimes more important than the content of the message (p. 71)
   a.   true*
   b.   false

131. Ken Chenault, CEO of American Express is an example of a leader with high emotional intelligence. (p. 72)
   a.   true*
   b.   false

132. Convergent thinking is another term often used to describe creativity. (p. 72)
   a.   true
   b.   false*

133. Creativity is the ability to develop new ideas or combine existing ones in novel ways. (p. 73)
   a.   true*
   b.   false

134. As opposed to less creative people, creative people are willing to take high risks where the chance of failure is strong. (p. 73)
   a.   true
   b.   false*

135. People tend to become more creative when they put on stress and pressure. (p. 73)
   a.   true
   b.   false*

136. According to Theresa Amabile, most people can be creative with experience and motivation. (p. 73)
   a.   true*
   b.   false

137. As leaders move up the organization, they rely less on technical skills and more on conceptual skills. (p. 74)
   a.   true*
   b.   false

138. Conceptual skills involve communication and conflict management. (p. 74)
   a.   true
   b.   false*

139. Once leaders learn new skills, they can quickly implement them in their organization. (p. 74)
   a.   true
   b.   false*

140. A leader's personality influences his or her preference, style and behavior. (p. 74)
   a.   true*
   b.   false

141. Over the years, researchers have identified five major personality dimensions. (p. 74)
   a.   true*
   b.   false

142. Emotional stability is the Big Five personality dimension most strongly linked to job performance. (p. 75)
   a.   true
   b.   false*

143. The Big Five personality dimensions are strongly linked to leadership. (p. 75)
   a.   true
   b.   false*

144. Extroversion is a required dimension for successful leadership. (p. 75)
   a.   true
   b.   false*

145. Extraversion is important for almost any job or position. (p. 75)
   a.   true
   b.   false*

146. Some degree of anxiety and worrying can be helpful for leaders. (p. 76)
   a.   true*
   b.   false

147. Locus of control is indicator of how much a person feels s/he has control over the environment. (p. 76)
   a.   true*
   b.   false

148. Leaders with internal locus of control tend to be more ethical in their decision making. (p. 76)
    a.   true*
    b.   false

149. People with external locus of control are proactive and rebound well from stressful situations. (p. 76)
    a.   true
    b.   false*

150. The need for control is at the heart of Type A. (p. 77)
    a.   true*
    b.   false

151. Being a Type A can be helpful to managers because they are better able to delegate tasks. (p. 78)
    a.   true
    b.   false*

152. The inability to delegate tasks is one of the key challenges Type A managers may face. (p. 78)
    a.   true*
    b.   false

153. Type A managers are more successful than Type B managers. (p. 79)
    a.   true
    b.   false*

154. Several of the Type A characteristics are similar to the high energy and motivation that is considered to be important in leadership. (p. 79)
    a.   true*
    b.   false

155. Type A and locus of control are closely related. (p. 79)
    a.   true
    b.   false*

156. High self-monitors read and use environmental cues better than low self-monitors. (p. 80)
    a.   true*
    b.   false

157. High self-monitors are particularly skilled at delegating tasks. (p. 80)
    a.   true
    b.   false*

158. High self-monitors emerge as leaders more often than low self-monitors. (p. 80)
    a.   true*
    b.   false

159. Research shows that low self-monitors resolve conflict cooperatively. (p. 80)
    a.   true
    b.   false*

160. The MBTI is a reliable tool to use to identify who is likely to be an effective leader. (p. 81)
    a.   true
    b.   false*

161. The MBTI helps in understanding how leaders think and make decisions. (p. 81)
   a.   true*
   b.   false

162. Sensation thinkers are good communicators and open to change. (p. 82)
   a.   true
   b.   false*

163. Intuitive feelers have personal charisma and relate well to others (p. 82)
   a.   true*
   b.   false

164. Intuitive thinkers are good change agents because they focus on possibilities. (p. 82)
   a.   true*
   b.   false

165. Sensation feelers respond well to change and focus on the future. (p. 82)
   a.   true
   b.   false*

166. Because they are good at managing relationships, high machs tend to be the most effective leaders. (p. 83)
   a.   true
   b.   false*

167. High Machiavellians are likely to be successful but not effective. (p. 83)
   a.   true*
   b.   false

168. Research indicates that the Chinese score higher on the Mach scale and are more willing that many Westerners to use social power to accomplish their goals. (p. 83)
   a.   true*
   b.   false

169. Moderate rather than high or low mach are likely to make the best managers. (p. 83)
   a.   true*
   b.   false

170. Research about why leaders fail indicates that the primary cause of failure is lack of technical expertise. (p. 84)
   a.   true
   b.   false*

171. Leaders who fail are most often rigid, isolated from others and uncaring. (p. 84)
   a.   true*
   b.   false

172. Steve Bennett of Intuit successfully re-energized his organization by paying attention to people and building and employee-friendly culture.
   a.   true
   b.   false*

173. Because personality traits are reliable, they should be used to make decisions regarding leader selection and promotion. (p. 86)
    a.   true
    b.   false*

174. The most appropriate use of personality traits is for self-awareness and development. (p. 86)
    a.   true*
    b.   false

175. Pernille Spiers-Lopez' s success at IKEA is primarily due to fact that she focuses on employees. (p. 100-101)
    a.   true*
    b.   false

176. Pernille Spiers-Lopez of IKEA has the relaxed and easy going style typical of Type Bs. (p. 100-101)
    a.   true
    b.   false*

CHAPTER 4

<u>Multiple Choice Questions</u>

1. _____ is the ability of one person to influence others. (p. 103)
   - a.   influence
   - b.   power*
   - c.   authority
   - d.   control

2. Power and influence differ in that: (p. 103)
   - a.   influence refers to changing the course of an action*
   - b.   influence implies effectiveness
   - c.   power is vested in a position
   - d.   influence is vested in a position

3. _____ is power vested in a formal position. (p. 103)
   - a.   control power
   - b.   persuasion
   - c.   authority*
   - d.   influence

4. Which one of the following is one of the typical reactions to power? (p. 103)
   - a.   control
   - b.   compliance*
   - c.   counter control
   - d.   influence

5. Zingerman's Community of Business (ZCoB) provides an example of: (p. 103)
   - a.   commitment*
   - b.   compliance
   - c.   control
   - d.   motivation

6. Kamal has send directives for his employees to complete a certain task. The employees eagerly undertake the task and complete it. The employees' reaction is an example of: (p. 103)
   - a.   commitment*
   - b.   compliance
   - c.   control
   - d.   motivation

7. Paulette has set goals for all of her team members. She informs them of the goals; although several members think the goals are not reasonable, they go along with them. The team members' reaction is an example of: (p. 104)
   - a.   commitment
   - b.   compliance*
   - c.   control
   - d.   lack of motivation

8. Lee has made several written and oral requests for his employees to undertake a new project. Although he has not received any feedback from his group, the task does not appear to be even started. This is an example of: (p. 104)
   a. counter control
   b. insubordination
   c. follower power
   d. resistance*

9. The leader's power increases when employees(p. 104)_____.
   a. are motivated
   b. comply with her decisions
   c. do not resist a decision
   d. are committed to her decisions*

10. Research about the effect of power distribution suggests that: (p. 104)
   a. centralized power allows organizations to perform well.
   b. concentrated power can be detrimental to performance.*
   c. leaders often give up power willingly.
   d. power sharing works well in most cultures

11. Nigel is an Australian manager who is heading a division of his company in Mexico. He has tried, without much success, to get his employees to participate and make suggestions regarding how to organize the work activities. The Mexican employees' reluctance to participate may be due to: (p. 105)
   a. the Mexican employees' lack of experience.
   b. the high-context Mexican culture.
   c. the high power distance in Mexico.*
   d. Nigel's incompetence.

12. The higher _____ and the lower the _____, the more likely it is that leaders will hold a high degree of power that they can use. (p. 105)
   a. power distance/tolerance for uncertainty*
   b. collectivism/power distance
   c. egalitarianism/task focus
   d. individualism/masculinity

13. In Japan and Indonesia people value: (p. 105)
   a. independence and freedom
   b. clear hierarchy and authority*
   c. creativity and innovation
   d. hard work and independence

14. Mexicans expect their leaders to: (p. 105)
   a. empower them
   b. be creative
   c. provide answers*
   d. give them independence

15. In _____ cultures, power bases are stable, and upward mobility is limited. (p. 105)
   a. individualistic
   b. socialized
   c. vertical power
   d. high power distance*

16. Researchers have identified _____ source of power related to individuals. (p. 106)
    a.   two
    b.   three
    c.   four
    d.   five*

17. Alan Greenspan, the chairman of the U.S. Federal Reserve, uses _____ and _____ as primary sources of power. (p. 106)
    a.   reward/punishment
    b.   coercive/reward
    c.   informational/legitimate
    d.   legitimate/expert*

18. _____ power is based on the formal position a person holds, while _____ is based on friendship and respect. (p. 106)
    a.   legitimate/referent*
    b.   authority/politics
    c.   persuasive/negotiation
    d.   managerial/personal

19. Nicolo gets his employees to go along with him by threatening to fire or demote them. Nicolo is using which of the sources of individual power? (p. 106)
    a.   Legitimate
    b.   Authority
    c.   Coercive*
    d.   Expert

20. All managers have access to which source of individual power? (p. 106)
    a.   Legitimate*
    b.   Authority
    c.   Coercive
    d.   Expert

21. Which of the following sources of individual power are available to everyone within an organization regardless of their position? (p. 106)
    a.   Legitimate
    b.   Authority
    c.   Coercive
    d.   Expert*

22. The power of celebrities to influence others is based on which source of individual power? (p. 106)
    a.   Legitimate
    b.   Referent*
    c.   Informational
    d.   Reward

23. In order for leaders to get commitment from their followers, they should rely on which of the following two sources of power. (p. 107)
    a.   Legitimate and referent
    b.   Referent and expert*
    c.   Expert and reward
    d.   Reward and authority

24. Using _____ as a source of power is most likely to lead to _____. (p. 107)
   a.   Coercive compliance
   b.   Reward/commitment
   c.   Expert/compliance
   d.   Referent/commitment*

25. Individuals with _____ power can influence others because they are liked and respected. (p. 108)
   a.   Legitimate
   b.   Referent*
   c.   Informational
   d.   Reward

26. Which one of the following is not one of the influence tactics? (p. 108)
   a.   Control*
   b.   Pressure
   c.   Exchange
   d.   Inspiration

27. If you are trying to influence your supervisor's decision regarding a project, which would be the most appropriate influence tactic to use? (p. 108)
   a.   pressure
   b.   personal appeal
   c.   consultation
   d.   rational persuasion*

28. The personal appeal influence tactic is most appropriate to use with _____. (p. 108)
   a.   inspiration
   b.   control
   c.   personal appeal*
   d.   pressure

29. Rational persuasion relies on _____ as a source of power whereas personal appeal relies on _____. (p. 108)
   a.   expert/referent*
   b.   referent/information
   c.   information/legitimate
   d.   legitimate/coercive

30. _____ is one of the influence tactics that rely on all sources of personal power. (p. 108)
   a.   Pressure
   b.   Personal appeal
   c.   Consultation*
   d.   Rational persuasion

31. Using _____ depends on having reward and information and is most appropriate to use with _____ (p. 108).
   a.   coalition building/bosses and colleagues
   b.   consultation/subordinates
   c.   ingratiation/bosses
   d.   exchange/subordinates and colleagues*

32. In early stages of their career, which base of power should young leaders develop? (p. 109)
    a.   Legitimate through power building
    b.   Credibility through expertise*
    c.   Reward through access to resources
    d.   Coercion by demonstrating toughness

33. What challenges do managers in mid careers face regarding power? (p. 109)
    a.   Building credibility
    b.   Sharing power
    c.   Using power ethically*
    d.   Giving fair rewards

34. Regarding the use of power, managers in late career stages must: (p. 109)
    a.   empower others
    b.   build their network
    c.   train their replacement
    d.   let go of power*

35. Research by Oana Branzei on cultural difference in use of influence tactics shows that: (p. 110)
    a.   people with less experience use more legitimate techniques.
    b.   the Japanese prefer rational persuasion and inspiration.*
    c.   women use pressure the most.
    d.   Romanians rely on consultation more than other cultures.

36. _____ sources of power are particularly important to teams. (p. 109)
    a.   Personal
    b.   Individual
    c.   Legitimate
    d.   Organizational*

37. The concept of _____ suggests that teams gain power based on their ability to remove obstacles for others. (p. 109)
    a.   strategic contingencies*
    b.   shared power
    c.   empowerment
    d.   coalition building

38. Which of the following is not one of the organizational sources of power? (p. 111)
    a.   centrality
    b.   dependency
    c.   substitutability
    d.   organicity*

39. A team that helps others in the organization by providing a service that is key to goal accomplishment will gain power. This is an example of: (p. 111)
    a.   centrality*
    b.   organicity
    c.   coping with uncertainty
    d.   boundary spanning

40. Teams can gain power by reducing uncertainty for others in their organization. Which of the following is not one of the uncertainty reduction methods? (p. 111)
   a.   Gathering information
   b.   Prediction of upcoming changes
   c.   Prevent changes from affecting the organization
   d.   Preventing change from happening*

41. The CEO of a company believes that diversity is a very important and strategic issue. She creates a team to make diversity related recommendations and has the team report directly to her on a regular basis. The CEO is using which organizational source of power to assure that the team has power? (p. 111)
   a.   centrality*
   b.   organicity
   c.   coping with uncertainty
   d.   boundary spanning

42. Team Alpha has developed considerable expertise and has a lot of departments that depend on it to get their job done. Team Alpha' source of power is: (p 111-112)
   a.   centrality
   b.   lack of substitutability *
   c.   coping with uncertainty
   d.   legitimate rewards

43. A team leader focuses on assuring that his team members have the latest expertise not available elsewhere in the organization. He is using which organizational source of power to assure that his team has power? (p. 112)
   a.   centrality
   b.   organicity
   c.   substitutability*
   d.   coalition building

44. Which of the following is not one of the ways to help increase the power of teams so that they can be effective? (p. 112)
   a.   Keep the team away from difficult challenges.*
   b.   Make the team central to mission.
   c.   Give the team meaningful tasks.
   d.   Provide the team with access to decision makers.

45. Top executives have access to how many additional sources of power? (p. 113)
   a.   Two
   b.   Three
   c.   Four*
   d.   Five

46. The individual power source of "rewards" is equivalent to which source of top executive power? (p. 113)
   a.   Distribution of resources*
   b.   Control of decision criteria
   c.   Centrality
   d.   Access to all levels

47. Raika is the CEO of a not-for-profit organization, is looking for a vice president and has decided to let a committee made-up of various people within her organization select the next VP. She drafts the job description and makes a detailed list of the type of characteristics, skills, experiences, and abilities the person should have. Raika's action is an example of: (p. 113)
    a.   empowerment
    b.   distribution of power
    c.   access to resources
    d.   control of decision criteria*

48. Whether an organization is traditional or informal structure, CEOs are strategically located for access to information and resources. This is an example of which of the executive sources of power? (p. 113)
    a.   Distribution of resources
    b.   Control of decision criteria
    c.   Centrality*
    d.   Access

49. A new executive who brings in his own team and puts people he trusts in key positions is using which source of executive power? (p. 113)
    a.   Distribution of resources
    b.   Control of decision criteria
    c.   Centrality
    d.   Access*

50. Power corruption is primarily due to: (p. 114)
    a.   corrupt leaders
    b.   too much power without accountability*
    c.   national culture
    d.   board of directors

51. What was the attitude of the framers of the U.S. Constitution regarding power? (p. 114)
    a.   Power should not be concentrated*
    b.   Leaders should have enough power to do their job
    c.   Democracy is important
    d.   Power is essential to leadership

52. One of the consequences of power, be it legitimate or excessive is to: (p. 114)
    a.   make leaders more legitimate
    b.   corrupt leaders
    c.   require eventual power sharing between leaders and followers
    d.   increase the distance between leaders and followers*

53. Causes of power corruption fall into two categories. These are: (p. 114)
    a.   group related and traits
    b.   individual leader and organizational factors*
    c.   cultural elements and political factors
    d.   legal and ethical factors

54. Leaders who are likely to abuse power often show which of the following characteristics? (p. 115)
    a.   Flexibility
    b.   Concern for employees
    c.   Focus on others
    d.   Unwillingness to share power*

55. Jason is a successful executive who believes he deserves the high salary and perks that he is getting. He rarely changes his mind or asks others' opinions and has a small group of employees he trusts and is highly distrustful of others. Jason shows many of the characteristics of: (p. 115)
- a. typical top level managers
- b. an extreme Type A
- c. a destructive narcissist*
- d. a powerful executive

56. Why are evil managers who abuse their power often successful? (p. 115)
- a. They have loyal followers.
- b. They manage their supervisor well.*
- c. Overall, they perform better than other managers.
- d. They surround themselves with highly competent followers.

57. Which one of the following is a sign of a destructive narcissistic manager? (p. 115)
- a. They work alone
- b. They don't get promoted
- c. They take care of their followers
- d. They divide the world between friends and enemies*

58. The key organizational factor in abuse of power is: (p. 115)
- a. a decentralized structure
- b. the organizational culture*
- c. the leadership succession plan
- d. the training and development plan

59. Which one of the following is not an organizational factor that contributes to power corruption? (p. 115-116)
- a. Formal and closed communication.
- b. Focus on short-term goals.
- c. Performance-based hiring.*
- d. Centralized decision making.

60. Keesha's employees rarely, if ever, disagree with her because they worry about her negative reactions and tantrums. This is an example of which of the factors in the corruption cycle? (p. 116)
- a. Compliance*
- b. Isolation
- c. Lack of accountability
- d. Flattery

61. Because of their power, employee compliance, and isolation leaders in the corruption cycle often: (p. 116)
- a. develop bad habits
- b. have the inability to make decisions
- c. worry about their constituents' reactions
- d. get an inflated view of themselves*

62. All but one of the following is a reason why followers comply with their leaders even when they are wrong. (p. 116)
- a. Desire to ingratiate themselves
- b. Weakness and incompetence
- c. Fear of reprisals
- d. Lack of caring*

63. Employee compliance, flattery, and unwillingness to speak out contribute to a corrupt leader's reliance on _____. (p. 116)
   a. empowerment
   b. financial measures
   c. coercive methods*
   d. communication

64. Donald Carty of American Airlines and Richard Scrushy of HealthSouth are examples of CEOs who: (p. 117)
   a. became whistle blowers
   b. abused their powers*
   c. took action to correct ethical violations
   d. made serious strategic mistakes

65. Which of the following is the most common and serious consequence of power corruption? (p. 118)
   a. Dissatisfied employees
   b. Poor decision making*
   c. Legal problems
   d. Low stock prices

66. Abusive and corrupt leaders intimidate their followers into silence and then consider the silence and lack of responsiveness as a sign of their followers' incompetence, therefore asking them even less for input. This is an example of: (p. 118)
   a. self-actualization
   b. self-fulfilling prophecy*
   c. the corruption cycle
   d. narcissistic destruction

67. The isolation and flattery that contribute to the corruption cycle often cause leaders to: (p. 118)
   a. seek outside input
   b. rely more on board of director members
   c. learn to make good decisions alone
   d. develop a separate sense of morality*

68. Power corruption and destructive managers can be prevented by which of the following factors? (p. 118)
   a. Centralized communication
   b. Reduce the role of outsiders in the organization
   c. Using objective performance measures*
   d. Ethics training for the leader

69. Many organizations find ways for employees to get direct and objective feedback from customers and other sources regarding their performance. This can help prevent corruption of leaders by: (p. 118)
   a. reducing dependence on leader*
   b. opening lines of communication
   c. creating internal audits
   d. allowing followers to discuss performance with their leader

70. At the BTW company, employees are constantly reminded that their focus should be on performance, productivity and customer service. This type of reminder can prevent power corruption because: (p. 119)
   a.   it opens lines of communication
   b.   it involves leaders in day-to-day activities
   c.   it provides objective measures of performance
   d.   it sets the right culture*

71. The new CEO of American Airlines, Gerard Arprey is focusing on correcting the corruption that was the part of the administration of his predecessor by: (p. 119)
   a.   rebuilding the company culture*
   b.   centralizing decision making
   c.   involving more outsiders in company activities
   d.   putting in place a clear code of ethics

72. The underlying theme of empowerment is: (p. 119)
   a.   delegating all power to employees
   b.   sharing power with those who need it to perform their job*
   c.   setting goals that everyone can achieve easily
   d.   centralizing decision making in the team

73. Which of the following is not one of the reasons empowerment tends to be effective? (p. 120)
   a.   It tends to increase employees' sense of self-efficacy.
   b.   It allows employees to internalize goals and builds commitment
   c.   It provides the leader with delegation training*
   d.   It brings power where it is needed

74. Which one following is an organizational factors that contribute to empowerment? (p. 120)
   a.   Appropriate selection and training for leaders
   b.   Appropriate selection and training for employees
   c.   Setting high performance standards*
   d.   Removing bureaucratic barriers

75. Mario has attended many leadership training programs where he has been exposed to empowerment methods. He often reminds his employees that he believes in empowerment and encourages them to take initiative and responsibility. However, employees feel that their suggestions are ignored and that they get in trouble when they make decision without checking with Mario. What is Mario doing wrong? (p. 120)
   a.   He is not communicating openly
   b.   He is not expressing confidence in employees
   c.   His performance standards are too high
   d.   He is not walking the talk*

76. Lin-may is eager to implement empowerment in her organization. She has encouraged her employees, expressed confidence in them, and given them responsibility. She has created a positive emotional atmosphere. What else must she do to make empowerment effective? (p. 120)
   a.   Lower the performance standards
   b.   Create clear hierarchy for reporting
   c.   Reward employees openly and personally*
   d.   Use only teams for decision making

77. Which of the following is <u>not</u> one of the organizational factors in empowerment? (p. 120-121)
    a.   Appropriate selection and training of leaders
    b.   Removing bureaucratic barriers
    c.   Expressing confidence in employees*
    d.   Fair policies

78. Top leaders of the New organization have told their managers and employees that they want to implement empowerment. They have decentralized the structures and changed the reward structure. After a few months, they see no change in the leaders' or employees' behaviors. Which organizational empowerment factor did they miss? (p. 121-122)
    a.   They did not train leaders and employees.*
    b.   They did not create a positive atmosphere.
    c.   They did not walk the talk.
    d.   They set low standards.

79. Ricardo Semler, CEO of Semco is an example of: (p. 122)
    a.   how a corrupt leader can negatively impact an organization
    b.   the importance of followers
    c.   the importance training in successful empowerment*
    d.   how teams can share power with their managers

80. The first steps for organization to start the empowerment process is to: (p. 122)
    a.   identify the potential blocks to empowerment*
    b.   train leaders
    c.   train followers
    d.   set up the right reward structure

81. Examples of use of empowerment in many organizations show that: (p. 123)
    a.   empowerment is frustrating to many employees
    b.   leaders are afraid to give up power
    c.   empowerment can lead to increased motivation*
    d.   followers are key to empowerment

82. The empirical research on empowerment has found: (p. 123)
    a.   mixed results for the impact of empowerment*
    b.   that empowerment is an effective and powerful tool
    c.   empowerment works well across many cultures
    d.   empowerment works best in collectivistic cultures

83. In the early part of his career Dick Grasso relied on which source of power? (p. 129-130)
    a.   legitimate
    b.   reward
    c.   expert*
    d.   reward

84. Dick Grasso used _____ as sources of power with superiors and stakeholders. (p. 129-130)
    a.   legitimate and referent
    b.   expert and referent*
    c.   referent and legitimate
    d.   coercive and reward

85. Dick used _____ as sources of power with employees and subordinates. (p. 129-130)
   a.   legitimate and referent
   b.   expert and referent
   c.   referent and legitimate
   d.   coercive and reward*

True/False Questions

86. Power is a necessary component of leadership. (p. 102)
   a.   true*
   b.   false

87. Power is the ability to influence others effectively. (p. 103)
   a.   true*
   b.   false

88. Power and authority are synonymous. (p. 103)
   a.   true
   b.   false*

89. Power and influence are primarily the domain of formal leaders within organizations. (p. 103)
   a.   true
   b.   false*

90. The employees at Zingerman's Community of Business (ZCoB) are an example of commitment. (p. 103)
   a.   true*
   b.   false

91. Commitment, control, and resistance are the three typical reactions to power and influence. (p. 103-104)
   a.   true
   b.   false*

92. A large majority of today's organizations rely on democratic practices to accomplish their goals. (p. 104)
   a.   true
   b.   false*

93. Research indicates that concentrated power can be detrimental to organizational performance. (p. 104)
   a.   true*
   b.   false

94. The more equal the power distance in organization, the higher the performance of the organization. (p. 104)
   a.   true*
   b.   false

95. Bulgarian employees listen to their managers mostly when they rely on referent power and friendship. (p. 105)
   a.   true
   b.   false*

96. The Chinese, Japanese, and Indonesians are all collectivistic cultures where employees are comfortable sharing power with their leader. (p. 105)
   a.   true
   b.   false*

97. The French and Germans expect their bosses to provide answers to their questions. (p. 105)
   a.   true*
   b.   false

98. Legitimate power is based on the position in the organization while expert power relies on the individual. (p. 106)
   a.   true*
   b.   false

99. Referent power is based on a person's ability to get access to information. (p. 106)
   a.   true
   b.   false*

100. Personal sources of power are likely to disappear when a manager loses his/her position in the organization. (p. 106)
   a.   true
   b.   false*

101. Alan Greenspan relies primarily on his expertise to influence others. (p. 106)
   a.   true*
   b.   false

102. The most likely reactions to using reward and coercion as source of power are compliance and resistance. (p. 107)
   a.   true*
   b.   false

103. When leaders rely on their expertise to influence followers, they are likely to simply comply rather than be committed to the leader's decision. (p. 107)
   a.   true
   b.   false*

104. People tend to be influenced by celebrities because they have referent power. (p. 107)
   a.   true*
   b.   false

105. Followers react to all sources of power the same way. (p. 107)
   a.   true
   b.   false*

106. Consultation and coalition building are two influence tactics that use all sources of power. (p. 108)
   a.   true*
   b.   false

107. In order to increase commitment, one of the most effective methods of persuasion is coalition building. (p. 108)
   a.   true
   b.   false*

108. It is most appropriate to use exchange as an influence tactic with subordinates and colleagues. (p. 108)
    a.   true*
    b.   false

109. To influence supervisors, rational persuasion is the most appropriate influence tactic. (p. 108)
    a.   true*
    b.   false

110. Because most of us are skilled at a few influence tactics, each person should stick with the tactics she/he is most comfortable with. (p. 108)
    a.   true
    b.   false*

111. Young leaders in early stages of their career should focus on building their power through demonstrating their expertise and competence. (p. 109)
    a.   true*
    b.   false

112. Leaders in the middle of their career must focus on how to give up power to others. (p. 109)
    a.   true
    b.   false*

113. The concept of strategic contingencies suggests that teams must address the needs of strategic stakeholders outside the organization. (p. 109)
    a.   true
    b.   false*

114. Teams acquire power in organizations by addressing strategic contingencies. (p. 109)
    a.   true*
    b.   false

115. Research by Oana Branzei shows in more masculine cultures, women tend to use ingratiation more often than men. (p. 110)
    a.   true*
    b.   false

116. Teams increase their power as they are able to remove obstacles for others in the organization. (p. 111-112)
    a.   true*
    b.   false

117. By staying away from difficult challenges, teams can gain power. (p. 111-112)
    a.   true
    b.   false*

118. Teams can rely on individual sources of power to maintain power and be effective. (p. 111-112)
    a.   true
    b.   false*

119. Top executives have and primarily use the same sources of power as individuals and teams. (p. 113)
    a.   true
    b.   false*

120. One of the sources of powers of executives is the ability to control the criteria by which decisions are made. (p. 113)
    a.   true*
    b.   false

121. The change in personnel in government after elections is an example of need for access as a source of executive power. (p. 113)
    a.   true*
    b.   false

122. Most organizations provide their top executives with a lot of power without much accountability. (p. 114)
    a.   true*
    b.   false

123. Organizations have many checks and balances in place to limit the power of their top level leaders. (p. 114)
    a.   true
    b.   false*

124. One of the benefits of power is that it increases the distance between leaders and followers. (p. 114)
    a.   true
    b.   false*

125. Both individual and organizational factors contribute to corruption that is caused by too much power. (p. 115)
    a.   true*
    b.   false

126. Managers who abuse power often have an inflated view of themselves. (p. 115)
    a.   true*
    b.   false

127. Managers who abuse power perform well because they surround themselves with highly competent followers. (p. 115)
    a.   true
    b.   false*

128. The factor in organizational structure that contributes to power corruption is the degree of centralization. (p. 116)
    a.   true*
    b.   false

129. Fear of reprisals or weakness are factors that cause employees to comply with a corrupt leaders. (p. 116)
    a.   true*
    b.   false

130. Follower compliance contributes to power corruption by increasing the leaders' inflated view of themselves. (p. 116)
    a.   true*
    b.   false

131. Richard Scrushy of HealthSouth, instituted effective ways to battle corruption. (p. 117)
    a.   true
    b.   false*

132. The flattery that many followers use to express their views to their leaders is a helpful tool to building good relations between them. (p. 117)
    a.   true
    b.   false*

133. Donald Carty of American Airlines had developed a separate sense of morality. (p. 118)
    a.   true*
    b.   false

134. Separating followers and leaders can help reduce power corruption. (p. 118)
    a.   true
    b.   false*

135. Because corrupt leaders intimidate followers who refuse to speak out and contribute to decision making, the leaders often are forced to use group decision making. (p. 118)
    a.   true
    b.   false*

136. The most common and serious consequence of power corruption is poor decision making. (p. 118)
    a.   true*
    b.   false

137. Because XYZ corporation has reduced its employees' dependence on managers for feedback and rewards, it is likely to see an increase in corruption of employees. (p. 118)
    a.   true
    b.   false*

138. The closer leaders are to day-to-day activities, the more likely they are to abuse their power. (p. 118-119)
    a.   true
    b.   false*

139. Followers who do not depend on their leader are less likely to contribute to the corruption cycle. (p. 119)
    a.   true*
    b.   false

140. The most effective way to prevent power corruption is to address the organizational culture and structure. (p. 119)
    a.   true*
    b.   false

141. The new CEO of American Airlines, Gerard Arprey is focusing on correcting the corruption that was the part of the administration of his predecessor by putting in place a clear code of ethics. (p. 119)
    a.   true
    b.   false*

142. Empowerment involves pushing decision making and implementation to the lowers possible level. (p. 119)
   a.　　　true*
   b.　　　false

143. Leaders who want to implement empowerment should set high performance standards and expect followers to meet those standards. (p. 120)
   a.　　　true*
   b.　　　false

144. One of the reasons empowerment can be effective is that it can enhance employees' belief in their abilities and provide them with a sense of control and accomplishment. (p. 121)
   a.　　　true*
   b.　　　false

145. Organizations that implement empowerment often have to lower their performance standards. (p. 121)
   a.　　　true
   b.　　　false*

146. The most important organizational factor in empowerment is decentralizing the structure. (p. 121)
   a.　　　true*
   b.　　　false

147. Changing HR practices and training are essential to the success of empowerment in organizations. (p. 121)
   a.　　　true*
   b.　　　false

148. Semco provides employees with freedom and empowerment and set high performance expectations. (p. 122)
   a.　　　true*
   b.　　　false

149. Semco and its CEO Ricardo Semler provide an example of how empowerment can work with little training but good intentions. (p. 122)
   a.　　　true
   b.　　　false*

150. Although there is not strong research support, many organizations believe that empowerment leads to higher employee motivation. (p. 123)
   a.　　　true*
   b.　　　false

151. Considerable research about empowerment shows its positive impact on organizations. (p. 123)
   a.　　　true
   b.　　　false*

152. Dick Grasso, the chairman of the New York Stock Exchange came under attack because his salary was too high. (p. 129-130)
   a.　　　true*
   b.　　　false

153. To gain power in the early stages of his career, Dick Grasso the chairman of the NYSE relied on reward and legitimate power. (p. 129-130)
   a.   true
   b.   false*

154. Dick Grasso, the chairman of the NYSE used the same source of power with subordinates and superiors. (p. 129-130)
   a.   true
   b.   false*

CHAPTER 5

<u>Multiple Choice Questions</u>

1. The first researcher who suggested that leadership can be best understood by taking a contingency approach was: (p. 131)
    a.   Lewin
    b.   Maslow
    c.   Stogdill*
    d.   Mayo

2. The contingency approach can be summarized as: (p. 131)
    a.   what works depends on the situation.*
    b.   there is a best way to lead.
    c.   the behavior approach along with some traits is most effective.
    d.   leadership is contingent on power.

3. Based on the resource allocation models, which one of the following is <u>not</u> one of the questions leaders should asked? (p. 134)
    a.   When should the group be used?
    b.   When should the leader rely on his/her own experience?
    c.   When should power be used fully?
    d.   When should the task be clarified?*

4. The resource allocation models suggest that: (p. 134)
    a.   the amount of resources determines the leader's effectiveness.
    b.   effective use of resources by the leader is key to effectiveness.*
    c.   allocating resources is the primary role of the leaders.
    d.   power and financial resources are the primary resource for leaders.

5. Which of the following is <u>not</u> one the requirements in use of effective use of resources? (p. 134)
    a.   Understanding the leadership situation.
    b.   Identifying the leader's style.
    c.   Matching the leader to the situation.
    d.   Training for leaders and followers.*

6. The first researcher to implement the contingency approach and develop a leadership theory based on the approach was: (p. 134)
    a.   Stogdill
    b.   Fiedler*
    c.   House
    d.   Vroom

7. According to the Contingency Model: (p. 134)
    a.   if the leader's style matches the situation, the leader will be effective.*
    b.   if followers respect the leader, the leader will be effective.
    c.   when the leader has power, he/she will be more effective.
    d.   if the leader is trained and experience, the group will be most effective.

8. The LPC stands for: (p. 134)
    a.   Leader Personality Construct.
    b.   Leader Personal Contingency.
    c.   Least Preferred Coworker.*
    d.   Lower Performance Conditions.

9. When asked to evaluate a coworker she does not like working with, Tatiana has a very negative view of that person. She describes him as incompetent, cold, and untrustworthy. Based on this description, Tatiana is most likely: (p. 134)
    a.   a low LPC*
    b.   a harsh person
    c.   a high LPC
    d.   a middle LPC

10. A low LPC leader draws self-esteem from: (p. 134-135)
    a.   power.
    b.   getting along with people.
    c.   managing conflict.
    d.   accomplishing tasks well.*

11. A high LPC leader draws self-esteem from: (p. 134-135)
    a.   power.
    b.   getting along with people.*
    c.   managing conflict.
    d.   accomplishing tasks well.

12. When Paul's group fails, he tends to be harsh in judging his subordinates and tends to blame and punish them. Paul is most likely: (p. 134-135)
    a.   a low LPC*
    b.   a harsh leader
    c.   a high LPC
    d.   a middle LPC

13. When asked to evaluate a coworker she does not like working with, Nilanjan describe the person in generally positive terms judging them to be loyal, sincere, and warm. Based on this description, Nilanjan is most likely: (p. 134-135)
    a.   a low LPC
    b.   a kind person
    c.   a high LPC*
    d.   a middle LPC

14. Low LPC individuals consider _____ of co-workers to be a key trait. (p. 134-135)
    a.   conflict management skills
    b.   competence*
    c.   loyalty
    d.   enthusiasm

15. High LPC individuals consider _____ of co-workers to be a key trait. (p. 134-135)
    a.   conflict management skills
    b.   competence
    c.   loyalty*
    d.   enthusiasm

16. Fiedler considers the LPC to be a _____ that people _____. (p. 134-135)
   a.   stable characteristic/cannot change*
   b.   behavior/can learn to change
   c.   skill/can be trained to do
   d.   value/learn early in life

17. _____ is another term used to describe middle LPC individuals. (p. 135)
   a.   Highly conforming
   b.   Task-oriented
   c.   Relationship-oriented
   d.   Socio-independent*

18. Mort Meyerson of Perot Systems, and Darlene Ryan of PharmaFab are both examples of leaders who are: (p. 135)
   a.   low-LPC
   b.   middle-LPC
   c.   high-LPC*
   d.   both high and low LPC

19. Marilyn Moats Kennedy of Career Strategies, and Marissa Peterson of Sun Microsystems, are both example of leaders who are: (p. 135)
   a.   low-LPC*
   b.   middle-LPC
   c.   high-LPC
   d.   both high and low LPC

20. According to Fiedler, there are several factors that describe the leadership situation. Which of the following is not part of situation? (p. 136)
   a.   leader-member relations
   b.   task structure
   c.   follower maturity*
   d.   position power

21. According to Fiedler, _____ is the most important factor in any leadership situation. (p. 136)
   a.   leader-member relations*
   b.   task structure
   c.   follower maturity
   d.   position power

22. According to Fiedler, the second most important factor in any leadership situation is _____.(p. 136)
   a.   leader-member relations
   b.   task structure*
   c.   follower maturity
   d.   position power

23. According to Fiedler, the least influential element of the leadership situation is_____. (p. 136)
   a.   leader-member relation
   b.   task structure
   c.   follower maturity
   d.   position power*

24. Nader is the manager a group of highly cohesive individuals whose primary job is to reconcile the budgets from other divisions. Based on Fiedler's classification, Nader faces which kind of situation? (p. 136-137)
    a.   Typical corporate management
    b.   High situational control*
    c.   High managerial power
    d.   Mid-level control

25. Jose's group works on designing advertising campaigns for different types of clients. Although the job is unstructured, Jose is likely to feel that he has a lot of control if: (p. 136-137)
    a.   he is smart.
    b.   he is task-oriented.
    c.   he is relationship-oriented.
    d.   he has experience doing the job.*

26. According to the Contingency Model, _____ will be effective in high and low situational control, while _____ will be effective in moderate situational control. (p. 137-138)
    a.   task-motivated/relationship-motivated*
    b.   relationship-motivated/task-motivated
    c.   middle LPC/low LPC
    d.   high LPC/middle LPC

27. According to the Contingency Model, task-motivated leaders will be most effective in which type of situation? (p. 137)
    a.   high-control*
    b.   moderate control
    c.   low control
    d.   all situations

28. According to the Contingency Model, relationship-motivated leaders will be most effective in which type of situation? (p. 137)
    a.   high-control
    b.   moderate control*
    c.   low control
    d.   all situations

29. Anwar is a task-motivated leader who is in a high situational control environment. Based on Fiedler's Contingency Model, he is likely to: (p. 137-138)
    a.   be tense, overbearing, and over controlling.
    b.   be confident, considerate, and focused on removing obstacles.*
    c.   considerate, open to suggestions and concerned with resolving conflicts.
    d.   directive, serious, and with little concern for others.

30. Sally is a relationship-motivated leader who is in a moderate situational control environment. Based on Fiedler's Contingency Model, she is likely to: (p. 137-138)
    a.   be tense, overbearing, and over controlling.
    b.   be confident, considerate, and focused on removing obstacles.
    c.   considerate, open to suggestions and concerned with resolving conflicts.*
    d.   directive, serious, and with little concern for others.

31. Which two U.S. presidents can be considered to be relationship-oriented? (p. 138-139)
    a.   Nixon and Carter
    b.   Carter and Ford
    c.   G.H. Bush and G.W. Bush
    d.   Reagan and Clinton*

32. Which two U.S. presidents can be considered to be task-oriented? (p. 138-139)
   a.   Nixon and Carter*
   b.   Carter and Ford
   c.   G.H. Bush and G.W. Bush
   d.   Reagan and Clinton

33. Hiro is leading a group of volunteer that is facing considerable difficulty. The members do not get along, they are doing a task with no structure that no one quite knows how to do.   All of Hiro's efforts at building cohesion have been wasted and he is frustrated and has decided to leave his followers to fend for themselves. Based on this description, Hiro is most likely: (p. 137-138)
   a.   a consultative leader
   b.   a socio-independent leader
   c.   a relationship-oriented leader*
   d.   a leader with task skills

34. Over 40 years of research studies about Fiedler's Contingency Model have found: (p. 139-140)
   a.   the model to be weak.
   b.   the model to be reliable.*
   c.   that the concept of contingency does not apply to most situations.
   d.   leadership to be a trait.

35. Your company is planning to use Fiedler's Contingency Model to train its leaders and managers. Based on the assumptions and finding of the theory, what will be the focus of the training? (p. 140-141)
   a.   Teaching leaders the different decision styles they need to be effective in different situations.
   b.   Getting leaders to be more sensitive to the needs of their followers so they can use them as resources when needed.
   c.   Train leaders to remove obstacles on their followers' path.
   d.   Helping leader be aware of their style and understand the situations they face.*

36. John has just come back from a leadership training based on Fiedler's Contingency Model. He has very much enjoyed the training and is planning to implement what he has learned. Which one of the following in John likely to do? (p. 140-141)
   a.   He will focus on gaining more experience in the job that he is doing so that he can increase his sense of control.
   b.   He will make sure that he has the power he needs to implement his decisions.
   c.   He will focus on understanding and changing his leadership situation when he is out of match.*
   d.   He will empower his employees any chance he gets and include them in decision-making.

37. The study by Richard Miller, Jeanne Butler, and Charles Cosentino about Least Preferred Leaders (LPL) and follower effectiveness shows: (p. 141)
   a.   that matching employees' personal style to the situation can help them be more effective.*
   b.   the Least Preferred Leader scale can be used instead of the LPC to predict leader effectiveness.
   c.   the LPL scale should be used on cross-cultural research instead of the LPC.
   d.   the LPL is more reliable than the LPC.

38. Which of the following is not one of the practical implications of the Contingency Model for managers? (p. 140-142)
    a.   Leaders must understand their style and the situation.
    b.   Leaders should focus on changing the situation.
    c.   Leaders can compensate for task ambiguity by getting more training.
    d.   Leaders can learn to change their style to fit different situations.*

39. Terry Semel and Libby Sartain are two of the leaders at Yahoo! Although they are both effective, they have very different styles. Semel is _____ while Sartain is _____. (p. 143)
    a.   task-oriented/relationship-oriented*
    b.   relationship-oriented/task-oriented
    c.   focused on human resources/focused on the financial bottom line
    d.   eager to make the company more relaxed/deliberate and detailed-oriented

40. Junki Yoshida, the founder and owner of Yoshida Group enterprise, is an example of:
    a.   the effectiveness of relationship-oriented leaders. (p. 142)
    b.   how different decision styles can be used in different situations.*
    c.   a leader's inability to switch styles based on the situation.
    d.   the importance of the quality of the leader-member relations in leadership effectiveness.

41. Which of the following principles is the basis for the Normative Decision Model? (p. 142)
    a.   Empowerment is always effective.
    b.   Western employees expect to participate in decision making.
    c.   Groups are wasteful and inefficient.*
    d.   Employee motivation results from the leader removing obstacles.

42. According to group dynamics research that is the basis for the Normative Decision Model: (p. 142)
    a.   groups make better decisions.
    b.   well trained groups make faster decisions that individuals.
    c.   leaders get better results when they rely on groups.
    d.   participation in decision-making leads to commitment.*

43. According to the Normative Decision Model, leaders should adjust their decision style depending on _____ and _____. (p. 142)
    a.   their personal style/the situation
    b.   the followers' maturity/goals of the organization
    c.   the need for a quality decision/likelihood that employee will accept the decision*
    d.   the complexity of the task the group is doing/the degree to which the group agrees with the leader

44. The Normative Decision Model proposes how many general decision styles? (p. 143-144)
    a.   two
    b.   three
    c.   four*
    d.   five

45. Which of the following is not one of decision styles used in the Normative Decision Model? (p. 143-144)
    a.   Autocratic
    b.   Individual*
    c.   Consultative
    d.   Group

46. In the _____ decision style, the leader makes the decision alone with or without information from the group. (p. 143-144)
   a.   autocratic*
   b.   individual
   c.   consultative
   d.   group

47. In the _____ decision style, the leader asks for information and ideas from the group members either individually or as group. (p. 143-144)
   a.   autocratic
   b.   individual
   c.   consultative*
   d.   group

48. In the _____ decision style, the leader exchanges ideas with followers who are equal partners in the decision process. (p. 143-144)
   a.   autocratic
   b.   individual
   c.   consultative
   d.   group*

49. Which of the following is not one of the several contingency factors in the Normative Decision Model? (p. 145)
   a.   Leader information
   b.   Goal congruence
   c.   Goal conflict*
   d.   Employee conflict

50. When there is no quality requirement and employee commitment is not needed, the most appropriate leader decision style is: (p. 146-147)
   a.   autocratic*
   b.   individual
   c.   consultative
   d.   group

51. Jade is new at her managerial position and does not have a lot of technical expertise. The quality of her team's work is very important to the organization and the commitment of her employees is essential. Based on the Normative Decision Model, Jade should use _____ as her primary decision style. (p. 146-147)
   a.   autocratic
   b.   individual
   c.   consultative
   d.   group*

52. When the leader has enough information, the quality of the decision is not important, the employees do not agree with each other or the goals of the organization, the most appropriate decision style is: (p. 146-147)
   a.   autocratic*
   b.   consultative
   c.   delegation
   d.   individual

53. When the employees' commitment is essential, they generally agree with the goals of the organization, and the leader does not have enough information, the most appropriate decision style is: (p. 146-147)
   a.　　autocratic
   b.　　consultative*
   c.　　delegation
   d.　　individual

54. The two weaknesses of the Normative Decision Making are: (p. 147-148)
   a.　　poorly define decision styles and poor application.
   b.　　it is too complex and it assumes leader can easily change styles.*
   c.　　it has weak theoretical bases and the decision styles are poorly defined.
   d.　　a simplistic view of leadership and low validity of measures.

55. Carlos has decided to implement the principles of the Normative Decision Model to managing his team. In order to be successful, he must do all of the following, except: (p. 147-148)
   a.　　allow his followers to participate in all decisions.*
   b.　　understand the situation and the decision style options.
   c.　　pay attention to followers' needs.
   d.　　be aware of the followers' level of commitment.

56. The leadership factor included in the Cognitive Resource Theory is: (p. 148)
   a.　　task or relationship orientation
   b.　　decision style
   c.　　power
   d.　　intelligence*

57. The primary contingency factor in the Cognitive Resource Theory is: (p. 148)
   a.　　situational control
   b.　　employee commitment
   c.　　stress*
   d.　　structure

58. Pierre is a highly intelligent leader who is not shy about telling his followers what to do. According to the Cognitive Resource theory: (p. 148-149)
   a.　　his followers are likely to be frustrated.
   b.　　his group is likely to benefit from his intelligence.*
   c.　　Pierre will only succeed if he has power.
   d.　　Pierre will be most effective in stressful situations that require complex analysis.

59. Based on the Cognitive Resource Theory, which type of leader is not likely to be best in a stressful situation? (p. 148-149)
   a.　　a task-oriented leader
   b.　　an autocratic leader
   c.　　a delegator
   d.　　a highly intelligence leader*

60. The Alpha team is facing a highly stressful situation, as the person responsible for assigning a leader to the team, based on Cognitive Resource Theory, whom should you appoint? (p. 148-149)
   a.　　A leader who consults with followers
   b.　　A leader who has experience with similar situations*
   c.　　A creative leader
   d.　　A leader who can make tough decisions without concern for people

61. Which cultural value may impact how U.S. and Western-developed contingency models apply to other cultures? (p. 149-150)
    a.   high-low context
    b.   individualism-collectivism*
    c.   tolerance of ambiguity
    d.   time orientation

62. Some cross-cultural researchers suggest that the concept of contingency does not fully apply in non-Western cultures. Due to the power of collectivism: (p. 149-150)
    a.   leaders must always be supportive and nurturing.*
    b.   leaders must play a directive role.
    c.   leaders' focus on the task is appropriate in most situations.
    d.   leaders are more consultative in collectivistic cultures.

63. Bill Gates, CEO of Microsoft, is an example of a _____ leader. (p. 165-166)
    a.   task-oriented*
    b.   relationship-oriented
    c.   cognitively complex
    d.   very empathetic

64. Mary Kay Ash, of Mary Kay Cosmetics, is an example of a _____ leader. (p. 165-166)
    a.   task-oriented
    b.   relationship-oriented*
    c.   highly intelligent
    d.   culturally aware

65. Mary Kay and Bill Gates are both effective because: (p. 165-166)
    a.   they are both intelligent.
    b.   they both case about their employees.
    c.   their style fits their leadership situation.*
    d.   they both have excellent financial skills.

True/False Questions

66. The concept of contingency suggests that what leadership style is effective depends on the situation. (p. 131)
    a.   true*
    b.   false

67. The contingency approach to leadership suggests that democratic style works best in most situations. (p. 131)
    a.   true
    b.   false*

68. Based on the resource allocation models, the effective use of resources transforms efforts into performance. (p. 133)
    a.   true*
    b.   false

69. The resource allocation models address the issue of how the leader should use resources. (p. 133)
    a.   true*
    b.   false

70. Fred Fiedler was the first researcher who implemented the contingency approach. (p. 134)
   a.   true*
   b.   false

71. Fiedler proposed that leadership effectiveness is a function of the match between the leader's style and the leadership situation. (p. 134)
   a.   true*
   b.   false

72. The LPC determines which behavior the leader should use. (p. 134)
   a.   true
   b.   false*

73. A low LPC person draws self-esteem from good interpersonal relations. (p. 134-135)
   a.   true
   b.   false*

74. A high LPC person draws self-esteem from accomplishing the task. (p. 134-135)
   a.   true
   b.   false*

75. High and low LPC individuals different focus is most obvious in times of crisis and when the person is under pressure. (p. 134-135)
   a.   true*
   b.   false

76. The middle LPC individuals are the least effective leaders. (p. 135)
   a.   true
   b.   false*

77. Fiedler believes that the LPC is a stable characteristic that cannot be easily changed. (p. 135)
   a.   true*
   b.   false

78. According to Fiedler, situational control is made up of three factors. (p. 136)
   a.   true*
   b.   false

79. According to Fiedler's Contingency Model, the quality of the relationship between the leader and followers is the most important element of the situation. (p. 136)
   a.   true*
   b.   false

80. Good relationships with followers provide the leader with high control over a situation. (p. 136)
   a.   true*
   b.   false

81. If the leader has power, he/she does not have to worry about other aspects of the situation. (p. 136)
   a.   true
   b.   false*

82. According to the Contingency Model, relationship-motivated leaders are most effective in high control situations. (p. 137-138)
   a.   true
   b.   false*

83. According to the Contingency Model, in chaotic, low control situations, task-oriented leaders are be effective. (p. 137-138)
    a.   true*
    b.   false

84. According to the Contingency Model, middle LPC are more effective than either low or high-LPCs (p. 137-138)
    a.   true
    b.   false*

85. Task-motivated leaders who are in high-situational control tend to relax and focus on helping their group. (p. 138)
    a.   true*
    b.   false

86. Task-motivated leaders who are in moderate-situational control focus on resolving group conflict. (p. 138)
    a.   true
    b.   false*

87. Relationship-motivated leaders who are in moderate-situational control are often considerate and open to ideas and suggestions. (p. 138)
    a.   true*
    b.   false

88. Relationship-motivated leaders who are in low-situational control, are often tense and nervous because of the group's conflict. (p. 138)
    a.   true*
    b.   false

89. U.S. Presidents Nixon and Reagan can both be considered to be task-oriented. (p. 138-139)
    a.   true
    b.   false*

90. The strongest criticism of Fiedler's contingency model has been regarding the meaning and validity of the LPC scale. (p 139)
    a.   true*
    b.   false

91. Based on the Fiedler's Contingency Model, task-oriented leaders are generally more effective than other leaders. (p. 139)
    a.   true
    b.   false*

92. According to Fiedler, leaders must learn to change their style in order to be effective in all situations. (p. 140)
    a.   true
    b.   false*

93. According the Fiedler, leaders will be more effective if they are aware of their styles and understand the leadership situations they face, and know how to change them as needed. (p. 140-142)
    a.   true*
    b.   false

94. Leaders can train themselves to change their LPC leadership style. (p. 140-142)
   a.   true
   b.   false*

95. The Normative Decision Model has a narrower focus than the Contingency Model. (p. 142)
   a.   true*
   b.   false

96. Both the Contingency Model and the Normative Decision Model recommend matching the leader and the situation. (p. 142)
   a.   true*
   b.   false

97. Both the Contingency Model and the Normative Decision Model assume that the leader can change his/her style to match the situation. (p. 142)
   a.   true
   b.   false*

98. The Normative Decision Model is based on the assumptions that groups are generally more efficient and that participation leads to commitment. (p. 142)
   a.   true
   b.   false*

99. The two central contingency factors in the Normative Decision Model are quality of the decision and need for acceptance and commitment by followers. (p. 142)
   a.   true*
   b.   false

100. The Normative Decision Model proposes four general decision making styles that are each effective in different types of situations. (p. 143-144)
   a.   true*
   b.   false

101. According to the Normative Decision Model, the consultative style of decision-making involves the leader allowing followers to make the decision. (p. 144)
   a.   true
   b.   false*

102. According to the Normative Decision Model, the autocratic decision style can involve either the leader making the decision without any information from followers, or the leader asking for information, but making the decision alone. (p. 144)
   a.   true*
   b.   false

103. To decide what decision style to use, leaders using the Normative Decision Model have to work through a decision tree with a eight contingency factors or questions. (p. 145)
   a.   true*
   b.   false

104. The Normative Decision Model assumes that consultation and participation require time and are not efficient. (p. 145)
   a.   true*
   b.   false

105. According to the Normative Decision Model, when the leader has sufficient information, it is still important in all cases, to involve follower in decision-making. (p. 146)
    a.   true
    b.   false*

106. According to the Normative Decision Model, the autocratic decision style is appropriate when followers are cohesive and are likely to support the leader and implement decisions. (p. 146)
    a.   true*
    b.   false

107. According to the Normative Decision Model, when the quality of the decision is not essential, the leader should use an autocratic decision style. (p. 147)
    a.   true*
    b.   false

108. According to the Normative Decision Model, when employees do not agree with each other, the leader should encourage them to debate and let them make the decision. (p. 147)
    a.   true
    b.   false*

109. According to the Normative Decision Model, when employees do not agree with the goals of the organization, the leader should make decisions alone. (p. 147)
    a.   true*
    b.   false

110. According to the Normative Decision Model, the leader should consult employees when he/she does not have sufficient information. (p. 147)
    a.   true*
    b.   false

111. According to the Normative Decision Model, the leader should use consultation when the followers agree with the goals of the organization. (p. 147)
    a.   true*
    b.   false

112. According to the Normative Decision Model, the need for employee commitment is a primary determinant for using consultation as a decision style. (p. 147)
    a.   true*
    b.   false

113. According to the Normative Decision Model, participation is not always the best style of decision making. (p. 148)
    a.   true*
    b.   false

114. The Cognitive Resource Theory (CRT) considers how leaders make decisions. (p. 148)
    a.   true
    b.   false*

115. The Cognitive Resource Theory adds to the other two resource theories by considering follower satisfaction. (p. 148)
    a.   true
    b.   false*

116. Intelligence and experience are the two leader characteristics in the Cognitive Resource Theory. (p. 148)
    a.   true*
    b.   false

117. The Cognitive Resource Theory suggests that more intelligent leaders use resources better than less intelligent leaders and are therefore more effective. (p. 148-149)
    a.   true
    b.   false*

118. According to the Cognitive Resource Theory, in low stress situations a leader's intelligence rather than his/her experience is most helpful. (p. 148-149)
    a.   true*
    b.   false

119. The Cognitive Resource Theory is one of the most researched resource utilization theories. (p. 149)
    a.   true
    b.   false*

120. Because they are well researched, the contingency theories of leadership generally apply well to other cultures. (p. 149-150)
    a.   true*
    b.   false

121. Tolerance for uncertainty is one of the factors that may impact whether the U.S. developed contingency theories apply to other cultures. (p. 149-150)
    a.   true
    b.   false*

122. Research in Japan indicates that a good leader in that culture is production oriented and nurturing. (p. 149-150)
    a.   true*
    b.   false

123. The concept of contingency in leadership may only apply in individualistic cultures. (p. 149-150)
    a.   true*
    b.   false

124. Bill Gates and Mary Kay Ash are both effective, although they have highly different styles. (p. 165-166)
    a.   true*
    b.   false

CHAPTER 6

<u>Multiple Choice Questions</u>

1. The exchange and relationship development and management contingency theories focus on: (p. 168)
   a.   how the leader uses relationships to be effective
   b.   the process by which a leader guides followers to become effective*
   c.   how a leader manages internal and external relationships
   d.   the contingency factors that affect the leader-follower exchange

2. The Path-Goal theory suggests that the role of the leader is to clear paths for followers allowing them to: (p. 168)
   a.   fulfill their needs and reach goals*
   b.   function without their leader when necessary
   c.   build a cohesive team
   d.   have time to address interpersonal conflicts

3. Which motivation theory is one of the concepts included in Path-Goal Theory? (p 168)
   a.   Maslow's need hierarchy
   b.   Goal setting
   c.   Expectancy theory*
   d.   ARG theory

4. According the Path-Goal Theory, the leader must motivate follower by: (p. 168)
   a.   strengthening the links among effort, performance, and outcomes*
   b.   encouraging them to do their best
   c.   addressing each follower's needs
   d.   being both a supportive and a task-oriented leader who focuses on followers

5. The concept of _____ is at the core of the Path Goal theory. (p. 168)
   a.   power
   b.   interpersonal relationships
   c.   exchange*
   d.   team building

6. The conceptual basis for the Path-Goal theory is: (p. 168)
   a.   the need theory of motivation
   b.   group dynamics theories
   c.   the influence theory of leadership
   d.   the expectancy theory*

7. While Fiedler's Contingency model assumes that leadership style is _____, Path-Goal relies on leader _____. (p. 168)
   a.   trait-like/behaviors*
   b.   cultural/styles
   c.   changeable/traits
   d.   learnable/power

8. Tran is applying Path-Goal theory to manage his team. He should focus on: (p. 168)
   a. improving relationships with followers
   b. creating career development paths for his team members
   c. empowering followers
   d. removing obstacle that can weaken motivation linkages*

9. In Path-Goal theory, _____ and _____ determine which leadership behavior should be used. (p. 168-169)
   a. power/leader-follower relationships
   b. nature of the task/follower characteristics*
   c. effort/performance
   d. group factors/organizational factors

10. According to Path-Goal theory, when _____, followers are likely to be frustrated. The leader must therefore provide _____. (p. 169)
   a. the group has conflict/facilitation
   b. the job is routine/direction
   c. the task is unclear/structure*
   d. the leader is autocratic/empowerment

11. According to Path-Goal theory, the leader must _____ when followers _____. (p. 169)
   a. be understanding/have conflict
   b. be considerate/face a routine task*
   c. be firm/disagree
   d. show empathy/complain

12. According to Path-Goal theory, when the task is unstructured, _____ can increase follower satisfaction. (p. 169)
   a. participative leadership*
   b. structuring
   c. autocratic
   d. task-oriented

13. According to Path-Goal theory, when the task is unstructured, achievement-oriented leadership: (p. 169)
   a. can help structure the task for followers
   b. can challenge followers and increase their self-confidence*
   c. can provide consideration for followers
   d. can clarify the task

14. Which one of the following is not one of the Path-Goal's assumptions? (p. 169)
   a. Leaders can correctly analyze the situation.
   b. Leaders can decide what behavior is required.
   c. Leaders can change their behavior.
   d. Leaders can change their power.*

15. The major weakness of the Path-Goal Theory is: (p. 170)
   a. not enough research*
   b. poor measures of leaders behavior
   c. unreliable hypotheses
   d. inability to measure motivation

16. Path-Goal makes a unique contribution to leadership theory by: (p. 170)
   a.   including follower's perception of the task.*
   b.   assuming that leaders can change their behavior.
   c.   presenting the concept of in-group.
   d.   by including culture in leadership.

17. Suzanna would like to improve her leadership effectiveness using Path-Goal theories of leadership. She should: (p. 170)
   a.   identify her in-group and out-group and how followers get in each group.
   b.   make sure that she has enough power.
   c.   understand her followers' need for autonomy and their perception of the task.*
   d.   make sure she is comfortable with a variety of decision styles.

18. Which of the following is not one of the recommendations based on the Path-Goal Theory? (p. 170)
   a.   The leader must understand followers and the task
   b.   The leader must consider followers' need for autonomy
   c.   When followers need to be challenged, leaders must avoid to be directive
   d.   When tasks are routine and boring, the leader must provide goals and structure*

19. Attributional theories focus on explaining: (p. 170)
   a.   how we interpret the cause of behavior.*
   b.   how we attribute power to others.
   c.   how we identify other people's attributes.
   d.   the attributes of leaders.

20. There are two reasons why understanding attribution may be helpful in leadership situations. These are: (p. 171)
   a.   evaluations and promotions
   b.   understanding internal and external causes of behavior
   c.   determining the cause of errors and taking corrective action*
   d.   assessing performance and establishing rules

21. One of the factors in the leader's attribution about followers' action is: (p. 171)
   a.   the extent to which the follower's action impacts the leader's goal accomplishment*
   b.   the leader's personality style
   c.   the followers' ability to set goals and stay on course
   d.   the organizational politics

22. According to attributional theories of leadership, leaders are more likely to blame follower when: (p. 171)
   a.   when the employees have performed well in the past
   b.   when the employee gets defensive*
   c.   when the employee's performance does not affect anyone else
   d.   when the issues are trivial

23. Jiang Li has made a mistake in her work and has talk to her manager and apologized for her error. She has always been a very good performer and done well as all of tasks that are assigned to her. Her mistake does not impact anyone in her team. Based on research on attribution and leadership, her manager is likely to: (p. 171)
   a.   fire Jiang Li.
   b.   blame Jiang Li for the mistake and hold her responsible.
   c.   let Jiang Li off easy and assume it was an honest error.*
   d.   not do much; most managers know that employees can't control everything.

24. Sandy has made an error in her work that has caused the loss of an important client. Although she did not intend to do so, she got very defensive when her managers asked her what happened. Based on research on attribution and leadership, her manager is likely to: (p. 171)
    a.   fire Sandy.
    b.   blame Sandy for the mistake and hold her responsible.*
    c.   let Sandy off easy and assume the client was difficult.
    d.   not do much; most managers know that employees can't control everything.

25. Mansour is a middle-eastern manager who works for a Swedish company. Hans, his new German supervisor extensively consults with Mansour before making decisions. However Mansour rarely contributes much and complains often that Hans is a weak leader. This exchange is likely due to: (p. 171)
    a.   Hans' pushiness.
    b.   Mansour's possible prejudice against Westerners.
    c.   Mansour's attribution about Hans' lack of confidence as a leader.*
    d.   Han's attribution about the need for empowerment in most cultures.

26. In the scenario above, which of the following is the most likely interpretation Hans is to make of Mansour's behavior? (p. 171)
    a.   Mansour is disloyal or incompetent*
    b.   Mansour does not understand Hans' directions
    c.   Mansour does not have enough skills
    d.   Mansour is prejudiced against Germans

27. Which of the following is not one of the attributional biases? (p. 172)
    a.   Stereotypes
    b.   Self-serving bias
    c.   Ego defensiveness
    d.   Social facilitation*

28. The self-serving bias is best defined as: (p. 172)
    a.   accepting credit for success and rejecting blame for failure*
    b.   evaluating others based on your own self-image
    c.   evaluating people based on the group to which they belong
    d.   blaming others for things that you have done

29. The leader who sees a female employee's hard-driving and competitiveness as overly aggressive, but considers the same behavior appropriate when performed by a male employee, is falling prey to which attributional bias? (p. 172)
    a.   Stereotypes*
    b.   Self-serving bias
    c.   Ego defensiveness
    d.   Social facilitation

30. Leaders can help reduce the potential for biases in their attributions about followers by doing which of the following?
    a.   Relying on their intuition and experience.
    b.   Using traits to evaluation followers.
    c.   Awareness and recognition of biases.*
    d.   Distancing themselves from followers.

31. The Leader-Member Exchange (LMX) model of leadership is based on the premise that: (p. 172)
   a.   leadership is a relationship between leaders and each follower*
   b.   leadership is an exchange process
   c.   leaders and followers must develop a relationship
   d.   leadership is a group phenomenon

32. An earlier version of the Leader-Member Exchange (LMX) model was called: (p. 173-174)
   a.   the Leader-Member Relationship model
   b.   the vertical dyad linkage model*
   c.   the transactional leadership model
   d.   the exchange relations model

33. According to Leader-Member Exchange (LMX) model, followers who are _____ will have the leader's trust and be expected to perform and grow. (p. 174)
   a.   more intelligent
   b.   in the in-group*
   c.   from the same culture
   d.   who ingratiate themselves with the leader

34. According to the Leader Member Exchange (LMX) model, regardless of the quality of the relationship between the leader and the follower, they: (p. 174)
   a.   take a while to establish a relationship
   b.   end up having conflict over the relationship
   c.   they eventually manage to work well together
   d.   establish a role of each follower*

35. According the LMX, the followers who have a high quality relationship with their leader are likely to do all but one of the following (p. 174)
   a.   perform well
   b.   be satisfied with their job
   c.   be carefully watched so that they make mistakes *
   d.   communicate often with their leader

36. Juan has had an excellent relationship with his boss who is grooming him to be his successor. In spite of good performance, Juan makes a serious mistake in one of his projects. According to Leader-Member Exchange (LMX), what is Juan's boss most likely to do? ((p. 174)
   a.   be highly disappointed in Juan
   b.   punish Juan very harshly
   c.   take the blame for Juan's mistake
   d.   overlook Juan's mistake*

37. Viktor has a hard time getting along with his boss and cannot seem to get on the right projects to show off his skills, and demonstrate his potential and performance. Based on Leader-Member Exchange (LMX) This is most likely because:
   a.   Viktor is from a different culture than his boss
   b.   Viktor is not in his boss's in-group*
   c.   Viktor does not have enough experience
   d.   Viktor's boss is a bad manager

38. Employees who do not have a high quality LMX are likely to experience one of the following. (p. 174)
   a.   assignment to challenging tasks
   b.   a lot of positive and negative communication from their leader
   c.   limited interaction with the leader*
   d.   high performance expectations

39. Which of the following is <u>not</u> one of the outcomes of a high quality leader-member exchange? (p. 174)
    a.   Little need for communication.*
    b.   High performance.
    c.   High satisfaction.
    d.   Better performance ratings for followers.

40. According to Leader Member Exchange (LMX), when followers are not close to the leader: (p. 174)
    a.   they become innovative.
    b.   the organization functions better.
    c.   the formal job description defines activities.*
    d.   they have independence and autonomy to do what is needed.

41. According to Leader Member Exchange (LMX), for both followers who are close to the leader and those who are not, the relationship with their leader: (p. 174)
    a.   is essential.
    b.   can lead to a self-fulfilling prophecy.*
    c.   can become irrelevant.
    d.   is a source of satisfaction and self-efficacy.

42. Leaders form positive relationship with three types of followers. Which of the following is not one of the followers? (p. 174)
    a.   those who are competent
    b.   those they trust
    c.   those who are willing to assume responsibility
    d.   those who are similar to the leader*

43. Which of the following is <u>not</u> a factor in the creation of positive relationships? (p. 174)
    a.   Trust between the leader and the follower
    b.   Follower competence
    c.   Follower ingratiation*
    d.   Follower willingness to assume more responsibility

44. In the Middle-East, leaders are likely to pick their trusted followers based on _____, while in the U.S., _____ is likely to be a primary factor. (p. 174)
    a.   friendship/similarity to the leader
    b.   obedience/team building ability
    c.   obligation/contacts
    d.   social class and birth/performance*

45. In ascriptive cultures such as the Middle East or France, a higher quality LMX depends primarily on: (p. 175)
    a.   trust*
    b.   performance
    c.   friendship
    d.   work structure

46. The concept of _____ does not readily apply to ascriptive cultures where loyalty to one's clan and family are a primary concern. (p. 175)
    a.   nepotism*
    b.   stereotypes
    c.   biases
    d.   racism

47. According to research conducted by Onne Janssen and Nico Van Yperen, followers who believe that their efforts lead to performance and improvement are more likely to: (p. 175)
   a.   challenge their leader
   b.   not need their leader
   c.   rely on organizational practices to improve
   d.   have a high quality relationship with their leader*

48. In the _____ stage of relationship development between leaders and followers, the leader provides challenges and opportunities to perform and followers demonstrate loyalty to their leader. (p. 176)
   a.   testing and assessment
   b.   socialization
   c.   development of trust*
   d.   creation of emotional bond

49. The relationship between leaders and followers develops in how many stages? (p. 176)
   a.   two
   b.   three*
   c.   four
   d.   five

50. Which of the stages of the development of the LMX only exits for those followers who have a high quality relationship? (p. 176)
   a.   Assessment
   b.   Development of trust*
   c.   Evaluation
   d.   Membership reconsideration

51. The Leader-Member Exchange Model needs further development in which of the following areas? (p. 176)
   a.   Leader characteristics
   b.   Exchange factors
   c.   Factors that lead to the development of relationships*
   d.   How organizational factors impact the leader's style

52. The development of individual exchange between leaders and followers: (p. 176)
   a.   is detrimental to organizations
   b.   can lead to identification of competent employees*
   c.   blocks the achievement of personal goals
   d.   allows for self-actualization of followers

53. Benefits of developing individual exchanges between leaders and their followers include: (p. 176)
   a.   quicker and more efficient decisions*
   b.   better performance
   c.   equal treatment of followers
   d.   ability to evaluate followers individually

54. Disadvantages of developing individual exchanges between leaders and followers include: (p. 176)
   a.   slow decision making
   b.   favoritism*
   c.   inefficiencies
   d.   poor performance

55. Alan Canton, president of Adams-Blake Co. found that _____ can become highly destructive (p. 177)
   a.   in-groups can turn into cliques and*
   b.   out-group members
   c.   the leader setting up in and out-groups
   d.   not having a positive LMX

56. Having an in and out-group can be highly productive if membership is based on: (p. 177)
   a.   trust and loyalty
   b.   friendship between the leader and the follower
   c.   compatibility and ability*
   d.   ability to disagree

57. The benefits of having a cohesive in-group include all <u>but one</u> of the following. (p. 177)
   a.   reducing unnecessary delays
   b.   efficient decision making
   c.   goal achievement
   d.   creativity*

58. One of the potential reasons why Michael Ovitz could not work with Michael Eisner of Disney and was not successful is that (p. 178)
   a.   he lacked experience
   b.   he did not become part of the inner circle*
   c.   he abused his power with subordinates
   d.   he made too many fast changes to the Disney management team

59. Maggie Widerotter of Wink Communication battles the potential negative consequence of having in-groups by (p. 178)
   a.   she goes out of her way to meet people she does not know well*
   b.   she does not set up in-groups at all
   c.   she delegates to all her employees equally
   d.   she includes everyone in her in-group

60. A _____ leadership team is likely to be cohesive and work well together. (p. 178)
   a.   diverse
   b.   competent
   c.   homogeneous*
   d.   top-level

61. A _____ leadership team is likely to lack creativity and disregard input from outsiders. (p. 178)
   a.   diverse
   b.   competent
   c.   homogeneous*
   d.   top-level

62. The key issue in keeping in-groups productive is (p. 178)
   a.   the leader's personality
   b.   followers' personality
   c.   how in-group members are selected*
   d.   the quality of the LMX

63. Which of the following is <u>not</u> one of the guidelines for developing groups for the leader? (p. 179)
   a.   Pick members based on competence and contribution
   b.   Keep rules for members in various groups ambiguous*
   c.   Keep membership fluid to allow movement from one group to another
   d.   Maintain a variety of groups

64. Terry has just learned about the LMX model and would like to make sure that her in-groups are productive and benefit followers and her organization. Which one of the following should she <u>avoid</u>? (p. 179)
   a.   Pick members based on competence and contribution
   b.   Keep membership fluid
   c.   Avoid differentiated in-groups and out-groups
   d.   Establish a group of competent followers and use them for all activities*

65. Which of the following is <u>not</u> one of the categories of factors that reduce the impact of leadership? (p. 179-179)
   a.   Follower characteristics
   b.   Task characteristics
   c.   Organizational characteristics
   d.   Leader characteristics*

66. Employees are not likely to need their leader to provide structuring behavior if: (p. 179)
   a.   they have information about the task through other means*
   b.   if they do not get along with the leader
   c.   if the leader does not have enough power
   d.   if the leader is not located in the same place as the employees

67. At the Brazilian company Semco, Ricardo Semler has set up a number of leadership substitutes. Which one of the following is <u>not</u> one of the substitutes? (p. 179-180)
   a.   thorough training
   b.   open book management
   c.   experienced workers
   d.   experienced managers*

68. Follower professionalism serves as a substitute for _____. (p. 179-180)
   a.   leader consideration behaviors*
   b.   organizational policies
   c.   leader structuring behaviors
   d.   leader's lack of power

69. Having a clear task that provides direct feedback to follower serves as a substitute for _____. (p. 179-180)
   a.   leader consideration behaviors
   b.   organizational policies
   c.   leader structuring behaviors*
   d.   leader's lack of power

70. A cohesive team can act as _____ for the leader's _____ behavior. (p. 180)
   a.   neutralizer/conflict resolution
   b.   substitute/structuring*
   c.   substitute/team building
   d.   neutralizer/consideration

71. The Alpha team is located in a building that is far apart from the rest of the organization, including the team's manager who is located over 100 miles away. The physical distance between the manager and followers acts as a _____ for leader _____. (p. 179-180)
   a.   substitute/consideration*
   b.   neutralizer/consideration
   c.   neutralizer/responsibility
   d.   substitute/lack of power

72. Ravi would like to use the substitute for leadership concepts to improve his leadership effectiveness. Which of he following should she focus on? (p. 179-180)
   a.   Increase the distance between himself and his followers.
   b.   Decrease his power.
   c.   Put in place rigid organizational policies.
   d.   Increase his team's cohesion.*

73. The substitute for leadership model has increasing applications to many organizations as they: (p. 181)
   a.   implement the use teams*
   b.   select leaders with certain traits
   c.   teach leaders to be both considerate and provide structure
   d.   move to other cultures

74. One of the oldest breweries in the U.S., D.G.Yuengling, applies modern leadership theories by: (p. 181)
   a.   teaching leaders how to use in-groups
   b.   providing cross-cultural training
   c.   using the concept of contingency leadership
   d.   setting up substitutes for leadership*

75. The implication of the leadership substitute model for leadership training is to: (p. 181)
   a.   train the leader to empower followers.
   b.   teach the leader to change situations.*
   c.   focus the leader on acquiring power
   d.   help the leader manage relationships with followers

76. The Situational Leadership model uses _____ and _____ as the two contingency factors. (p. 181)
   a.   task structure/leader power
   b.   organizational culture/group cohesion
   c.   follower ability/follower maturity*
   d.   leader traits/situational control

77. Which one of the following is one of the behaviors used in Situational Leadership? (p. 181)
   a.   Structuring
   b.   Consideration
   c.   Participation
   d.   Delegating*

78. Which of the following is not one of the factors used by W.L. Gore to achieve its unique structure and culture? (p. 182)
   a.   Designating formal leaders.*
   b.   Keeping each plant to less than 200.
   c.   Allowing employees to select their own projects.
   d.   Celebrating failures.

79. One of the weaknesses of the situational leadership model is that: (p. 183)
   a.   the concept of maturity is poorly defined*
   b.   there are no clear measures
   c.   it is not easily used in real-life settings
   d.   it is intuitively unappealing

80. The contingency-based theories of leadership differ on all <u>but one</u> of the following factors? (p. 184)
   a.   Effectiveness criteria
   b.   Leader characteristics
   c.   Leader use of power*
   d.   Task structure

81. Regardless on what factors they use, all the contingency theories agree that: (p. 184)
   a.   leaders should change their style to match the situation.
   b.   different leadership is needed in different situations.*
   c.   leadership effectiveness is about group performance.
   d.   power should always be considered.

82. The theory that considers how leaders perceive their followers' actions, make judgments, and decide on a course of action is: (p. 171)
   a.   Path-Goal theory
   b.   Attributional models*
   c.   Leader-Member Exchange
   d.   Substitutes for Leadership

83. The theory that recommends that leaders remove obstacles to motivate their followers is: (p. 168)
   a.   Path-Goal theory*
   b.   Attributional models
   c.   Leader-Member Exchange
   d.   Substitutes for Leadership

84. The theory that suggests there are some situations where leaders' role is limited is: (p. 179)
   a.   Path-Goal theory
   b.   Attributional models
   c.   Leader-Member Exchange
   d.   Substitutes for Leadership*

85. The theory that suggests that leaders develop a unique relationship with each follower is: (p. 173)
   a.   Path-Goal theory
   b.   Attributional models
   c.   Leader-Member Exchange*
   d.   Substitutes for Leadership

86. Commander Abrashoff was effective because he shifted focus from _____ to _____. (p. 195-196)
   a.   obedience/performance*
   b.   structuring/consideration
   c.   conflict/cohesion
   d.   power sharing/effectiveness

87. The relationship development and management theories assume that leaders are able to change their behavior as needed. (p. 168)
    a.   true*
    b.   false

88. The concept of power is at the core of the Path-Goal theory. (p. 168)
    a.   true
    b.   false*

89. The theoretical basis for Path-Goal theory is the need theory of motivation. (p. 168)
    a.   true
    b.   false*

90. According to Path-Goal theory, the leader must focus on satisfying employees by removing obstacles they face. (p. 168)
    a.   true*
    b.   false

91. Based on Path-Goal theory, when the task is unclear, the leader must show understanding. (p. 168)
    a.   true
    b.   false*

92. Based on Path-Goal theory, if followers have done the task many times before, the leader must be considerate and understanding. (p. 169)
    a.   true*
    b.   false

93. One of the factors that Path-Goal theory recommends leaders pay attention to is their followers need for autonomy. (p. 169)
    a.   true*
    b.   false

94. Path-Goal has received strong research support. (p. 170)
    a.   true
    b.   false*

95. Path-Goal theory adds to other leadership theories by considering follower satisfaction. (p. 170)
    a.   true*
    b.   false

96. The attributional model of leadership considers how the leader decides what is causing his or her personal success. (p. 171)
    a.   true
    b.   false*

97. Attributions can be made to internal or external factors. (p. 171)
    a.   true*
    b.   false

98. Leaders tend to be harsher on employees and blame them for errors when the leader's success depends on the employees' good performance. (p. 171)
    a.   true*
    b.   false

99. One way employees can avoid being blamed for their errors, is to put up a strong defense. (p. 171)
   a.   true
   b.   false*

100. The better an employee's track record, the less likely s/he is to be blamed for and error. (p. 171)
   a.   true*
   b.   false

101. Because they involve cognition, attributional processes are not affected by culture. (p. 171)
   a.   true
   b.   false*

102. The potential for bias and error greatly increases when people have to make attributions across cultures. (p. 171)
   a.   true*
   b.   false

103. Attributional biases happen only when communicating across different cultures. (p. 171)
   a.   true
   b.   false*

104. Attributions are always subject to bias. (p. 172)
   a.   true*
   b.   false

105. Although attributional theories have a limited scope in leadership, they help explain an important aspect of the leader's role. (p. 172)
   a.   true*
   b.   false

106. Two-way communication can help leaders avoid attributional biases. (p. 172)
   a.   true*
   b.   false

107. Using judgments based on intuition and experience can help leaders avoid attributional biases in evaluating their followers. (p. 172)
   a.   true
   b.   false*

108. The Leader-Member Exchange (LMX) model suggests leaders develop two groups of followers; those in the in-group and those in the out-group. (p. 173)
   a.   true*
   b.   false

109. The Leader-Member Exchange (LMX) model suggests that leaders do not have the same relationship with all their followers. (p. 174)
   a.   true*
   b.   false

110. High quality LMX relationship sometimes even extends to social networks outside of work. (p. 174)
   a.   true*
   b.   false

111. For followers who are not close to the leader, the formal job description often defines their activities (p. 174)
   a.   true*
   b.   false

112. According to Leader Member Exchange (LMX), followers who are not close to the leader often rebel and improve their performance to prove their worth to the leader. (p. 174)
   a.   true
   b.   false*

113. The followers who are similar to the leader on several dimensions are the ones who are most likely to develop a high quality LMX. (p. 174)
   a.   true
   b.   false*

114. In most cultures, leaders pick the followers they trust based on competence and performance. (p. 175)
   a.   true
   b.   false*

115. Researchers Onne Janssen and Nico Van Yperen found that how followers set up their goals can impact the quality of their relationship with their leader. (p. 175)
   a.   true*
   b.   false

116. In ascriptive cultures such as France, the quality of the LMX often depends on the followers' performance. (p. 175)
   a.   true
   b.   false*

117. The development of a relationship between leaders and followers typically takes place in three stages. (p. 176)
   a.   true*
   b.   false

118. The development of trust stage of relationship development mostly exists for out-group members. (p. 176)
   a.   true
   b.   false*

119. Most countries in the world try to avoid nepotism in their organizational practices. (p. 176)
   a.   true
   b.   false*

120. The development of LMX is a natural part of any interaction. (p. 177)
   a.   true*
   b.   false

121. Alan Canton, president of Adams-Blake co., found that in-groups were a valuable part of the structure of his organization. (p. 177)
   a.   true
   b.   false*

122. Having in-groups allows for quick and creative decision-making (p. 177)
   a.   true
   b.   false*

123. The case of Michael Eisner and Michael Ovitz at Disney provides an example of the potential negative consequences of in-groups. (p. 178)
   a.   true*
   b.   false

124. Maggie Widerotter of Wink communication believes that in-groups help her organization be more efficient. (p. 178)
   a.   true
   b.   false*

125. To avoid the potential negative impact of in-groups, leaders must make a conscious effort to seek out all followers. (p. 178)
   a.   true*
   b.   false

126. Because the development of individual relationships with followers tends to bias the leader, it is recommended that leaders avoid one-on-one relationships. (p. 178)
   a.   true
   b.   false*

127. Research indicates that people tend to become friends and be attracted to those who unlike them. A leader's inner circle is therefore likely to be very different than him/herself. (p. 178)
   a.   true
   b.   false*

128. The Leader-Member Exchange (LMX) model applies well to non-Western cultures. (p. 178)
   a.   true
   b.   false*

129. The advantages of in-groups that have members who are similar can be offset by lack of creativity and limited decision making. (p. 178)
   a.   true*
   b.   false

130. Leaders should find a competent group of followers and maintain them as part of their in-group for most of the tasks that they need performed. (p. 179)
   a.   true
   b.   false*

131. Leaders should periodically evaluate the criteria for membership in their in-group. (p. 179)
   a.   true*
   b.   false

132. Research shows that leaders are essential in all situations. (p. 179)
   a.   true
   b.   false*

133. Professionals who have experience in their task often do not rely on their leader. (p. 179)
   a.   true*
   b.   false

134. Organizational rigidity can reduce the need for the leader to provide task structure. (p. 179-180)
    a.   true*
    b.   false

135. The Brazilian firm Semco uses training and cohesive teams as substitutes for leadership. (p. 179)
    a.   true*
    b.   false

136. Ricardo Semler and his company Semco are example of use of leadership neutralizers. (p. 179)
    a.   true
    b.   false*

137. Having factors that substitute for leadership is a negative situation. (p. 180)
    a.   true
    b.   false*

138. Follower experience and training is a substitute for leader structuring behavior. (p. 180)
    a.   true*
    b.   false

139. Followers' lack of value for goals is a neutralizer for leadership. (p. 180)
    a.   true*
    b.   false

140. Direct feedback from the task neutralized the leader. (p. 180)
    a.   true
    b.   false*

141. A cohesive team can act as a substitute for leader consideration. (p. 180)
    a.   true*
    b.   false

142. The substitute for leadership has potential application self-managed teams. (p. 180)
    a.   true*
    b.   false

143. The leaders at D.G.Yuengling & Son, one of the oldest breweries in the U.S., recognize the need to set up various substitutes for leadership. (p. 181)
    a.   true*
    b.   false

144. Although the Situational Leadership model is popular in corporate leadership training, it has little empirical support. (p. 181)
    a.   true*
    b.   false

145. W.L. Gore assigns "natural leaders" to lead its creative teams. (p. 182)
    a.   true
    b.   false*

146. Regardless on what factors they use, all the contingency theories agree that leaders should change their behaviors to match the situation. (p. 183-184)
    a.   true
    b.   false*

147. Different contingency theories use different criteria for leadership effectiveness. (p. 183-184)
   a.   true*
   b.   false

148. Commander Michael Abrashoff is effective because he focuses on applying rules fairly. (p. 195-196)
   a.   true
   b.   false*

149. Commander Michael Abrashoff removed obstacles which increased his crew's motivation and satisfaction. (p. 195-196)
   a.   true*
   b.   false

CHAPTER 7

<u>Multiple Choice Questions</u>

1. The concept of employee participation is party of many management and leadership theories. Which one of the following does not include the concept of participation? (p. 200)
    a.   Theory X and Theory Y
    b.   Leader behavior research
    c.   Contingency models
    d.   Trait approach*

2. Ford Motor Co. is an example of a company that: (p. 200)
    a.   has moved fully towards team-based management
    b.   combines teams with more traditional structures*
    c.   continues to be successful without using teams
    d.   has found the use of team highly challenging

3. Research indicates that organizations can reap many benefits from employee participation and involvement. Which of the following is <u>not</u> one of the typical programs used in today's organizations? (p. 201)
    a.   group decision making
    b.   teams
    c.   social audits*
    d.   profit sharing

4. Space X company provides an example of a company that: (p. 201)
    a.   has moved fully towards team-based management
    b.   combines teams with more traditional structures*
    c.   continues to be successful without using teams
    d.   has found the use of team highly challenging

5. Royal Philips Electronics is counting on _____ to _____. (p. 201)
    a.   management/implement teams
    b.   employees/convince management about use of teams
    c.   teams/revive the company*
    d.   top leadership/move towards teams

6. Genencor International started its employee participation program: (p. 201)
    a.   when they build new headquarters*
    b.   after the leadership team took a trip to Japan
    c.   after they hired a new CEO
    d.   as a routine part of doing business

7. _____ and _____ are two of the criteria managers should use to determine when to involve employees in decision making. (p. 202)
    a.   Culture/cost
    b.   Efficiency/effectiveness
    c.   Leader style/financial issues
    d.   Task complexity/time*

8. Nelson has been a successful manager for over 30 years. He has considerable expertise and makes most of the decision by himself. He supervises over 200 people who are spread-out across 20 states. Using employee participation may be a challenge for Nelson because of: (p. 202)
     a.   time and complexity of the task.
     b.   the leader's style and the geographic dispersion.*
     c.   follower commitment and readiness.
     d.   environmental factors and culture.

9. Li Wei is under pressure to make a quick decision on a project where she has considerable expertise and experience. Her team is inexperience and generally supportive, and she needs the members' strong commitment to implement her decision. In this situation, Sun-lee should: (p. 202)
     a.   make the decision by herself.
     b.   allow for employee participation.*
     c.   seek more information.
     d.   delegate the decision to the group.

10. The case of Kiwi Airlines is an example of: (p. 203)
     a.   successful participation.
     b.   a leader not being ready for participation.
     c.   lack of employee training in participation.
     d.   too much participation by employees.*

11. Which of the following cultural values can affect how much employees participate in decision making? (p. 203-204)
     a.   Collectivism*
     b.   Tolerance for ambiguity
     c.   Ascription
     d.   Time orientation

12. The more _____ a culture, the less likely it is that employees will participate in decision making. (p. 203-204)
     a.   collectivist
     b.   ascriptive
     c.   power oriented*
     d.   flexible

13. _____ combined with _____ often create a challenge in implementing participation and teams in countries such as the U.S. and Australia. (p. 203-204)
     a.   High power distance/competitiveness
     b.   High performance orientation/short time orientation
     c.   High individualism/low power distance*
     d.   Low context/high tolerance for ambiguity

14. In spite of cultural and other differences, one of the keys to successful implementation of teams is: (p. 204)
     a.   followers' involvement
     b.   organizational policies
     c.   slow implementation
     d.   leader's belief in participation*

15. Which of the following is one of the goals of delegation? (p. 205)
     a.   Help the leader with excessive workload.*
     b.   Share power with employees.
     c.   Empower employees.
     d.   Increase the leader's power.

16. Which one of the following is not one of the benefits of delegation? (p. 205)
    a.   Develop followers.
    b.   Increase follower involvement in the task.
    c.   Increase follower motivation.
    d.   Increase leader's power.*

17. John has found that delegating tasks allow him to manage his own workload and stress. What other potential benefit does delegation offer John? ((p. 205)
    a.   Enrich the job of his followers.*
    b.   Create a more cohesive team.
    c.   Save his followers' time.
    d.   Increase leader's power.

18. Researchers Evert Van de Vliert and Peter Smith studied whether a country's wealth and climate may impact the extent of delegation. Their research suggests that: (p. 206)
    a.   leaders in harsh climates rely more on their followers.
    b.   leaders in less developed rely less on their followers.*
    c.   the higher the uncertainty avoidance, the more employee participation.
    d.   leaders in temperate climates rely the most on their followers.

19. It is important for managers to understand the difference between _____ and _____.
(p. 205)
    a.   development/enrichment
    b.   teams/group
    c.   leadership/leadership substitutes
    d.   delegation/dumping*

20. Alberto is an over-worked manager who is trying to reduce his workload. He decides to assign all the tasks that he does not like and take a long time to his subordinates. What is Alberto doing? ((p. 205)
    a.   delegating his tasks wisely
    b.   dumping on his subordinates*
    c.   developing his subordinates
    d.   reducing his workload while training his subordinates in good management practice

21. Shane wants to delegate a task to one of his followers. What guidelines should he follow? (p. 205-207)
    a.   Delegate the task and leave the employee alone to finish it.
    b.   Monitor to make sure he can pull back if employee makes a mistake.
    c.   Clarify the goals and expectation, and monitor the employee.*
    d.   Delegate the task, but make sure he keeps the authority to do it.

22. Leaders should generally not delegate which type of tasks or decisions? (p. 206-207)
    a.   Strategic decisions
    b.   Personnel decisions*
    c.   Manufacturing tasks
    d.   Quality control

23. Selena has a new project for a key client that she needs to delegate to one of her employees. This is a complex and important project. Which of the following employee should she pick? (p. 207)
    a. James who is competent, but not motivated, so that she can motivate him.
    b. Tanya who has performed poorly in many different instances, so that she can give her a chance to improve.
    c. Beverly who is new and does not have much experience or expertise, so that she can see how she performs.
    d. Ken who is competent and eager, but has recently failed at a task, so that she can give him a chance to recover.*

24. Not delegating tasks may be valid and acceptable _____, but not effective _____. (p. 208)
    a. in the short-term/when the leader takes a long-term view.*
    b. for leaders who are Type As/most other leaders.
    c. for leaders who have expertise/for less experienced leaders.
    d. in complex situations/for simple tasks.

25. Which one of the following is <u>not</u> one of the typical excuses managers use for not delegating? (p. 208)
    a. My followers are not ready
    b. I can do the job quicker myself
    c. The organization does not allow it*
    d. My followers do not have enough skills

26. Which underlying factor may be a contributing factor to leader's inability to delegate? (p. 208)
    a. follower's personality
    b. leader's personality*
    c. organizational policies
    d. organizational culture

27. _____ are more likely to find it difficult to delegate task to their followers. (p. 208)
    a. Experienced managers
    b. Relationship-orientated leaders
    c. Leaders who have trouble developing positive LMX
    d. Type A leaders*

28. How many factors distinguish teams from groups? (p. 209)
    a. two
    b. three
    c. four
    d. five*

29. Which one of the following distinguishes teams from groups? (p. 209)
    a. Team members are accountable to a manager.
    b. Team members share leadership.*
    c. Team members have frequent conflict.
    d. Team members accomplish their goals.

30. Teams have all the following characteristics, <u>except</u>: (p. 209)
    a. members share a common goal.
    b. members trust one another.
    c. members are accountable to a manager.*
    d. the team achieves synergy.

31. Rackspace, a web hosting company, achieves its exceptional customer service by: (p. 209)
    a.   training its leaders and managers
    b.   relying on self-managed teams*
    c.   delegating tasks to the best employees
    d.   building a relationship between leaders and followers

32. As compared to group where leadership is _____, in teams, leadership is _____. (p. 209)
    a.   temporary/permanent
    b.   assigned/shared*
    c.   required/unnecessary
    d.   primary/secondary

33. In teams members often share _____. (p. 210)
    a.   a culture*
    b.   norms
    c.   history
    d.   personal experiences

34. The XYZ team manages its own work, has members with different expertise, share leadership, has power to implement its own decisions while it coordinates activities with other teams. Based on this description, the XYZ team is: (p. 210)
    a.   an effective team
    b.   an advanced team
    c.   a self-managed team*
    d.   a self-leadership team

35. Which one of the following is not one of the characteristics of self-managed teams? (p. 210)
    a.   power to manage their work
    b.   members with different expertise
    c.   absence of outside manager
    d.   ability to determine their work without consulting with others*

36. Self-managed teams use leadership based on: (p. 210)
    a.   cooperation
    b.   consideration
    c.   shared responsibility
    d.   facilitation*

37. Which of the following is not one of the factors that contribute to the success of teams? (p. 211)
    a.   careful selection of team members
    b.   commitment to a team goal
    c.   complex tasks
    d.   competition*

38. _____ is one of the key factors in effective teams. (p. 211)
    a.   Building trust*
    b.   A good leader
    c.   Clear rules
    d.   A goal handed down from upper management

39. Robert wants to increase the trust among his team members. What should he do? (p. 211)
    a.   Create friendly competition among the members.
    b.   Set up formal communication mechanisms.
    c.   Reward cooperation.*
    d.   Assign a formal leader.

40. Teams require specialized training. Which one of the following is not the type of specialized training that may help teams? (p. 212)
   a.   Team building.
   b.   Coordination training.
   c.   Assertiveness training
   d.   Leadership training.*

41. Self-guided correction is one of the skills that effective teams need. It means (p. 212)
   a.   team members monitor and correct their own behavior*
   b.   the team is able to correct mistakes of other teams
   c.   the leader guides the members in correcting mistakes
   d.   the organization guides the members to self-correct their behavior

42. Superleaders are individual who: (p. 213)
   a.   are visionary.
   b.   encourage followers to lead themselves.*
   c.   establish clear exchange relationships that allow followers to reach their goals.
   d.   provide clear and consistent reward to their followers.

43. Isabelle wants to become a self-leader. She has learned to set her own goals. What else can she do? (p. 213)
   a.   Develop a positive and motivating thought pattern.*
   b.   Find a mentor to guide her.
   c.   Make sure the organization rewards her for her effort.
   d.   Provide a vision for others.

44. Superleadership is similar to which of the other theories of leadership? (p. 213)
   a.   Fiedler's Contingency Model
   b.   The LMX model
   c.   The substitutes for leadership*
   d.   Situational leadership

45. Superleaders _____ instead of _____. (p. 213)
   a.   keep information/sharing information
   b.   make sure everyone is on board/letting employees develop their own goals
   c.   provide a vision/letting the team set goals
   d.   encourage creativity/conformity*

46. Which one of the following is not one of the strategies for the development of super and self-leaders? (p. 214)
   a.   Listen more; talk less
   b.   Ask questions; don't provide answers
   c.   Share information; don't hoard information
   d.   Be decisive; don't consult too much*

47. The leadership traits identified by IBM to revive the company include which of the following? (p. 213)
   a.   Being a visionary.
   b.   Developing people and enabling growth.*
   c.   Being able to take charge.
   d.   Having both task and people skills.

48. Which term is most often used when describing the role leaders in teams? (p .216)
    a.   Facilitator*
    b.   Visionary
    c.   Superleader
    d.   Team member

49. Which one of the following is <u>not</u> one of the roles of leaders in a team environment? (p .216)
    a.   Obtaining resources for the team
    b.   Helping team set boundaries
    c.   Setting goals for the team*
    d.   Assessing the team's ability

50. The use of teams in the U.S. was triggered by: (p .216)
    a.   globalization.
    b.   the growth of the Chinese economy.
    c.   failure of the U.S. management methods.
    d.   the successful use of teams in Japan.*

51. Instead of team-based management, Australian researchers have proposed the concept of
    _____ to involve individuals in teams in Western cultures. (p .217)
    a.   collaborative individualism*
    b.   superleadership
    c.   participation
    d.   transformational leadership

52. For teams to work in Western cultures, researchers suggest that individuals should _____
and _____. (p .217)
    a.   become collectivist/build consensus
    b.   build trust/empower the team
    c.   be cooperative/focus on the individual*
    d.   focus on task/care about people

53. Decision making power at Whole Foods rests with: (p. 227-228)
    a.   the CEO, John Mackey
    b.   teams that run each department*
    c.   the top level executives
    d.   individual

54. Whole Foods has developed a "Declaration of Interdependence" that focuses on: (p. 227-228)
    a.   the role of followers
    b.   the connectedness of all company stakeholders*
    c.   the dependence between leaders and their followers
    d.   the role of shareholders

<u>True/False Questions</u>

55. Most modern leadership and management theories address employee participation. (p. 200).
    a.   true*
    b.   false

56. Participation is on a continuum from traditional organizational to team-based organizations. (p. 200)
    a.   true*
    b.   false

57. The concept of participation is a relatively new idea in leadership and management. (p. 200)
   a.   true
   b.   false*

58. Most organizations use a combination of traditional structures and teams. (p. 200)
   a.   true*
   b.   false

59. Companies either use teams or they don't. (p. 200)
   a.   true
   b.   false*

60. Space X and Ford Motor co. are two companies that have moved toward completely team-based structures. (p. 200-201)
   a.   true
   b.   false*

61. Employee participation and involvement has clear benefits for organizations. (p. 201)
   a.   true*
   b.   false

62. Genencor International managers believe that employee participation programs often costs too much. (p. 201)
   a.   true
   b.   false*

63. Participation often provides solutions to most business problems. (p. 201)
   a.   true
   b.   false*

64. Royal Philips Electronics has made cross-boundary teams part of its revival strategy. (p. 201)
   a.   true*
   b.   false

65. Participation should be used when the task is complex, there is no time pressure, the organization is ready, and employee commitment is needed. (p. 202)
   a.   true*
   b.   false

66. Participation can only succeed if both leaders and followers are committed to it. (p. 202)
   a.   true*
   b.   false

67. In order for participation to be successfully implemented, it is important that followers be committed to its implementation. However, leadership commitment is less essential. (p. 202)
   a.   true
   b.   false*

68. Kiwi airlines provides an example of successful participation. (p. 203)
   a.   true
   b.   false*

69. Cultural values impact expectations for participation. (p. 203-204)
   a.   true*
   b.   false

70. Because of collectivism, Mexican employees often expect to participate in decision making. (p. 203-204)
   a.   true
   b.   false*

71. Although the Japanese culture is high on power distance, the country has a tradition of employee participation in decision making. (p. 203-204)
   a.   true*
   b.   false

72. Because the French are argumentative, they expect their leaders to involve them in decision making. (p. 203-204)
   a.   true
   b.   false*

73. In the U.S, low power distance facilitates participation. (p. 203-204)
   a.   true*
   b.   false

74. Culture determines which aspects of teams are expected and rewarded. (p. 203-204)
   a.   true*
   b.   false

75. Delegation and participation are the same concept. (p. 205)
   a.   true
   b.   false*

76. Delegation can be a useful tool in employee training and development. (p. 205)
   a.   true*
   b.   false

77. Researchers have found that a country's climate and level of development can impact the extent to which leaders delegate to followers. (p. 206)
   a.   true*
   b.   false

78. Leaders should delegate the tasks that they do not like and do not want to do. (p. 206)
   a.   true
   b.   false*

79. Once they train their followers well, it is appropriate for leaders to delegate all tasks including personnel related decisions. (p. 206)
   a.   true
   b.   false*

80. Once leaders have a sub-group of followers they know and can trust, they should delegate tasks to that subgroup. (p. 207)
   a.   true
   b.   false*

81. Leaders should delegate both a task and the authority to complete it. (p. 207)
   a.   true*
   b.   false

82. In order to build employee autonomy, once they delegate a task, leaders should leave their followers alone until the task is completed. (p. 207)
   a.   true
   b.   false*

83. Leaders should closely monitor employees after they delegate a task and make sure that they pull back the task if the employee makes a mistake. (p. 207)
   a.   true
   b.   false*

84. Leaders should not delegate if they can do the task themselves more quickly. (p. 207)
   a.   true
   b.   false*

85. Even if followers do not fully have the skills they need, the leader should delegate tasks to them to train them. (p. 207)
   a.   true*
   b.   false

86. One of the primary reasons leaders fail to delegate is that they feel their followers are not ready. (p. 208)
   a.   true*
   b.   false

87. Because followers' mistakes often are blamed on the manager, manager should avoid delegating tasks that they think their followers are not ready to do. (p. 208)
   a.   true
   b.   false*

88. An underlying factor that my prevent managers from delegating is the personality traits of their followers. (p. 208)
   a.   true
   b.   false*

89. Teams create a formal structure through which participation in decision making can be achieved. (p. 208)
   a.   true*
   b.   false

90. Teams are easy to implement in most organizations. (p. 209)
   a.   true
   b.   false*

91. Teams go beyond accomplishing goals to achieving synergy. (p. 209)
   a.   true*
   b.   false

92. Rasckspace, the web hosting company, relies on teams to achieve exceptional customer service. (p. 209)
   a.   true*
   b.   false

93. Team members often perform because of their exceptional commitment to their leader. (p. 209)
   a.   true
   b.   false*

94. Teams often have assigned leaders whereas groups share leadership. (p. 209)
    a.   true
    b.   false*

95. Groups have shared norms; teams have a shared culture. (p. 210)
    a.   true*
    b.   false

96. The primary role of team leaders is to set goals and make decisions regarding how to implement them. (p. 210)
    a.   true
    b.   false*

97. Self-managed teams are different from other teams in that they share leaders and are not accountable to an outside manager. (p. 210)
    a.   true*
    b.   false

98. Self-managed teams do not need to coordinate their activities and decisions with others in the organization. (p. 210)
    a.   true
    b.   false*

99. Having members with similar skills is essential to effective self-managed teams. (p. 210)
    a.   true
    b.   false*

100. Building effective teams is relatively quick once you pick the right members (p. 211)
    a.   true
    b.   false*

101. To be effective, teams must have right power and authority to accomplish its task and implement its ideas. (p. 211)
    a.   true*
    b.   false

102. To make teams effective, members only need to receive the same training as everyone else in the organization. (p. 212)
    a.   true
    b.   false*

103. Each team member must be trained only in his/her own area, so that she/he can provide the expertise to the team. (p. 212)
    a.   true
    b.   false*

104. In self-guided correction, team members monitor and correct their own behavior. (p. 212)
    a.   true*
    b.   false

105. Superleadership is the process of leading people to lead themselves. (p. 213)
    a.   true*
    b.   false

106. Superleadership relies on the receiving feedback and rewards from others. (p. 213)
   a.   true
   b.   false*

107. Superleaders set up substitutes that reduce their followers' dependence on the leader. (p. 213)
   a.   true*
   b.   false

108. IBM's new leadership believes that the company's success depends on leaders who can take charge. (p. 213)
   a.   true
   b.   false*

109. Super and self-leaders must learn to encourage follower conformity. (p. 214)
   a.   true
   b.   false*

110. Superleaders must ask questions rather than provide answers. (p .214)
   a.   true*
   b.   false

111. Teams are making leaders obsolete. (p .215)
   a.   true
   b.   false*

112. Dr. Nancy Hudson, vice president of Pfizer's global research and development helps her team stay on track through many failures by supporting them and putting people first. (p. 215)
   a.   true*
   b.   false

113. New roles for leaders in teams include continuing to do actual work. (p .216)
   a.   true*
   b.   false

114. Team leaders must be able to direct the team forcefully, when the team is confused. (p .216)
   a.   true*
   b.   false

115. Team-based Japanese style management is successfully implemented in the U.S. (p .216)
   a.   true
   b.   false*

116. Whole Foods is an example of a company that started with traditional structures and moved towards a team-based structure. (p. 227-228)
   a.   true
   b.   false*

117. The concepts of empowerment and team decision making are at the heart of Whole Foods management and success. (p. 227-228)
   a.   true*
   b.   false

CHAPTER 8

Multiple Choice Questions

1. The modern approach to charismatic leadership is primarily associated with which of the following researchers? (p. 230)
   a.   Bass and House*
   b.   Stogdill and Fiedler
   c.   Kirkpatrick and Locke
   d.   Vroom and Yetton

2. Theories of charismatic leadership are closely related to which of the other models of leadership? (p. 230)
   a.   contingency models
   b.   resource utilization models
   c.   exchange and relationship development models*
   d.   behavior models

3. Which of the following is one of the advantages of the charismatic approach to leadership over the contingency approaches? (p. 230)
   a.   They focus on middle level managers.
   b.   They show the importance of the task.
   c.   They highlight the importance of the emotional links.*
   d.   They allow us to measure traits more accurately.

4. The word charisma has Greek origins and means: (p. 230)
   a.   leadership
   b.   a divine gift*
   c.   power and inspiration
   d.   talented

5. Which one of the following is not one of the required elements of charismatic leadership? (p. 231)
   a.   Characteristics of the leader
   b.   Characteristics of followers
   c.   The situation
   d.   The organization*

6. Charismatic leaders and their followers: (p. 231)
   a.   have a complex exchange relationship.
   b.   are often very similar to each other.
   c.   tend to be distant from each other.
   d.   share an intense emotional bond.*

7. What do Michael Saylor of Micro Strategy and Howard Charney of Grand Junction Networks, have in common? (p. 231)
   a.   They both facilitate more than direct
   b.   They are both charismatic
   c.   They both have abused their charisma
   d.   They are both task-focused*

8. Which one of the following is not one of the characteristics of charismatic leaders? (p. 231)
    a.   High self-confidence
    b.   Strong conviction about ideas
    c.   High energy and enthusiasm
    d.   High task focus*

9. Mahatma Gandhi and Martin Luther King are both examples of charisma leaders. They both demonstrated: (p. 231)
    a.   little self-doubt about their direction and action.*
    b.   the ability to allow followers to participate in decision making.
    c.   the ability to organize tasks.
    d.   excellent delegation skills.

10. The charismatic leader's _____ motivates followers and creates a self-fulfilling prophecy. (p. 231)
    a.   communication skills
    b.   task focus
    c.   high level of energy
    d.   high self-confidence*

11. The charismatic leader's _____ helps defines and frame their vision and the mission of the group and the organization. (p. 231)
    a.   communication skills*
    b.   task focus
    c.   high level of energy
    d.   high self-confidence

12. Nelson Mandella, Mahatma Gandhi, and Aung San Suu Kyi were all imprisoned for their beliefs. Their imprisonment is an example of how charismatic leaders: (p. 232)
    a.   express themselves.
    b.   show their commitment.
    c.   are role models.*
    d.   they believe in what they do.

13. Hatin Tyabji of VeriFone Inc., considers _____ to be the first principle of leadership. (p. 233)
    a.   charisma
    b.   enthusiasm
    c.   passion
    d.   authenticity*

14. Dan Cathy, president and COO of Chick-fill-A is passionate about customer service. He tells his customers that he works in customer service. Cathy's behavior is an example of how charismatic leaders: (p. 233)
    a.   express themselves.
    b.   show their commitment.
    c.   are role models.*
    d.   believe in what they do.

15. John F. Kennedy carefully built the myth of Camelot around his family. Steve Case, the founder of American Online, lunches on turkey sandwiches and Sun Chips. These are examples of how charismatic leaders: (p. 233)
    a.   communicate.
    b.   show their passion.
    c.   express their confidence.
    d.   manage their image.*

16. Researchers suggest that by offering an appealing vision of the future charismatic leaders are able to: (p. 233)
   a.   impress their followers.
   b.   change how followers perceive what needs to be done.*
   c.   convince followers that.
   d.   recruit good followers.

17. Followers will only follow a charismatic leader if: (p. 234)
   a.   they believe change is needed.*
   b.   they are motivated.
   c.   they have clear rewards waiting for them.
   d.   they are confident.

18. As leaders perform well and demonstrate competence and loyalty to the group, and develop a bond with followers, they are allowed to move the group in new directions. This process is called: (p. 234)
   a.   transformational leadership.
   b.   charismatic leadership.
   c.   idiosyncracy credit.*
   d.   conformity and deviance.

19. Charismatic leaders are more likely to emerge: (p. 234)
   a.   in collectivistic culture.
   b.   in formal organizations.
   c.   when followers are loyal.
   d.   in times of crisis.*

20. When there is a perceived need for change, charismatic leaders are often successful by: (p. 235)
   a.   using fear to motivate their followers.
   b.   articulating a new vision.*
   c.   establishing clear rewards.
   d.   promoting cooperation.

21. The internal organizational conditions that facilitate the emergence of charismatic leadership include all but one of the following: (p. 235)
   a.   early or late stages of the organizational life cycle.
   b.   complex and ambiguous tasks.
   c.   flexible and organic structures.
   d.   ascriptive cultures.*

22. _____ are ideal situations for the emergence of charismatic leadership. (p. 236)
   a.   Well-established organizations
   b.   Complex and ambiguous tasks.*
   c.   Eiffel tower cultures.
   d.   Ascriptive cultures.

23. In which type of cultures are charismatic leaders more likely to emerge? (p. 236)
   a.   In horizontal collectivistic cultures that are egalitarian.
   b.   In high power distance cultures where followers are used to strong leadership.
   c.   In cultures that have a tradition of prophetic salvation.*
   d.   In cultures that are more emotional and value interpersonal relationships.

24. In Confucian cultures such as Japan and China, charismatic leaders emerge based on: (p. 236)
    a.   an intense emotional bond with followers.
    b.   religious fervor.
    c.   assertiveness and direct communication.
    d.   image of competence and moral courage.*

25. Communication with followers is universally valued as a positive leadership characteristic.
However, in _____ leaders are effective when they communicate non-aggressively and softly,
while in _____ effective leaders are bold and assertive. (p. 237)
    a.   China/India*
    b.   Mexico/U.S.
    c.   Iran/Brazil
    d.   Vietnam/Cambodia

26. Although _____ is an important component of leadership in the U.S., it is generally not
valued in many other cultures. (p. 237)
    a.   team building
    b.   risk-taking*
    c.   decisiveness
    d.   intelligence

27. Charismatic leadership has the potential for abuse because: (p. 237)
    a.   charismatic leaders are often unethical.
    b.   power tends to corrupt leaders.
    c.   of the emotional bond with followers.*
    d.   follower are often weak.

28. The primary difference between ethical and unethical charismatic leaders is that: (p. 237)
    a.   unethical charismatic leaders abuse their followers.
    b.   unethical charismatic leaders focus on their own goals.*
    c.   unethical charismatic leaders do not provide a vision.
    d.   Unethical charismatic leaders set unrealistic goals.

29. Based on research by Howell, unethical charismatic leaders are also called _____, while
ethical charismatic leaders are also called _____. (p. 238)
    a.   devious/direct
    b.   ineffective/effective
    c.   immoral/moral
    d.   personalized/socialized*

30. Which of the following is not one of the potential liabilities of charismatic leaders? (p. 238)
    a.   They often fail to manage details
    b.   They don't develop their successors.
    c.   They fail to reach their goals.*
    d.   They creative disruptive in-group and out-groups.

31. Research on charismatic leadership indicates that: (p. 238)
    a.   it has the potential for both negative and positive impact on an organization.*
    b.   it tends to address many of the problems today's organizations face.
    c.   it is a good training tool for leadership.
    d.   it is appropriate in Western cultures as the primary leadership tool to improve
           organizational performance.

32. Katherine DeCelles and Michael Pfarrer's research about the link between charisma and corporate corruption suggests that: (p. 239)
   a.   external pressure for performance leads to corruption regardless of charisma.
   b.   charismatic leaders are better able to convince followers to behave unethically.*
   c.   environmental uncertainty forces leaders to set clear rules of behavior which prevent power abuse.
   d.   external pressures and uncertainty reduces the followers' reliance on the leader and makes it difficult for the leader to implement anything.

33. Research on charismatic leadership indicates that: (p. 239)
   a.   it is difficult the measure
   b.   it does not have a lot of reliability
   c.   it is a power and undeniable part of leadership in Western cultures*
   d.   it does not apply to non-Western cultures

34. Transformational leadership address which of the following questions? (p. 240)
   a.   Who is a better leader?
   b.   How do leaders use their resources ethically?
   c.   What roles do followers play in transforming the leader?
   d.   How do leaders create and sustain change?*

35. _____ and _____ are both different types of transactional leadership. (p. 240)
   a.   Follower maturity/power
   b.   Individualized attention/charisma
   c.   Contingent reward/management by exception*
   d.   Intellectual stimulation/inspiration

36. The contingency models such as Fiedler's, the Normative Decision, or Path-Goal all focus on _____. (p. 240)
   a.   how leaders use their resources
   b.   the transaction between leaders and followers*
   c.   the relationship between leaders and followers
   d.   the role followers play in leadership effectiveness

37. While the contingency models are effective and can help leaders become more effective, they fail to explain: (p. 240)
   a.   why leaders fail
   b.   how to train leaders
   c.   how to create change*
   d.   why followers lose motivation

38. The concept of contingency reward is part of which theory of leadership? (p. 240)
   a.   Contingency Model
   b.   Normative Decision
   c.   Substitutes for leadership
   d.   Transactional leadership*

39. The case of the Rocky Flats nuclear site in Colorado provides an example of successful use of _____. Employees were given specific performance goals and generous rewards when they reach those goals. (p. 241)
   a.   contingent reward*
   b.   leader member exchange
   c.   leader authoritarian decision making
   d.   management by exception

40. Management by exception (MBE) involves: (p. 241)
   a.   little interaction between leaders and followers, except when things go wrong.*
   b.   the leader leaving followers alone and empowering employee to make decisions.
   c.   providing direction only in challenging situations rather on a routine basis.
   d.   managing exceptional followers only.

41. Contingent reward can have positive impact on followers and performance; however, _____ often leads to frustration and dissatisfaction. (p. 241)
   a.   transactional leadership
   b.   management by exception*
   c.   the leader's task focus
   d.   transformational leadership

42. Transformational leadership concepts were proposed: (p. 241)
   a.   to implement Japanese management methods in Western countries.
   b.   to address the need to revitalize organizations.*
   c.   as a replacement for transactional leadership theories.
   d.   to address the challenges of cultural differences.

43. How many factors are part of transformational leadership? (p. 242)
   a.   Two
   b.   Three*
   c.   Four
   d.   Five

44. Transformational leadership factors include all <u>but one</u> of the following. (p. 242)
   a.   Charisma and inspiration
   b.   Intellectual stimulation
   c.   Individual consideration
   d.   Internal clarification*

45. The _____ factor of transformational leadership develops followers trust, overcomes their resistance to change and makes it possible for them to consider and undertake change. (p. 242)
   a.   Charisma and inspiration*
   b.   Intellectual stimulation
   c.   Individual consideration
   d.   Internal clarification

46. The _____ factor of transformational leadership empowers followers and challenges them to come up with novel solutions. (p. 242)
   a.   Charisma and inspiration
   b.   Intellectual stimulation*
   c.   Individual consideration
   d.   Internal clarification

47. The _____ factor of transformational leadership motivates followers and encourages to perform better. (p. 243)
   a.   charisma and inspiration
   b.   intellectual stimulation
   c.   individual consideration*
   d.   internal clarification

48. Transformational leadership behaviors address which of the elements of the definition of leadership? (p. 243)
   a. External adaptation*
   b. Internal functioning
   c. Follower satisfaction
   d. Goal achievement

49. Additional research is needed to further develop the transformational leadership theory. Areas that need particular attention include all the following except: (p. 243)
   a. in the measurement of transformational leadership behaviors.
   b. regarding how to teach leaders the various transformational behaviors.
   c. the relationship of transformational leadership to other personality traits.
   d. the basic propositions of the model.*

50. Antonio has been through a training to become a transformational leader. He has learned to provide a vision and project confidence. Based on that training, what else should he do? (p. 244)
   a. Create clear reporting structures.
   b. Motivate employees using rewards and punishment.
   c. Treat everyone equally and fairly.
   d. Establish a personal relationship with followers.*

51. Sir Richard Branson, founder of the Virgin Group believes that _____ is at the heart of good leadership. (p. 245)
   a. controlling operations
   b. establishing a clear vision and communicating well
   c. encouraging people and hearing their input*
   d. assuring succession for his company

52. To be effective, change-oriented and visionary leaders must: (p. 246)
   a. develop teamwork and shared responsibility.*
   b. make sure that followers follower the leader's vision.
   c. set a clear course and stick with it.
   d. delegate tasks rather than empower followers.

53. Researcher Noel Tichy recommends that leaders communicate their vision through story telling. He suggests that leaders need to develop three types of stories about:
   a. their own background, their values, their goals.
   b. who they are, who the group is, and where the group is going.*
   c. the history of the organization, the nature of the competition, and the goal.
   d. the culture of the group, the nature of the industry, their vision.

54. Kouzes and Posner believe that all but one of the following are essential in motivating and inspiring followers. (p. 246)
   a. setting clear standards
   b. being around followers
   c. telling stories
   d. getting followers to adopt the leader's vision*

55. Which one of the following is not an element of a clear vision? (p. 246)
   a. Clear and understandable
   b. Easy to achieve*
   c. Idealistic
   d. Appeals to emotions

56. Amy has just finished reading Kouzes and Posner's book on what followers what and has learned about the practices of exemplary leaders. Based on those researchers' ideas, which of the following is Amy likely to focus on: (p. 246)
- a. challenging existing ideas and encouraging followers to experiment.*
- b. overcoming resistance to change and stimulating followers intellectually.
- c. cultivating dramatic symbols and developing obedience and loyalty.
- d. express high self-confidence and build her image.

57. Researchers Kouzes and Posner propose that in order to truly motivate followers must do all <u>but</u> <u>one</u> of the following: (p. 246)
- a. expect the best from followers.
- b. personalize recognition of followers.
- c. keep rules and standards fuzzy.*
- d. celebrate success together and often.

58. Practices of exemplary leadership include: (p. 247)
- a. holding information as to not confuse followers
- b. creating a shared vision*
- c. assuring that past practices stay in place to provide a sense of continuity
- d. encouraging competition to motivate followers

59. _____ is the major contribution of change-oriented and visionary leadership approaches. (p. 248)
- a. They are well researched
- b. They provide easy ways to measure effectiveness
- c. They apply well across cultures
- d. They address interesting and visible aspects of leadership*

60. The primary shortcoming of the change-oriented and visionary leadership approaches is that: (p. 248)
- a. they seem to suggest one best way to lead*
- b. they are hard to understand
- c. they have little practical value
- d. they apply only to Western cultures

61. Andrea Jung's success at Avon can be mostly attributed to: (p. 256-257)
- a. her financial expertise
- b. her enthusiasm and focus on people*
- c. her negotiation skills
- d. her credibility

62. Andrea Jung's had to overcome some of cultural background and learned to be: (p. 256-257)
- a. tougher in the corporate world*
- b. more focused on people
- c. a better negotiator
- d. upbeat and positive

<u>True/False Questions</u>

63. The concept of charisma was first proposed by Max Weber. (p. 230)
- a. true*
- b. false

64. Charismatic leadership theories are closely related to contingency models of leadership. (p. 230)
   a.   true
   b.   false*

65. The research on charismatic leadership has revived the interest in leadership. (p. 230)
   a.   true*
   b.   false

66. Although charismatic leadership theories have revived the interest in leadership, they do not have much to add to the contingency views of leadership. (p. 230)
   a.   true
   b.   false*

67. Charismatic and transformational leadership highlight the importance of middle level managers. (p. 230)
   a.   true
   b.   false*

68. Charismatic leaders have a strong emotional effect on their followers. (p. 230)
   a.   true*
   b.   false

69. Charisma in Greek means, special leader (p. 230)
   a.   true
   b.   false*

70. The leader's personality and traits are the only necessary elements of charismatic leadership. (p. 231)
   a.   true
   b.   false*

71. Steve Case, founder of America Online shows the high self-confidence typical of charismatic leaders. (p. 231)
   a.   true*
   b.   false

72. Charismatic leaders often manage the impression they make by manipulating symbols. (p. 232)
   a.   true*
   b.   false

73. Gandhi and Nelson Mandella's imprisonment are example of how charismatic leaders role model the behaviors they expect of their followers. (p. 232)
   a.   true*
   b.   false

74. Publicly admitting self-doubt is one factor that endears charismatic leaders with their followers. (p. 232)
   a.   true
   b.   false*

75. Followers are as critical as the leaders in creating charismatic leadership. (p. 234)
   a.   true*
   b.   false

76. Because followers of charismatic leaders are loyal to their leader, they do not have high performance expectations. (p. 234)
   a.   true
   b.   false*

77. Charismatic leaders are given credit that they use to deviate from the group norm and move the group to a new direction. (p. 234)
   a.   true*
   b.   false

78. Charismatic leadership is more likely to happen in times of crisis. (p. 234)
   a.   true*
   b.   false

79. Charismatic leaders often achieve their status without being formally designated. (p. 235)
   a.   true*
   b.   false

80. Charismatic leadership is more likely to emerge when an organization is stable and in need of change. (p. 235)
   a.   true
   b.   false*

81. Charismatic leaders emerge in situations where rewards can be clearly tied to performance. (p. 235)
   a.   true
   b.   false*

82. Cultures within the Judeo-Christian tradition with beliefs in a savior make the emergence of charismatic leadership more likely. (p. 236)
   a.   true*
   b.   false

83. Because of its culture, China has seen the rise of may charismatic leaders. (p. 236)
   a.   true
   b.   false*

84. Although GLOBE researchers have found that although charismatic leadership exists in most cultures, the term has different meanings in different cultures.
   a.   true*
   b.   false

85. GLOBE studies indicate that enthusiasm is a universal aspect of leadership. (p. 237)
   a.   true
   b.   false*

86. Some cultures tolerate and even value ruthlessness in leaders. (p. 237)
   a.   true
   b.   false*

87. Integrity and trustworthiness are universally valued traits in leaders. (p. 237)
   a.   true*
   b.   false

88. According to GLOBE research findings, a leader's ability to clearly, directly and assertively communicate his or her vision is valued in most cultures. (p. 237)
    a.   true
    b.   false*

89. Unethical charismatic leaders focus on their personal goals rather than on organizational goals. (p. 237)
    a.   true*
    b.   false

90. Personalized charismatic leaders work for the personal welfare of their followers. (p. 238)
    a.   true
    b.   false*

91. Charismatic leadership has become a central concept in much of recent leadership theory. (p. 238)
    a.   true*
    b.   false

92. Charismatic leadership is essential for organizational effectiveness and success. (p. 238)
    a.   true
    b.   false*

93. DeCelles and Pfarrer have found that environmental factors rather than charisma are a factor in corporate corruption. (p. 239)
    a.   true
    b.   false*

94. Researchers have found ways to train leaders to become charismatic. (p. 240)
    a.   true
    b.   false*

95. Charismatic leadership is one of the elements of transactional leadership. (p. 240)
    a.   true
    b.   false*

96. Transactional leadership theories explain how leaders and followers agree to reach goals. (p. 240)
    a.   true*
    b.   false

97. The use of contingent reward is a part of most leadership theories. (p. 240)
    a.   true*
    b.   false

98. All leaders should be trained to use contingent reward and apply it to managing their followers. (p. 240-241)
    a.   true*
    b.   false

99. Management by exception is an effective method of managing professional employees. (p. 241)
    a.   true
    b.   false*

100. In both laissez faire and Management by Exception, the leader only interacts with followers to correct or punish. (p. 241)
   a.   true*
   b.   false

101. Transformational leadership concepts were proposed to address the need to revitalize organizations. (p. 241)
   a.   true*
   b.   false

102. Intellectual stimulation allows the leader to encourage followers to pursue new ideas. (p. 242)
   a.   true*
   b.   false

103. Individual consideration is what motivates followers to carry through major changes in organizations. (p. 242)
   a.   true*
   b.   false

104. Charisma and inspiration encourage followers to come up with new ideas. (p. 242)
   a.   true
   b.   false*

105. Intellectual stimulation, charisma, and individual consideration are all necessary components of transformational leadership. (p. 243)
   a.   true*
   b.   false

106. Transactional leadership behaviors allow for external adaptability while transformational leadership behaviors maintain internal health. (p. 24)
   a.   true
   b.   false*

107. Transformational leadership concepts are extensively researched and tested. (p. 243)
   a.   true*
   b.   false

108. Some research suggests that individualistic cultures may be more receptive to transformational leadership than collectivistic cultures. (p. 243)
   a.   true
   b.   false*

109. Transformational leadership tends to be inaccurately proposed as a cure-all to organizational problems. (p. 243)
   a.   true*
   b.   false

110. Transformational leadership has as much potential for abuse as charismatic leadership. (p. 244)
   a.   true
   b.   false*

111. Transformational leaders typically set high expectations and create a supportive environment. (p. 244)
   a.   true*
   b.   false

112. Leaders who want to implement transformation leadership concepts in their organizations must provide a vision and establish personal relationships with followers. (p. 244)
   a.   true*
   b.   false

113. Two of the key themes that ties together several change oriented theories is the importance of vision and empowerment. (p. 245)
   a.   true*
   b.   false

114. Sir Richard Branson, CEO of the Virgin group has been successful by using many of the negative aspects of transformational leadership (p. 245)
   a.   true
   b.   false*

115. Researcher Noel Tichy recommends that leaders communicate their vision through telling three types of stories about themselves, the group, and the group's direction. (p. 246)
   a.   true*
   b.   false

116. Exemplary and visionary leaders need to commit themselves to one idea and stick with that. (p. 246)
   a.   true
   b.   false*

117. Rob Waldron was successful as CEO of Jumpstart by developing his own vision and assuring that followers adopted that vision. (p. 247)
   a.   true
   b.   false*

118. Practices of exemplary leadership include creating a shared vision and role modeling. (p. 247)
   a.   true*
   b.   false

119. Change-oriented and visionary leadership concepts have received considerable research support. (p. 248)
   a.   true
   b.   false*

120. One of the major weaknesses of visionary leadership is their lack of inclusion of contingency factors. (p. 248)
   a.   true*
   b.   false

121. One of the major contributions of visionary leadership concepts is the emphasis on passion and credibility. (p. 248)
   a.   true*
   b.   false

122. Andrea Jung follows a long string of strong female leaders who have led Avon. (p. 256-257)
   a.   true
   b.   false*

123. Two of Andrea Jung's distinguishing characteristics are her passion for her business and her focus on people. (p. 256-257)
    a.   true*
    b.   false

CHAPTER 9

<u>Multiple Choice Questions</u>

1. The difference between micro and macro level leadership is in the _____ and _____.
(p. 259-260)
    a.   definition/process
    b.   level/scope*
    c.   type/focus
    d.   performance level/definition

2. In micro leadership, the leader focuses on _____ factors, while macro leaders focus on
_____ issues. (p. 259-260)
    a.   internal/external*
    b.   people/task
    c.   financial/performance
    d.   teams/departments

3. Which of the following is <u>not</u> considered to be part of the upper echelon leadership of an
organization? (p. 259)
    a.   president
    b.   chief operating officers
    c.   top management team
    d.   top department leader*

4. The job of upper echelon leaders requires an equal focus on: (p. 260)
    a.   internal/external*
    b.   people/task
    c.   financial/performance
    d.   teams/departments

5. How many strategic forces are the domain of strategic leadership? (p. 261)
    a.   two
    b.   four
    c.   six*
    d.   eight

6. Which one of the following is <u>not</u> of the strategic forces that impact organizations? (p. 261)
    a.   culture
    b.   environment
    c.   technology
    d.   management*

7. Structure is best defined as: (p. 261)
    a.   the way human resources are organized.*
    b.   the process by which inputs are transformed into outputs.
    c.   common set of beliefs.
    d.   the internal factors that affect an organization.

8. The Jagged Edge Mountain Gear company provides an example of: (p. 262)
    a.   the role of strategic planning.
    b.   the key role of the CEO.
    c.   the importance of the fit among strategic factors.*
    d.   the link between upper level leadership and strategy.

9. The essence of strategic leadership and management is: (p. 262)
    a.   managing people and the task at the same time.
    b.   the simultaneous management of all strategic forces.*
    c.   providing a motivating vision to everyone.
    d.   dealing with internal and external uncertainty.

10. The primary role of strategic leaders is to _____. (p. 262)
    a.   provide a vision/ and find resources.
    b.   set goals and find financial resources.
    c.   manage the external stakeholders and keep them informed.
    d.   formulate and implement strategy.*

11. When do upper echelon leaders have a primary responsibility to formulate strategy for an organization? (p. 262)
    a.   When an organization is looking for strategic redirection.*
    b.   When a successful strategy is in place.
    c.   When the environment is uncertain.
    d.   When stakeholders have power to make decisions that impact the organization.

12. Anne Mulcahy of Xerox has been able to run Xerox around by: (p. 263)
    a.   leading by example.*
    b.   focusing on employees.
    c.   by managing the environment.
    d.   picking the right managers to be around her.

13. Two general sets of factors moderate the power and discretion of executives. These include: (p. 263-264)
    a.   employees and other managers.
    b.   environmental factors and stakeholders.
    c.   external factors and organizational factors.*
    d.   leadership factors and market issues.

14. Anthony has just become the CEO of a company that has been around for over 100 years and has been steadily declining. As Anthony takes on his new job, he finds that he has considerable power and influence to make decisions and implement them. Anthony's discretion is an example of: (p. 263-264)
    a.   the typical powers of CEOs
    b.   the increase of CEO discretion in times of crisis.*
    c.   how older companies still have traditional power structures.
    d.   the effectiveness of the fit between CEO characteristics and organizational factors.

15. In successful companies, the well established culture and procedures often _____. (p. 265)
    a.   reduce the impact of teams
    b.   provide increased discretion to the leader
    c.   increase the power of the leader
    d.   act as substitutes for the CEO*

16. A sense of crisis sets the stage for: (p. 265)
    a.   poor performance.
    b.   emergence of charismatic CEOs.*
    c.   a decrease in CEO discretion.
    b.   stakeholders to exercise more power.

17. The _____ the organization, the _____ the power and discretion of its top leader. (p. 265)
   a.   more complex/less
   b.   diverse/more
   c.   smaller/more*
   d.   uncertain/less

18. As organizations grow and mature, the leader's influence is often replaced with: (p. 265)
   a.   the influence of teams.
   b.   the power of middle management.
   c.   the presence of a strong culture.*
   d.   individual decision making.

19. Mickey Drexler, former CEO of the Gap, had considerable power and discretion while he was with the company because: (p. 266)
   a.   he is an effective CEO.
   b.   he was well liked by his employees.
   c.   the company board of directors was weak and ineffective.
   d.   the company was new and in need of revival.*

20. The _____, the less the power and discretion of the CEO. (p. 266)
   a.   less uncertainty in the environment
   b.   stronger the TMT*
   c.   younger the organization
   d.   more cohesive the organization

21. The cases of Carl Vogel, former CEO of Charter Communication, and Carly Fiorina, former CEO of HP, are examples of: (p. 266)
   a.   the role culture in CEOs' behavior and decisions.
   b.   the impact of a powerful board of directors.*
   c.   the negative effect of a poor economy on CEO performance.
   d.   the negative impact of arrogance on CEOs

22. As a general rule, the power and discretion of the CEO increase when: (p. 266)
   a.   the TMT members are similar to the leader.*
   b.   the CEO has considerable international experience.
   c.   the company goes public
   d.   a board of director is put in place to help the CEO

23. Researchers Yan Zhang and Nandini Rajagopalan found that when it comes to top management succession: (p. 267)
   a.   most CEOs need little training when they come from another company with similar products or services.
   b.   selecting internal candidates to be CEO is associated with better performance when the organization is unstable.*
   c.   selecting outside well-know leaders provides the organization with a better chance of survival in times of crisis.
   d.   organizations are better off with an outside new CEO when they want to change direction.

24. The XYZ organization is headed by the 60 year old Roger Smith who has been with the company for 25 years and CEO for the past 5 years. XYZ has performed well under his leadership. Based on research about upper echelon leaders, which of the following is most likely to happen? (p. 267)

    a.   Roger will continue performing well by changing course as the need for change arises.

    b.   Roger's performance is likely to go down, since most CEOs are not effective beyond 5 years.

    c.   Roger is likely to engage in international venture because most people in his generation have international experience.

    d.   Rogers is likely to lead XYZ the same way he has been for the past 5 years, without making major changes.*

25. Which of the following personality characteristics have been found to affect CEOs' decision making and strategic choices? (p. 268)

    a.   Big Five

    b.   Machiavellian scale

    c.   MBTI*

    d.   Fiedler's LPC

26. There are two common themes among all the individual characteristics that affect how CEOs make strategic choices. These are: (p. 268)

    a.   individualism and collectivism.

    b.   Type A and MBTI.

    c.   challenge seeking and need for control.*

    d.   external orientation and degree of self-focus.

27. Entrepreneurship, openness to change, transformational leadership, and futuricity are all part of which characteristic of upper echelon leaders? (p. 268)

    a.   external orientation

    b.   individualism

    c.   challenge seeking*

    d.   risk-taking

28. How open a leader is to change and how willing he/she is to take risks is most important and relevant: (p. 268)

    a.   in small organizations.

    b.   during the formulation of strategy.*

    c.   in times of crisis when high-risk decisions often pay off.

    d.   in certain environment.

29. Tolerance for diversity, extent of centralization, degree of employee participation, and organicity are all part of which characteristic of upper echelon leaders? (p. 269)

    a.   internal orientation

    b.   collectivism

    c.   need for control*

    d.   risk-aversion

30. The CEO of the WC organization, Anna Lopez, has created a decentralized organization, encourages participation and diversity of opinion, and has put in place few uniform policies and procedures. Based on this information, Anna is most likely: (p. 269)

    a.   an internally focused CEO

    b.   a collectivist leader

    c.   a CEO with low need for control*

    d.   a leader who likes risk-taking

31. Mickey Drexler, former CEO of the Gap, and Carly Fiorina, former CEO of HP are both examples of:
     a.   arrogant leaders who can't work with others. (p. 269)
     b.   creative CEOs who are open to change.
     c.   CEOs of large companies that failed because of their leadership.
     d.   CEOs who have a high need for control.*

32. Zhen does not like change much and empowers his employees to make their own decisions. Which strategic leadership type is he? (p. 270-271)
     a.   High-control innovator
     b.   Participative innovator
     c.   Status quo guardian
     d.   Process manager*

33. Maleeni enjoys new situations and likes taking risks and believes that leaders should delegate decision making to the lowest possible level. Which strategic leadership type is she? (p. 270-271)
     a.   High-control innovator
     b.   Participative innovator*
     c.   Status quo guardian
     d.   Process manager

34. Stephen has always enjoyed new challenges and feels most comfortable when he has a tight control of his employees. Which strategic leadership type is he? (p. 270-271)
     a.   High-control innovator*
     b.   Participative innovator
     c.   Status quo guardian
     d.   Product manager

35. Ashley is most comfortable when she is fully in charge of her group and likes to keep things as they are. Which strategic leadership type is she? (p. 270-271)
     a.   High-control innovator
     b.   Participative innovator
     c.   Status quo guardian*
     d.   Process manager

36. Mickey Drexler of J. Crew is an example of a (p. 271)
     a.   High-control innovator*
     b.   Participative innovator
     c.   Status quo guardian
     d.   Process manager

37. Janie and Victor Tsao, founders of Linksys, are examples of: (p. 271)
     a.   High-control innovator
     b.   Participative innovator
     c.   Status quo guardian*
     d.   Process manager

38. Which one of the strategic leaders implements the latest high-technology innovations in his/her organization, builds a strong dominant culture, and hires managers who are similar to him/her? (p. 272)
     a.   High-control innovator*
     b.   Participative innovator
     c.   Status quo guardian
     d.   Process manager

39. Which one of the strategic leaders tries to protect the organization from the impact of outside forces, encourages a fluid culture, and emphasizes efficiency? (p. 272)
- a. High-control innovator
- b. Participative innovator
- c. Status quo guardian
- d. Process manager*

40. Which one of the strategic leaders will focus on efficiency and protecting the organization from change and build a centralized and homogeneous organization? (p. 272)
- a. High-control innovator
- b. Participative innovator
- c. Status quo guardian*
- d. Process manager

41. Which of the strategic leaders will open his/her organization to the outside, engage in high risk strategies, and empower employees to make decisions? (p. 272)
- a. High-control innovator
- b. Participative innovator*
- c. Status quo guardian
- d. Process manager

42. Jon Brock, CEO of InBev, represents which type of strategic leader? (p. 273)
- a. High-control innovator
- b. Participative innovator
- c. Status quo guardian
- d. Process manager*

43. Ricardo Semler, CEO of Semco, is an example of which type of strategic leader? (p. 273)
- a. High-control innovator
- b. Participative innovator*
- c. Status quo guardian
- d. Process manager

44. Culturally endorsed leadership theories (CLTs) were proposed by _____. (p. 275)
- a. GLOBE researchers*
- b. Hofstede
- c. Trompenaars
- d. Hall

45. According the culturally endorsed leadership theories, which cultures most value leaders who are inspirational and provide a vision? (p. 275)
- a. Middle Easterners and Southern Europeans
- b. Latin Americans and Nordic Europeans*
- c. Eastern Asians and Africans
- d. Southwestern Asians and Germans

46. As a manager who practices participation and empower, your style of leadership is likely to be most appreciated by: (p. 275)
- a. Eastern Europeans
- b. Middle Easterners
- c. Nordic Europeans*
- d. Asians

47. Which of the following terms best represent the typical characteristics of French upper management, or "cadre"? (p. 275)
   a.   Participative, creative, and highly technical
   b.   Stubbornness, control, and practical application
   c.   Empowerment, focus on efficiency, flexible
   d.   Intellectual brilliance, excellent communication and analytical skills*

48. The common thread among many female executives is: (p. 276)
   a.   the fear of failure
   b.   employee empowerment*
   c.   lack of international experience
   d.   strong financial skills

49. Which of the following is <u>not</u> one of the processes leaders use to influence their organization. (p. 276-277)
   a.   direct decisions
   b.   laissez-faire*
   c.   selection of other leaders
   d.   role modeling

50. Jeff Bezos, CEO of Amazon.com, decided to focus his organization on staying on top of technological developments. This is an example of how CEOs affect their organization through: (p. 277)
   a.   allocation of resources*
   b.   selection of other leaders
   c.   role modeling
   d.   technology management

51. Ming Tsao rarely openly comments on or criticizes his managers and employees' actions. Instead, he carefully selects those he believes have potential, invites them to attend meetings and social events, and allows them to spend more time with him. Ming's behavior is an example of which processes by which upper echelon leaders influence their organization? (p. 277)
   a.   direct decisions
   b.   role modeling
   c.   informal reward system*
   d.   promotions

52. In the examples provided in your book, Feargal Quinn, the CEO of the Irish supermarket chain Superquinn, Stan Shih, CEO of Acer, and Bob Moffat, head of IBM's personal computers all rely on _____ to influence their employees and organizations. (p. 278)
   a.   direct decisions
   b.   role modeling*
   c.   informal reward system
   d.   promotions

53. In 2003, the average executive compensation package for large U.S. companies was: (p. 279)
   a.   under $2 million
   b.   between $2 and 5 million
   c.   between $5 and 7 million
   d.   over $7 million*

54. Since 1995, the average executive salary has close to doubled while the salary of other white and blue collar workers has increased: (p. 279)
    a.   less than 5%*
    b.   between 5% and 10%
    c.   between 10 and 15%
    d.   close to 20%

55. What do Michael Eisner of Disney, Christopher Galvin of Motorola, and Peter Karmanors of Compuware have in common? (p. 279)
    a.   They are all CEOs of profitable companies.
    b.   They all got considerable pay increases while their company performed poorly.*
    c.   They all have been accused of ethical violations regarding corporate governance.
    d.   They were all fired for poor performance.

56. Which of the following is not a factor in determining a CEO's compensation? (p. 280)
    a.   Company size
    b.   Competition within the industry
    c.   Internationalization
    d.   Company performance*

57. One argument in support of the high executive packages is that: (p. 280)
    a.   higher pay leads to higher performance
    b.   the high salaries are needed to prevent CEOs from abusing their power
    c.   CEO jobs are demanding and unstable*
    d.   U.S. CEOs are among the best in the world

58. Prior to the late 2000, Procter and Gamble had a reputation for: (p. 291-292)
    a.   encouraging employee creativity and non-conformity.
    b.   providing clear guidelines for everything employees did.*
    c.   poor products and low innovation.
    d.   external promotions that discouraged long time employees.

59. A.G. Lafley, current CEO of Procter and Gamble, is credited with the company's revival and high performance. Lafley's style is best described as: (p. 291-292)
    a.   quiet and determined team builder.*
    b.   energetic and loud change master.
    c.   inspirational and charismatic.
    d.   focus on financial performance.

60. How does Lafley regard power? (p. 291-292)
    a.   Power is not necessary for performance.
    b.   Power must be shared with all employees.
    c.   Building a power based starts with expertise and must be backed-up with force if necessary.
    d.   Power is determined by influence rather than control.*

True/False Questions

61. CEOs have considerable impact on the direction and strategy of organizations. (p. 259)
    a.   true*
    b.   false

62. The definition of leadership is different at different levels of leadership. (p. 259)
    a.   true
    b.   false*

63. The difference between micro and macro leadership is in the nature of the process. (p. 259-260)
    a.   true
    b.   false*

64. There is usually one person who is the top leader of an organization. (p. 259)
    a.   true
    b.   false*

65. Dealing with external constituents is central to the function of upper echelon leaders. (p. 260)
    a.   true*
    b.   false

66. Both micro and macro leaders are effective when they reach their goal. (p. 260)
    a.   true*
    b.   false

67. There are four strategic forces that are the domain of strategic management (p. 261)
    a.   true
    b.   false*

68. The environment is the most important of the strategic force. (p. 261)
    a.   true
    b.   false*

69. Technology is the process by which inputs are transformed into outputs. (p. 261)
    a.   true*
    b.   false

70. The environment is made up of all the factors outside an organization that have the potential to affect it. (p. 261)
    a.   true*
    b.   false

71. The structure of an organization refers to how leadership is organized. (p. 261)
    a.   true
    b.   false*

72. Strategic leaders must balance the various strategic forces and create a fit among them. (p. 262)
    a.   true*
    b.   false

73. The Jagged Edge Mountain Gear company provides an example of a company where strategic forces are not in balance and do not fit one another. (p. 262)
    a.   true
    b.   false*

74. Upper echelon leaders often formulate, but do not implement strategy. (p. 262)
    a.   true
    b.   false*

75. Upper echelon leaders often have unlimited power and influence in all aspects of decision making in their organization.   (p. 262)
    a.   true
    b.   false*

76. Anne Mulcahy was able to turnaround Xerox through role modeling hard work and determination. (p 263).
   a.   true*
   b.   false

77. The leader's role becomes more prominent when an organization faces an uncertain environment. (p. 263-264)
   a.   true*
   b.   false

78. Because mergers often create a sense of crisis and lead to internal chaos, employees rely less on their leaders. (p. 263-264)
   a.   true
   b.   false*

79. CEOs of very large organizations have considerable more impact on their organization. (p. 265)
   a.   true
   b.   false*

80. CEOs often have stronger impact in young organizations. (p. 265)
   a.   true*
   b.   false

81. Carly Fiorina, former CEO of Hewlett-Packard had considerable power and influence because her organization was very successful. (p. 265)
   a.   true
   b.   false*

82. Oprah Winfrey's strong influence over her company is an example of the impact of founders in young organizations. (p. 266)
   a.   true*
   b.   false

83. Powerful boards or TMTs are often needed to provide balance to the growing power of CEOs. (p. 266)
   a.   true*
   b.   false

84. The task-relationship dimensions used in micro level leadership have strong applications to upper level leadership. (p. 266)
   a.   true
   b.   false*

85. Research indicates that CEOs who have external locus of control tend to be more externally oriented and more innovative in their strategic choices. (p. 267)
   a.   true
   b.   false*

86. CEOs who are risk-takers and open to change perform better than those who are not. (p. 268)
   a.   true
   b.   false*

87. CEOs who encourage diverse opinions and put in place few rules often perform better than those who tightly control their organization. (p. 268)
   a.   true
   b.   false*

88. Designer David Rockwell is an example of a challenge seeker. (p. 269)
   a.   true*
   b.   false

89. CEOs who control their organization tightly are often successful in implementing various projects such as increasing diversity. (p. 269)
   a.   true*
   b.   false

90. Mickey Drexler of J.Crew and A.G. Lafley of P&G both are high control leaders. (p. 269)
   a.   true
   b.   false*

91. A high-control innovator has a high need for control and seeks challenge. (p. 269)
   a.   true*
   b.   false

92. A status-quo guardian seeks challenge and needs high control. (p. 270-271)
   a.   true
   b.   false*

93. A participative innovator delegates control inside his/her organization and is a risk-taker. (p. 270-271)
   a.   true*
   b.   false

94. A process manager delegates control inside the organization and is a risk-taker. (p. 270-271)
   a.   true
   b.   false*

95. Jamie and Victor Tsao, founders of Linksys, are participative innovators. (p. 271)
   a.   true
   b.   false*

96. Mickey Drexler, former CEO of the Gap, is an example of a status quo guardian. (p. 271)
   a.   true
   b.   false*

97. High-control innovators will seek innovative strategies that stay close to their current business. (p. 272)
   a.   true*
   b.   false

98. Status-quo guardians will protect their organization from the outside and hire people who are similar to them. (p. 272)
   a.   true*
   b.   false

99. Participative innovators are open to new strategies and decentralize decision making. (p. 272)
   a.   true*
   b.   false

100. Process managers avoid risk and centralize decision making. (p. 272)
   a.   true
   b.   false*

101. Jon Brock, CEO of InBev, represents a process manager. (p. 273)
   a.   true*
   b.   false

102. Ricardo Semler, CEO of Semco, is an example of a participative innovator. (p. 273)
   a.   true*
   b.   false

103. The type of strategic leader that will be effective depends on various organizational factors. (p.273)
   a.   true*
   b.   false

104. The more participative strategic leaders who encourage participation and empowerment are usually better and more effective CEOs. (p.273)
   a.   true
   b.   false*

105. The French upper management tend to have considerable power and authority. (p.274)
   a.   true*
   b.   false

106. Some research suggests that upper echelon female leaders tend to have a lower need for control than their male counter parts. (p. 274)
   a.   true*
   b.   false

107. Cross-cultural research shows different patterns of leadership based on culture, but those differences do not apply to upper echelon leadership. (p. 274)
   a.   true
   b.   false*

108. CLTs suggest that Anglos and Latin American value leaders who have a vision are inspirations more than Middle Easterners. (p. 275)
   a.   true*
   b.   false

109. The French upper echelon leaders are generally more open to change and non-hierarchical that leaders at other level of French organizations. (p. 275)
   a.   true
   b.   false*

110. Female upper echelon leaders, such as Meg Whitman, CEO of eBay, often focus less on power acquisition than their male counterparts. (p. 276)
   a.   true*
   b.   false

111. One of the most powerful ways upper echelon leaders is through direct decisions regarding vision, mission, strategy, and structure. (p. 276)
   a.   true*
   b.   false

112. One of the ways Jeff Bezos, CEO of Amazon.com influences the direction of his organization is by deciding where resources will go. (p. 277)
   a.   true*
   b.   false

113. CEOs often control the formal, but not the informal reward system their organization. (p. 277)
   a.   true
   b.   false*

114. Role modeling is often in ineffective way for CEOs to try to influence the behavior of others in their organizations. (p. 278)
   a.   true
   b.   false*

115. The CEO of large U.S. companies has consistently been as much as twice as high as CEOs in other industrialized countries. (p. 279)
   a.   true*
   b.   false

116. The increase in executive salaries in the U.S. is based on productivity and is match by similar percentage increases in the salary of white and blue collar workers. (p. 279)
   a.   true
   b.   false*

117. Data on executive salaries and firm performance shows a clear relationship between the two. (p. 279)
   a.   true
   b.   false*

118. The more global a company, the higher the compensation of its CEO. (p. 280)
   a.   true*
   b.   false

119. Many poorly performing upper echelon leaders continue to keep their jobs in spite of poor performance. (p. 280)
   a.   true*
   b.   false

120. In almost all cases, poorly performing CEOs are eventually fired because of their lack of performance. (p. 280)
   a.   true
   b.   false*

121. Many CEOs are simply not held accountable for their poor performance or even unethical behavior. (p. 280)
   a.   true*
   b.   false

122. A.G. Lafley, CEO of Procter and Gamble, successfully turned his company around by focusing on people and on the company's best brands. (p. 291-292)
    a.   true*
    b.   false

123. A.G. Lafley is a example of the typical power U.S. executives hold and how they use it. (p. 291-292)
    a.   true
    b.   false*

CHAPTER 10

1. The definition of leadership includes three factors. Which one of the following is <u>not</u> part of the definition of leadership? (p. 296)
   a.   Leadership is a group phenomenon.
   b.   Leadership assumes effectiveness.*
   c.   Leadership requires followers.
   d.   Leadership is goal oriented.

2. Leadership effectiveness includes two elements. They are: (p. 296)
   a.   internal health and external adaptability.*
   b.   task and consideration.
   c.   followers and the task.
   d.   power and authority.

3. The current views of leadership are deeply rooted in the concept of: (p. 296)
   a.   power
   b.   behaviors and traits
   c.   situational factors
   d.   contingency*

4. Charismatic, transformational, and change oriented leadership theories focus attention on: (p. 296)
   a.   the importance of the emotional bond between leaders and followers.*
   b.   the role of balance between task and people.
   c.   followers as well as leaders.
   d.   the contingency factors that affect leadership.

5. Culture can impact leadership on three levels. Which one of the following is <u>not</u> one of the levels of culture? (p. 296)
   a.   national
   b.   ethnic
   c.   organizational
   d.   individual*

6. Which one of the following individual difference characteristic has shown promise and requires further development as it relates to leadership? (p. 297)
   a.   Type A
   b.   MBTI
   c.   Emotional Intelligence*
   d.   Values

7. Which of the following is <u>not</u> one of the ways understanding the organizational context can help our understanding of leadership? (p. 297)
   a.   Clarify the impact of individual differences.
   b.   When situational demands are clear, people tend to respond to them; so understanding situations is helpful.
   c.   Help the debate between leadership and management
   d.   Clarify the role of teams and organizational structures.*

8. In cross-cultural research, the _____ approach focuses on understanding a particular culture. (p. 298)
   a.   cross-cultural research
   b.   global research
   c.   emic*
   d.   etic

9. In cross-cultural research, the _____ approach focuses generalizing across different cultures. (p. 298)
   a.   cross-cultural research
   b.   global research
   c.   emic
   d.   etic*

10. Which one of the following areas in cross-cultural leadership research is already established and does not require development further development? (p. 298)
   a.   Whether culture influences leadership.*
   b.   Whether leadership exists in all cultures.
   c.   What leadership ideals are in different cultures.
   d.   How to lead culturally diverse group.

11. Disappearing loyalty, changing values about work, and the push for work and life balance are all part of which category of change in the leadership context? (p. 298-299)
   a.   Structural changes.
   b.   Changing demographics.
   c.   New work ethic.*
   d.   Emphasis on flexibility.

12. The push towards empowerment, use of teams, telecommuting, and outsourcing are all part of which category of change in the leadership context? (p. 298-299)
   a.   Structural changes.*
   b.   Changing demographics.
   c.   New work ethic.
   d.   Emphasis on flexibility.

13. The 21st century employees are often _____ than _____. (p. 298-299)
   a.   less well trained/ previous generations
   b.   more loyal to themselves/to the organization*
   c.   dependent on the leader/on the team
   d.   less focused on personal life/on organizational success.

14. Wipro is a company located in _____. (p. 300)
   a.   The U.S.
   b.   Canada
   c.   Singapore
   d.   India*

15. Wipro and AES are both examples of: (p. 300)
   a.   poorly led companies.
   b.   how ethical problems can cross national borders.
   c.   how organizations deal creatively with the changing context.*
   d.   new models of leadership effectiveness.

16. The new work ethic requires leaders to: (p. 301)
    a.   accommodate different working styles.*
    b.   assure that all employees are evaluated the same way.
    c.   focus on developing complex HR practices.
    d.   realize the importance of strategic leadership.

17. The common theme in the new roles for leaders is: (p. 301)
    a.   changing the top down hierarchy.*
    b.   becoming knowledge workers.
    c.   replacing leaders with teams
    d.   strengthening the role of the leader as a strategic force.

18. Greenleaf and Collins both suggest that leaders: (p. 302)
    a.   should let followers do their own thing without interference.
    b.   are no longer really needed in complex, team-based organizations.
    c.   should be humble and focus on their followers.*
    d.   become cross-culturally savvy.

19. Which one of the following is not one of the actions leaders can take to help create the fit between the individual and the organization? (p. 302-303)
    a.   Clarify values and culture.
    b.   Understand followers' values.
    c.   Look for common ground between individuals and their organization.
    d.   Encourage individuals to change to have a better fit with their organization.*

20. Which one of the following is one of the new research areas in leadership? (p. 303-304)
    a.   Transformational leadership.
    b.   Role of emotions.*
    c.   Leadership traits.
    d.   Leader behaviors.

21. According to new research, authentic leaders are those who: (p. 304)
    a.   don't lie.
    b.   are self-aware and act on principle.*
    c.   focus on developing their followers
    d.   act as servants to their followers.

22. Future leaders must do all but one of the following. (p. 304)
    a.   Be self-aware.
    b.   Commit to continuous learning.
    c.   Balance their life and their work.
    d.   Be motivated to be in charge.*

True/False Questions

23. The three elements of leadership are: group phenomenon, followers, and goals. (p. 296)
    a.   true*
    b.   false

24. Leadership effectiveness depends on internal health and goal achievement. (p. 296)
    a.   true
    b.   false*

25. A set of individual traits can predict leadership. (p. 296)
   a.   true
   b.   false*

26. Power can be both a key requirement and a detriment to leadership. (p. 296)
   a.   true*
   b.   false

27. Modern leadership research has established that teams are generally more effective than individuals. (p. 296)
   a.   true
   b.   false*

28. Most of the leadership theories developed in the West can eventually be applied to other cultures. (p. 297)
   a.   true
   b.   false*

29. Further research is needed to integrate micro and macro level leadership concepts. (p. 297)
   a.   true*
   b.   false

30. The remaining issue in research on cross-cultural leadership is whether culture truly affects leadership. (p. 298)
   a.   true*
   b.   false

31. Knowledge workers and focus on learning organizations are part of the changing context of leadership. (p. 299)
   a.   true*
   b.   false

32. Changing demographics affects expectations that organizations have regarding their leaders' performance. (p. 300)
   a.   true
   b.   false*

33. Knowledge workers are often highly loyal to their organizations. (p. 300)
   a.   true
   b.   false*

34. Because of increased information, today's workers have less access to accurate information than previous generations. (p. 300)
   a.   true
   b.   false*

35. In order to deal with the changing context of organizations, Wipro focuses on organizational and individual learning as one of the key challenges. (p. 301)
   a.   true*
   b.   false

36. AES deals with its changing business context by remaining flexible. (p. 301)
   a.   true*
   b.   false

37. Greenleaf sees the leader as an authority figure who empowers followers. (p. 302)
    a.   true
    b.   false*

38. Continued demographic changes and globalization both require leaders to increase their knowledge of culture.
    a.   true*
    b.   false

39. Creating a fit between the individual and the organization is one of the key factors in effectiveness. (p. 302-303)
    a.   true*
    b.   false

40. Self-awareness continues to be one of the keys to effective leadership. (p. 302-303)
    a.   true*
    b.   false

41. Once leaders develop a style that work for them, they can focus on perfecting that style. (p. 304)
    a.   true
    b.   false*